IMAGES
of America

MAINE IN WORLD WAR I

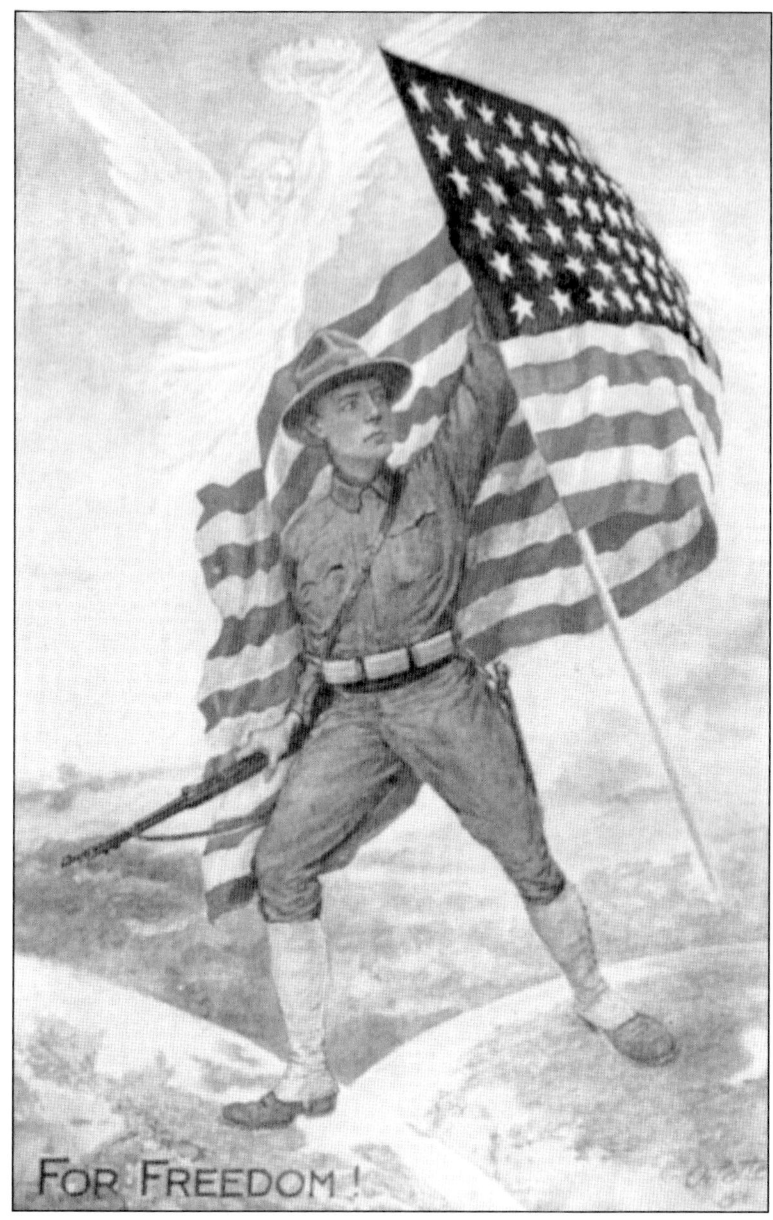

The hero of World War I was the American infantryman, commonly known as the doughboy. In *Testament of Youth*, Vera Brittain's memoir of service as an English nurse in France, she described the moment she first saw American troops: "Look! Look! Here are the Americans! I pressed forward with the others to watch the United States physically entering the War, so god-like, so magnificent, so splendidly unimpaired in comparison with the nerve racked men of the British Army. So these were our deliverers at last, marching up the road in the spring sunshine. There seemed to be hundreds of them, and in the fearless swagger of their proud strength they looked a formidable bulwark against the peril looming from Amiens." (MHPC.)

On the Cover: The *Evening Express* sponsored this Army and Navy recruiting station in Portland. See page 19. (MHPC.)

IMAGES
of America

MAINE IN WORLD WAR I

Jason C. Libby and
Earle G. Shettleworth Jr.

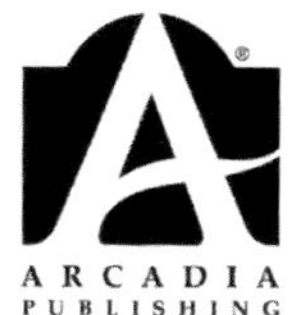

ARCADIA
PUBLISHING

ISBN 978-1-4671-2663-2

Published by Arcadia Publishing
Charleston, South Carolina

Printed in the United States of America

Library of Congress Control Number: 2017932368

For all general information, please contact Arcadia Publishing:
Telephone 843-853-2070
Fax 843-853-0044
E-mail sales@arcadiapublishing.com
For customer service and orders:
Toll-Free 1-888-313-2665

Visit us on the Internet at www.arcadiapublishing.com

This book is dedicated to Earle G. Shettleworth Sr. (1899–1986), who, in 1918, bought a Liberty Bond, volunteered to work in a shipyard, and enlisted in the Army Air Corps.

Contents

ACKNOWLEDGMENTS

The authors wish to thank the following individuals for their assistance in using images from institutional collections: Betsy Paradis of the Bangor Public Library; Paige Lilly of the Castine Historical Society, Kirk F. Mohney and Claudette Coyne of the Maine Historic Preservation Commission, Lt. Jonathan Bratten of the Maine Army National Guard; Jamie Kingman Rice and Sophia Yaloruis of the Maine Historical Society, Nathan Lipfert and Anne Witty of the Maine Maritime Museum, Samuel Howes of the Maine State Archives, Melanie Mohney and Adam Fisher of the Maine State Library, Bernard Fishman and Angela Goebel-Bain of the Maine State Museum, David Richards of the Margaret Chase Smith Library, and the Poland Spring Preservation Society. In addition, we wish to acknowledge the following individuals who provided photographs from their personal collections: Margaret Gardiner, Brennan Gauthier, Brian Harden, Joseph LePage, Jason C. Libby, Richard Shaw, Julie Bond Stegna, and Kenneth E. Thompson Jr. Willie Granston located several images for us. University of Southern Maine professor Libby Bischof's website devoted to Maine's World War I monuments was a valuable resource.

Unless otherwise noted, all images appear courtesy of the Maine Historic Preservation Commission. Images from other collections are noted in the following manner: Bangor Public Library (BPL), Castine Historical Society (CHS), Margaret Gardiner (Gardiner), Brennan Gauthier (Gauthier), Brian Harden (Harden), Joseph LePage (LePage), Jason C. Libby (Libby), Maine Army National Guard (MANG), Maine Historical Society (MHS), Maine Maritime Museum (MMM), Maine State Archives (MSA), Maine State Library (MSL), Maine State Museum (MSM), Margaret Chase Smith Library (MCSL), Poland Spring Preservation Society (PSPS), Richard Shaw (Shaw), Julie Bond Stegna (Stegna), and Kenneth E. Thompson Jr. (Thompson).

Introduction

One hundred years ago last spring, on April 6, 1917, America entered World War I. The European nations had been in conflict since the summer of 1914, but the United States had remained neutral until 1917, when German U-boats began sinking American ships in the North Atlantic, and Germany sought a military alliance with Mexico. At that point, Pres. Woodrow Wilson asked Congress for a declaration of war.

With the same patriotic fervor that Maine had responded to a call for troops in the Civil War, more than 35,000 men and women across the state joined the military in 1917–1918 to fight in "a war to end all wars" that promised to "make the world safe for democracy." The entire University of Maine Band joined the 103rd Infantry Regiment, as did a squad of warriors from the Passamaquoddy Nation, including the chief's own son, who was killed in action on November 10, 1918. The Maine National Guard, which included the Coastal Artillery Corps and the Naval Militia, the Army, the Navy, and the Naval Reserve comprised the bulk of those who served in the war. However, there were hundreds of men who served in the Marines as well as in the Coast Guard, which had come under the direction of the Navy. Other men volunteered for the Maine Home Guards, which served in the absence of the National Guard unit that had been federalized.

Maine civilians supported the war by purchasing $118.4 million in government bonds and $8.4 million in war savings stamps. Private sector relief programs operated by the American Red Cross, YMCA, YWCA, and the Salvation Army also received generous contributions from the public. Women's groups raised money, made bandages and clothes, and some volunteered to serve as nurses in the Red Cross or in military hospitals. The Boy Scouts and other youth organizations planted gardens, sold war savings stamps, and collected supplies to send overseas. By the end of the war, every man, woman, and child in the state had donated an average of $147 to the war effort. In addition, the public generously donated books, clothing, and other comforts of home to our armed forces and their allies.

Maine also provided vital support to the United States and its allies through farming and manufacturing. Aroostook County farms produced large quantities of potatoes, while other farms across the state raised wheat, corn, and beef to feed the troops. Factories produced goods that the military required, including tents, blankets, boots, shoes, overcoats, and cloth for uniforms.

Shipyards such as the Bath Iron Works and the Portsmouth Naval Shipyard as well as smaller shipbuilding facilities launched merchant ships, destroyers, patrol boats, and submarines. Many of these vessels were used to escort soldiers and sailors from the same home they had sailed from. Other industrial facilities manufactured armor plates, munitions, marine engines, wood for the construction of airplanes, lathes, and a host of items necessary to wage war.

Overseas, Mainers more than "did their part" on the Western Front. Maine's first son to give his life was Cpl. Harold Andrews of Portland, serving in the engineers. When his position was overrun on November 30, 1917, he put down his shovel and seized a rifle before he was killed in action. Maine's National Guard outfits—the 103rd Infantry, 101st Trench Mortar Battery, and 56th Pioneer Infantry—served with distinction on the Western Front. The 103rd never lost ground and captured the most prisoners of any outfit in the 26th Division. One of the first National Guardsmen to die in France was Pvt. Ralph Spaulding, who was killed in action on February 13, 1918. The 103rd Infantry was a "fighting regiment," taking part in five major campaigns in 1918, including the summer offensives where it was the first unit to go "over the top." As an indication of the toughness of the outfit, it was still attacking on November 11, 1918, as the Armistice went into effect. Less than 50 percent of the men who left Maine with the unit in 1917 came home unscathed in 1919.

The 56th Pioneer Infantry Regiment—nicknamed the "Milliken Regiment" after Gov. Carl E. Milliken—arrived in France in time to take part in America's bloodiest battle of all time: the Meuse-Argonne. Following the Armistice, the 56th advanced into Germany to serve as part of the Army of Occupation. In the ranks of the 56th was future Maine governor William Tudor Gardiner. Another future governor, Sumner Sewall, flew biplanes for the American Air Service and shot down enough German planes to earn the coveted title of "Ace." Thousands of men joined the coast artillery outfits protecting the Maine coast during the war, with hundreds later serving in France as part of the 54th Artillery, 101st Engineers, and 103rd Field Artillery.

The secretary of the Maine Committee on Public Safety raised a company of chauffeurs, truck drivers, and mechanics dubbed the 303rd Motor Truck Company, which supported the famed 1st Infantry Division, "the Big Red One," in its campaigns in 1918. It was one of the first truck units to cross into Germany after the Armistice. Similarly, men from the Maine Central Railroad enlisted together to form Company C, 14th Engineers (Railway), and played a vital role in building and running light railways across the Western Front. Over 1,000 Mainers perished in the Great War from enemy fire and disease. The war left its mark across the state with veterans returning with missing limbs or with poor lungs from the horrific poison gas attacks they had endured.

After 19 months of American participation, World War I ended on November 11, 1918, the Armistice Day that we now observe as Veterans Day. It would be several months before most of Maine's soldiers and sailors would return home. Rather than solving Europe's problems, the war led to an even greater conflict two decades later. Shaped by the hardships of the Depression, America's Greatest Generation rose to meet the challenge of World War II in order to preserve the freedoms that we cherish today.

Although those who participated in the war are gone, legacies remain. Monuments and memorials dot the countryside and towns and span the river between Maine and New Hampshire Moreover, Mainers were involved in the formation of the American Legion, an organization that unlike its predecessor, the Grand Army of the Republic from after the Civil War, carries on its mission of supporting veterans and promoting patriotism in the 21st century.

One

Prelude to War

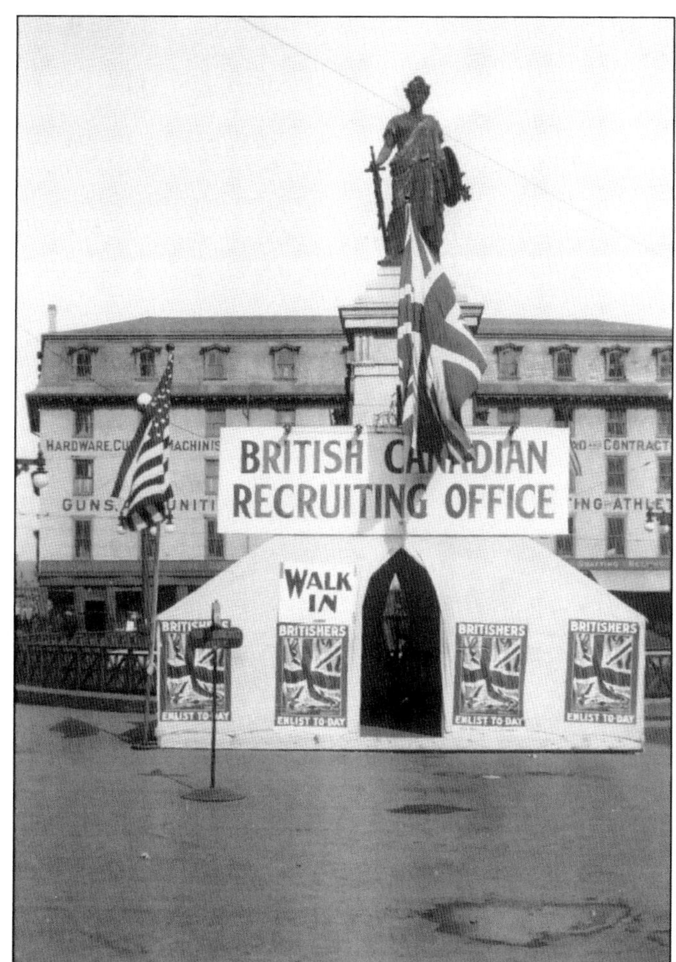

While the United States remained neutral in World War I from 1914 to 1917, many Americans supported the allies by making financial and material contributions to English, French, and Belgian relief organizations. Some Americans went a step further by joining the British or Canadian military, which recruited soldiers and sailors in Portland's Monument Square in 1916.

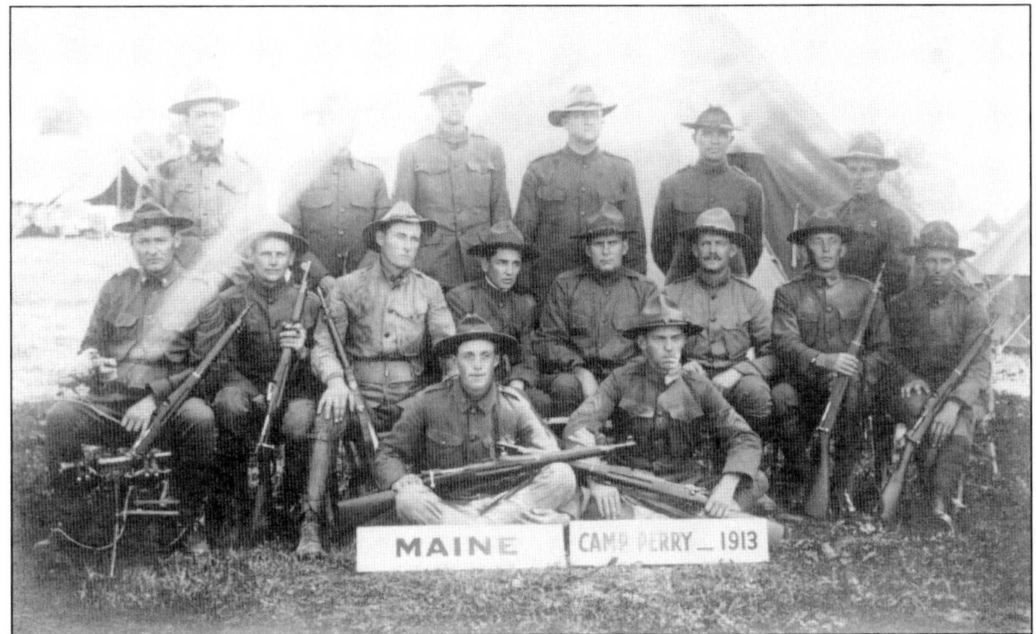

The 1913 Maine Rifle Team was composed of members of the 2nd Maine Infantry Regiment and the Coastal Artillery Corps. National Guard units throughout the country sent their best qualifiers to an annual competition at Camp Perry in Ohio. Of these 16 Maine soldiers, 10 would serve in World War I, and 2 became colonels in World War II. (Libby.)

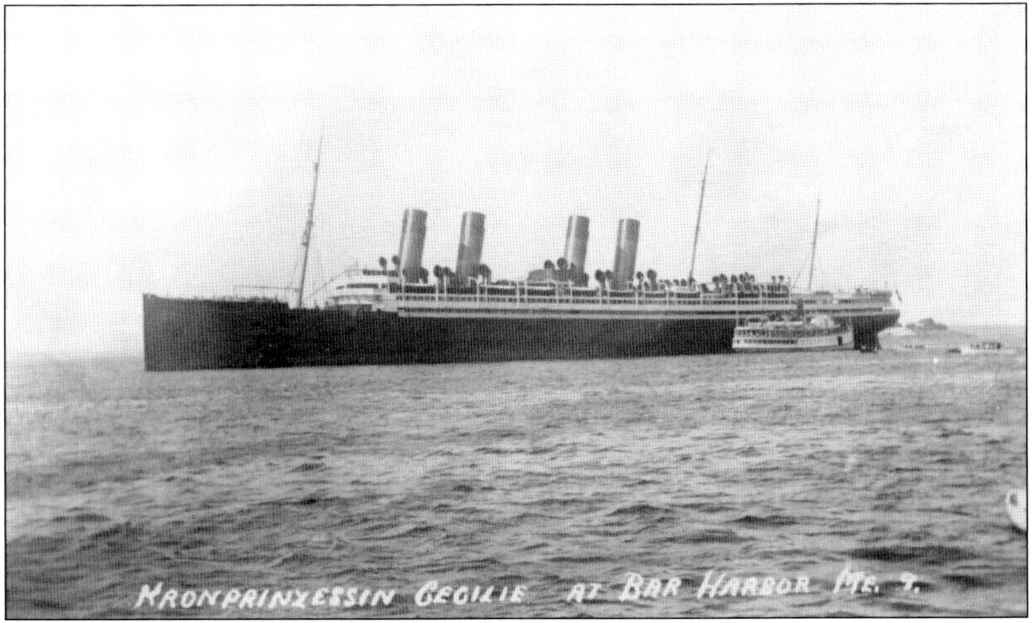

The SS *Kronprinzessin Cecilie* was a German ocean liner that was at sea when war broke out. Ordered to a neutral port, the vessel arrived in Bar Harbor on August 4, 1914, with 1,200 passengers and $11 million in gold and silver. The ship was interned, seized when the United States entered the war, and then renamed the USS *Mount Vernon* to serve as an American troop transport.

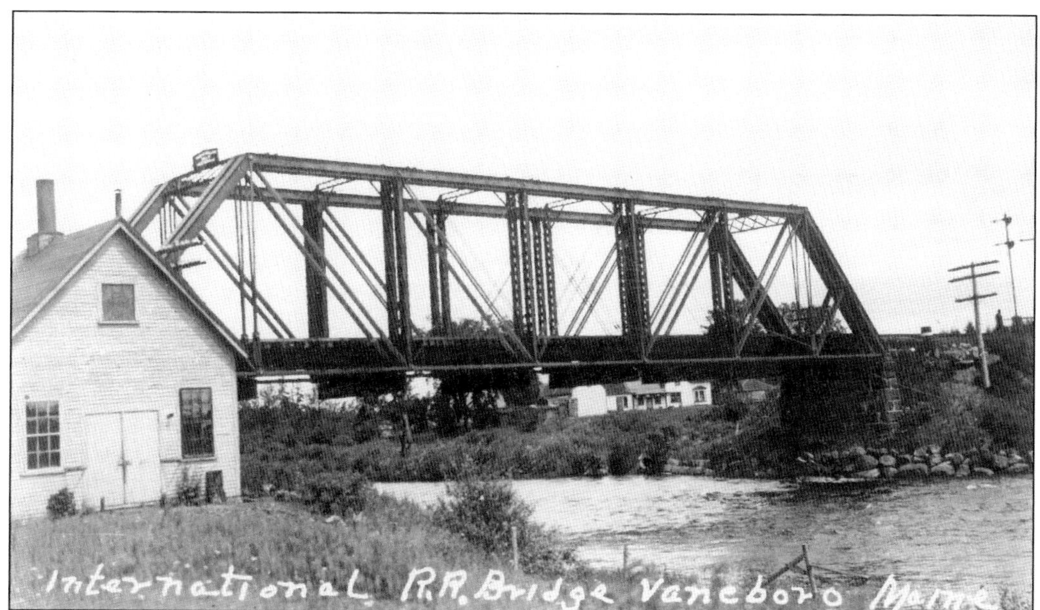

On February 2, 1915, Werner Horn, a member of the German army, attempted to blow up the St. Croix–Vanceboro Railway Bridge. Entering the United States from Mexico, he traveled to Vanceboro on the Canadian border and placed a suitcase of explosives on the St. Croix side. Although the explosives detonated, the bridge was minimally damaged, and Horn was caught and extradited to Canada.

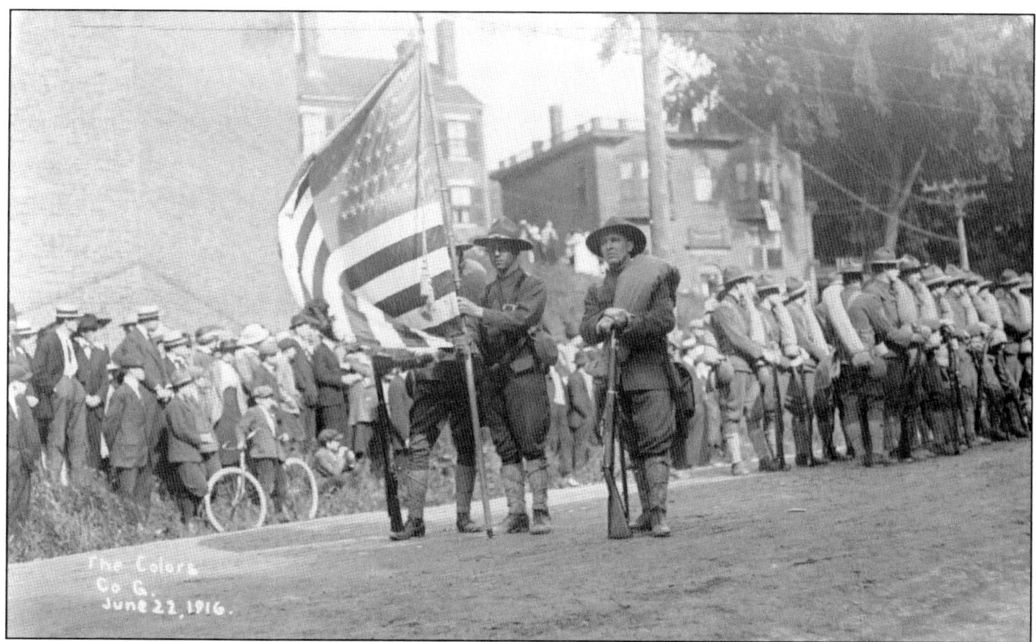

On June 22, 1916, Company G and a machine gun company left Bangor for duty on the Texas-Mexican border. Early that morning, the two units assembled at the armory on Court Street and marched through the city to board a waiting train at the Maine Central Railroad Station. Here, a soldier holds the colors that led the parade.

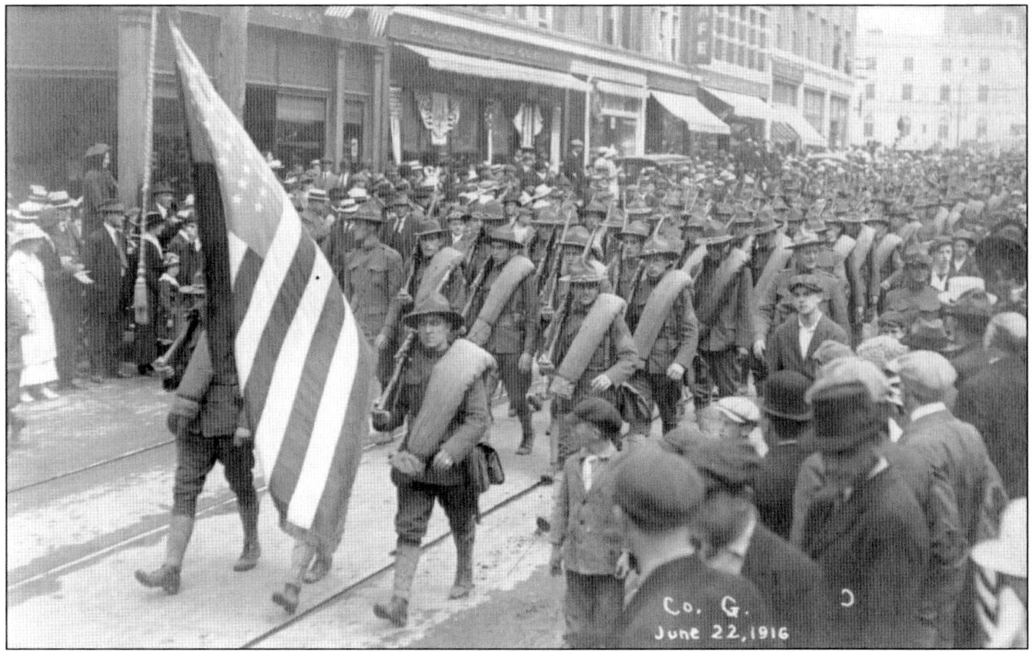

Thousands lined the parade route in Bangor on June 22, 1916, to bid farewell to the two military units bound for Texas. The *Bangor Daily News* reported the next day that "no one recalls when so many have been in the streets at such an early hour in the morning, and at no time within memory has there been such enthusiasm and loyalty for the soldiers."

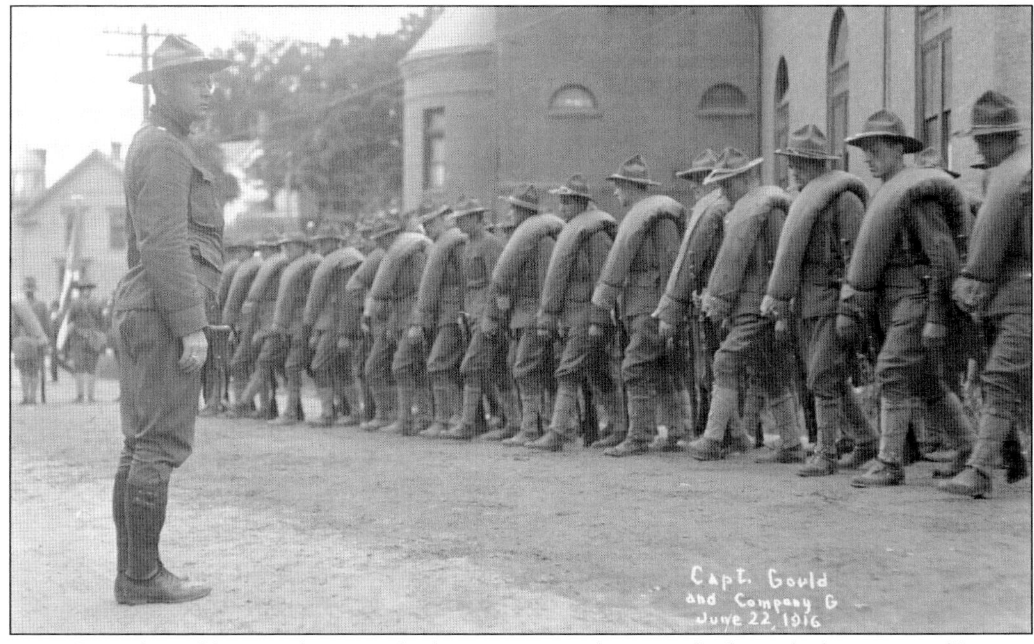

Capt. Daniel Gould is seen here overlooking troops as they parade through the streets of Bangor in 1916. Gould, a Canadian-born Bangor lawyer, was actively involved in the 2nd Maine Infantry regiment for many years. Later, when the war began and the regiment was federalized, Gould continued to serve as captain of Company G until he was transferred to another regiment.

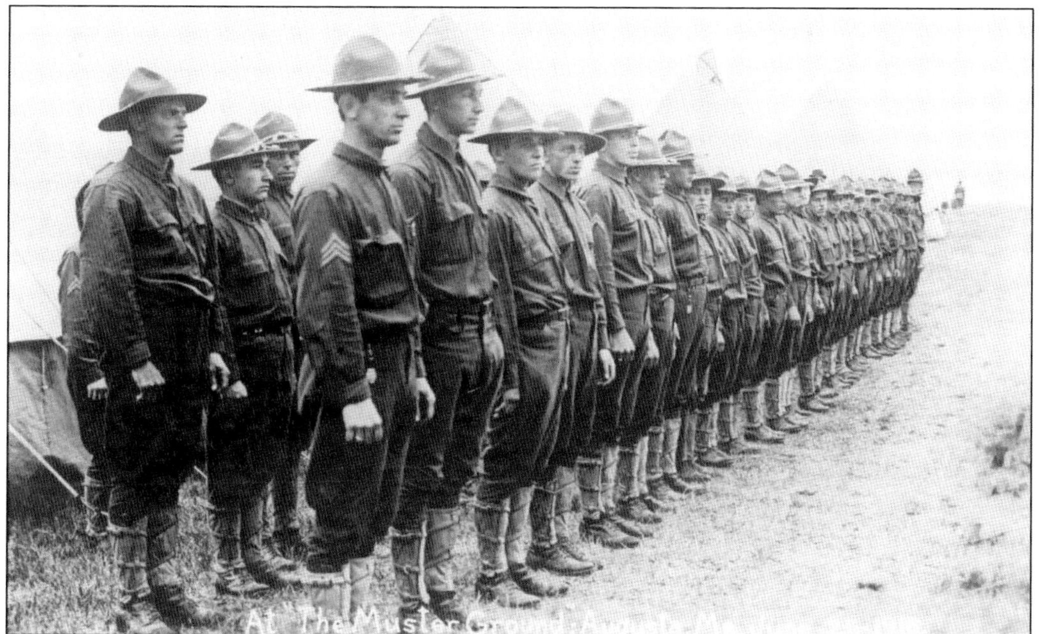

Soldiers of the Second Regiment of the Maine National Guard stand at attention at Camp Keyes in Augusta on June 25, 1916, the day before they are to take the oath to join the new US National Guard, which was created by the Army Reorganization Act. In taking the oath, they became members of the Federal army for the purpose of serving on the Texas-Mexico border.

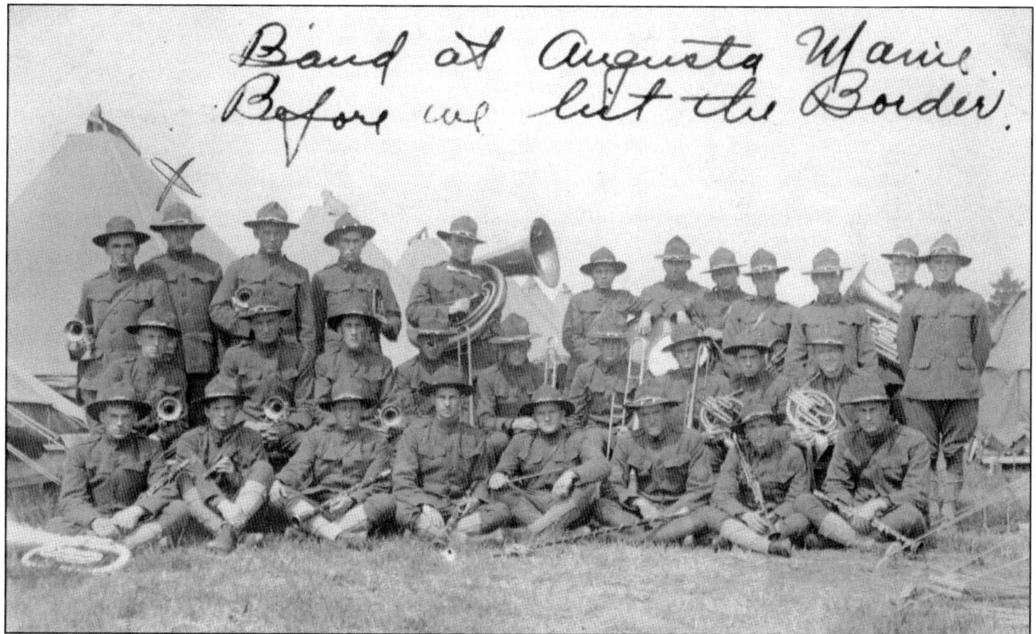

On June 26, 1916, about 5,000 Mainers visited Camp Keyes in Augusta to show their support for the National Guard. The visitors were serenaded by the Guard band, comprised of University of Maine students with an average age of twenty. The following day, the *Kennebec Journal* commented that "from now on, if the Maine troops are called to help protect the border, the college boys will be in line with them."

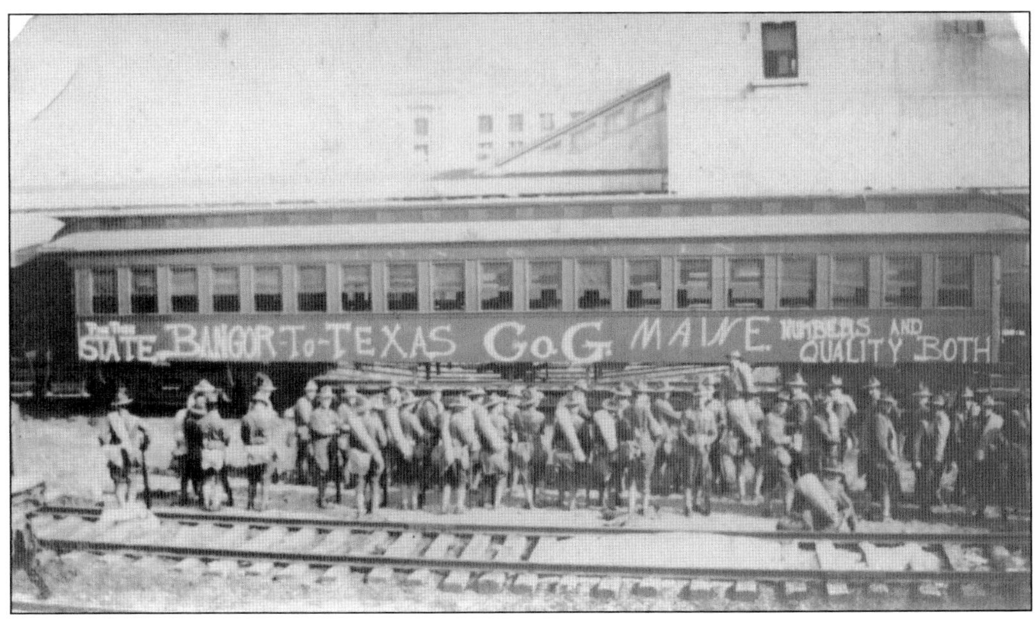

A railcar which had been graffitied by an artistic member of Company G, awaits boarding. With the increased seriousness of the crisis, the federal government called for more troops to be sent to the border. Railroad officials stated that they could move approximately 25,000 troops daily to the Texas-Mexico border. As the Maine troops assembled at Camp Keyes, guardsmen from New York, Massachusetts, New Jersey, and Connecticut had already begun traveling to the border with additional troops from Vermont, Delaware, West Virginia, and Florida mobilized and readied. Meanwhile, over two million rounds of ammunition along with other necessary military equipment were sent to the border for the potential showdown. Tensions declined after a series of talks between the two governments, and by October, the Maine troops were sent home to a grateful state. (Both, Shaw.)

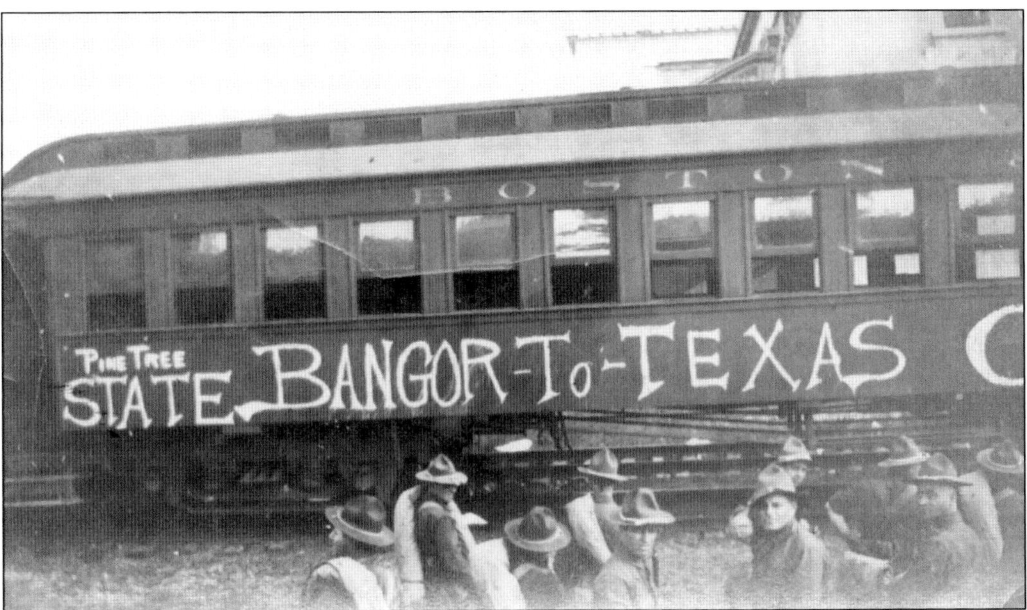

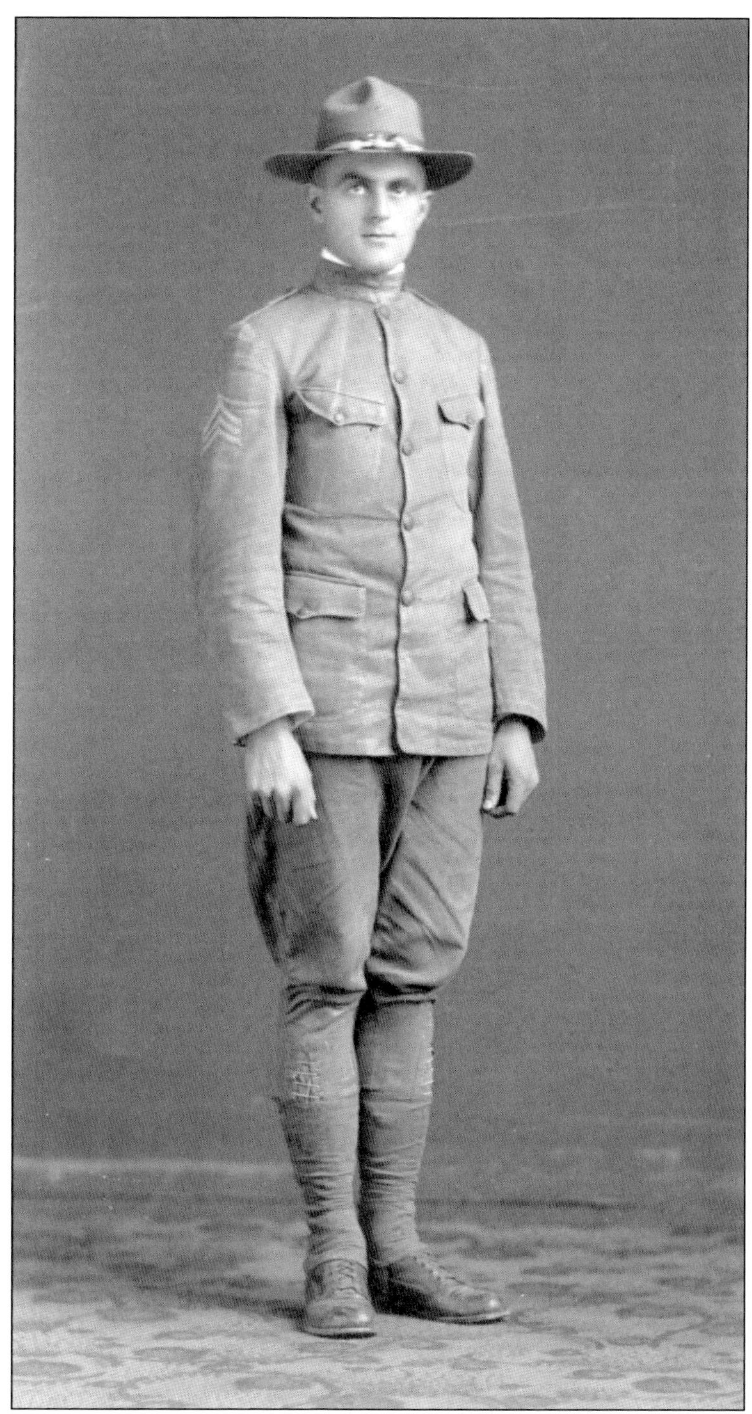

Born in the central Maine town of Newport, Lewis O. Barrows graduated from the University of Maine in 1916 and immediately joined the Second Regiment, Maine Infantry. A member of the regimental band, Sergeant Barrows participated in the Mexican border campaign. Returning to civilian life, he ran the family drug store and became involved in Republican politics, which resulted in serving two terms as governor from 1937 to 1941. (Libby.)

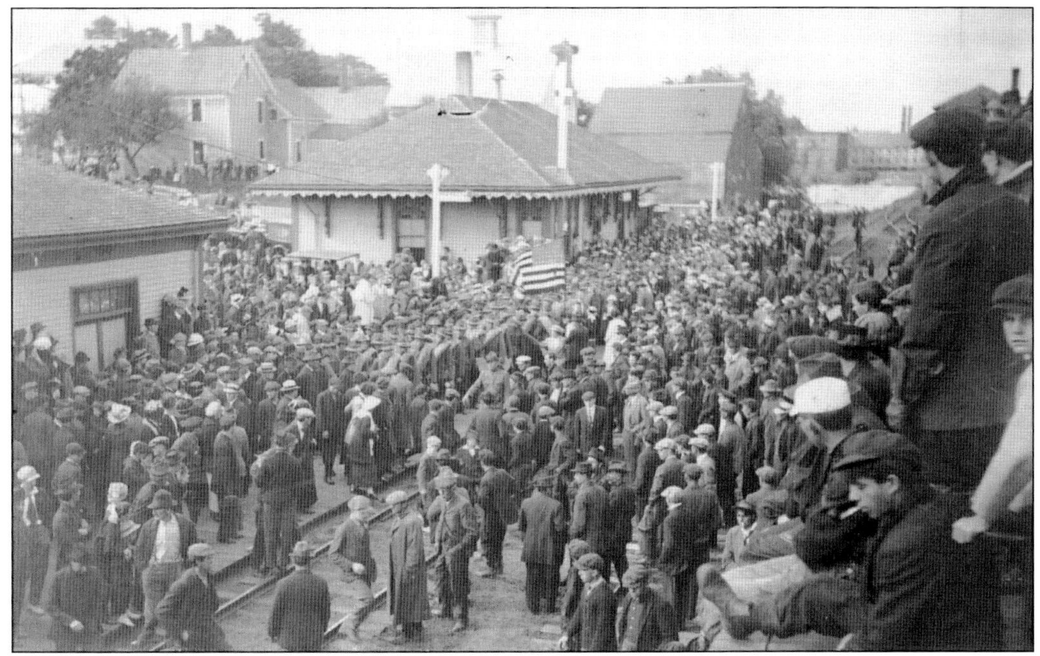

A large crowd gathered early on the morning of June 22, 1916, at the Maine Central Railroad Station in Dexter to say farewell to Company A, bound for duty on the Mexican border. Among the well-wishers seeing off the 7:15 a.m. train were the local band and 400 employees of the Fay and Scott machine shop and foundry, of whom 50 were members of Company A.

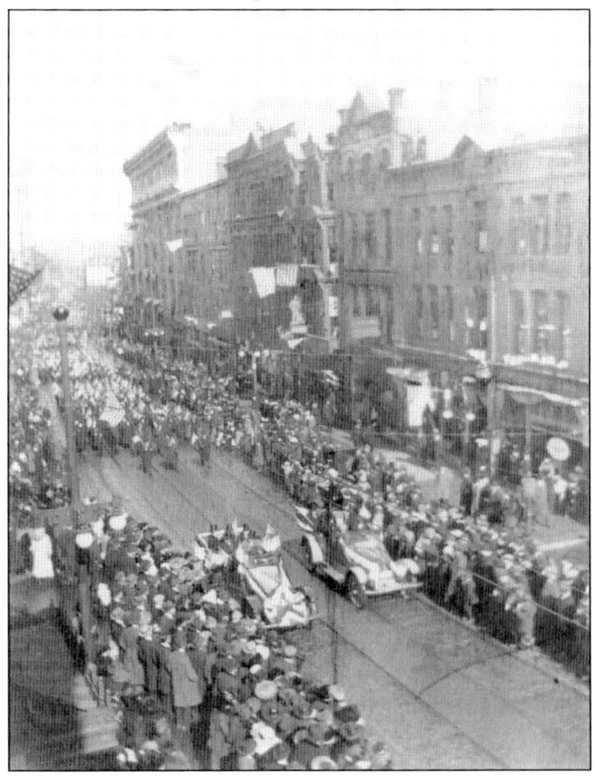

As America's entrance into the European conflict became likely, Maine communities staged Preparedness Parades to encourage support for the coming war. One of the largest of these events was held in Portland on March 16, 1917, with 8,000 people attending. Leading the procession up Congress Street were two cars carrying city officials. The next morning, the Eastern Argus declared the parade the "greatest demonstration of patriotism in Maine history."

Two

Preparations for War

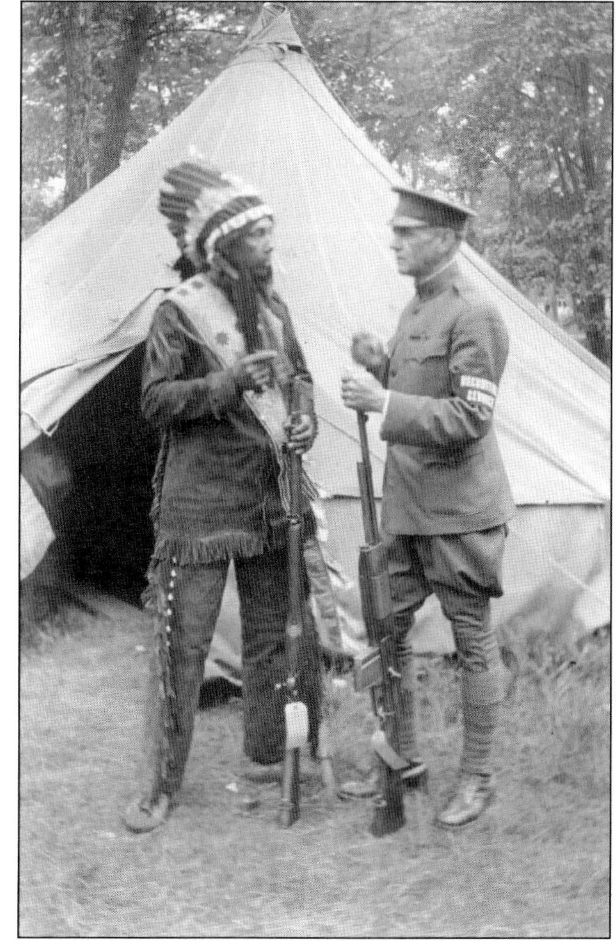

The Passamaquoddy Nation answered the call, even though as Native Americans they were not even eligible to vote. Here, a recruitment officer visits with tribal governor Peter Neptune, whose own son Moses, a member of Company I of the 103rd Infantry Regiment, was killed on November 10, 1918. By the close of the war, two dozen Passamaquoddy had served in either the American Expeditionary Forces or the Canadian Expeditionary Forces.

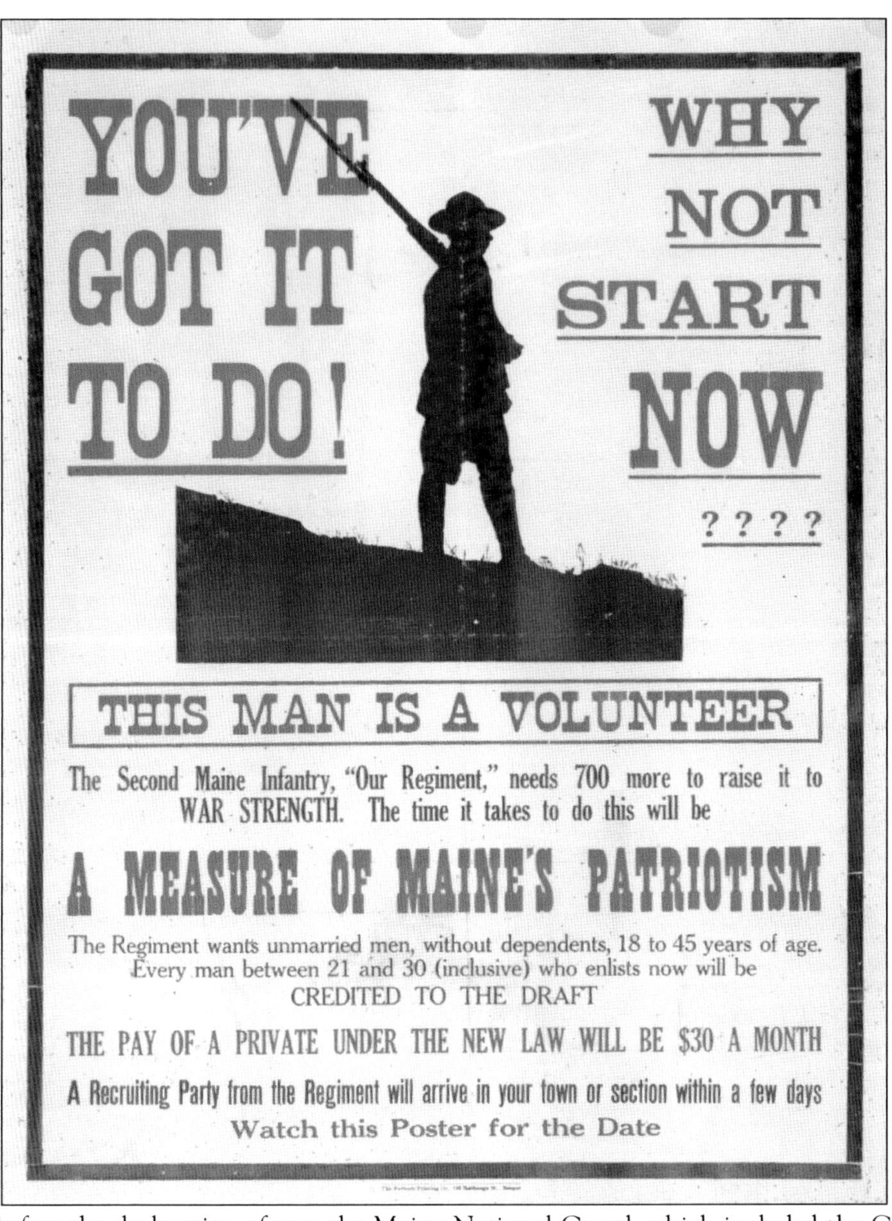

Even before the declaration of war, the Maine National Guard, which included the Coastal Artillery Corps, as well as the regular Army and Navy, were encouraging men to enlist. Immediately following the declaration, the adjutant general amended the qualifications for enlistees, which included age limit increases to 40 years of age and the replacement of an educational test for the requirement that a candidate be able to speak and understand English. By the close of 1917, more than 10,000 Mainers had enlisted in the war, which met the enlistment quota of 7,064 men and was second among all states in proportion to its population. This recruitment poster focused on enlisting men into the 2nd Maine Infantry Regiment of the National Guard. The 2nd Maine regiment traces its lineage to the Civil War and service beginning at the First Battle of Bull Run. Throughout the early 20th century, the regiment continued to operate with companies based in Dexter, Rumford, Livermore Falls, Norway, Skowhegan, Dover, Bangor, Waterville, Eastport, Farmington, Houlton, and Augusta. (MSM)

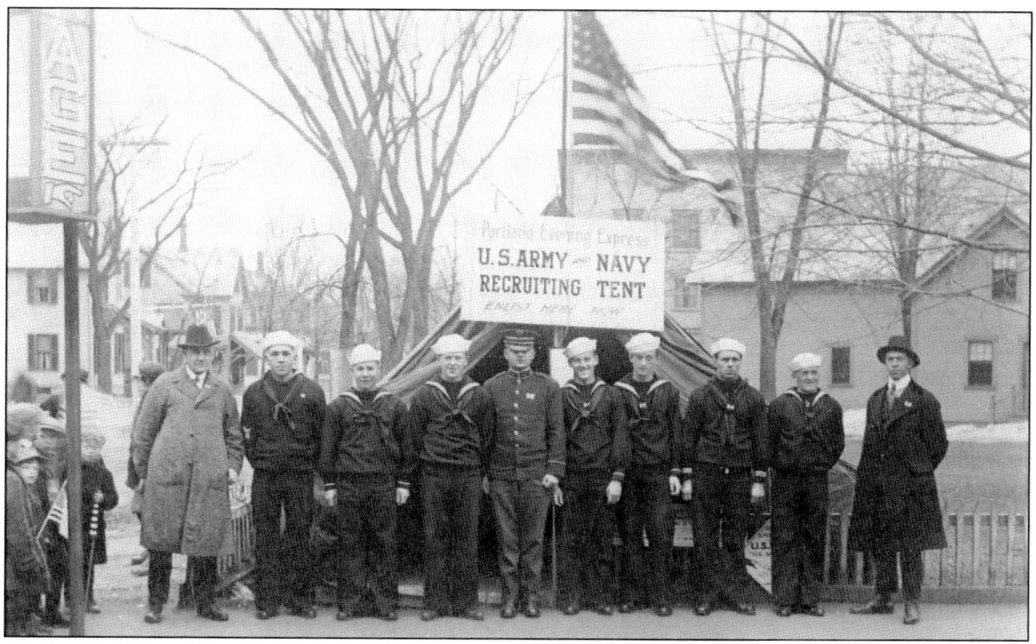

At the outbreak of the war, a local newspaper, the *Evening Express*, sponsored this Army and Navy recruiting station in Portland. When this photograph was taken, the tent was staffed primarily by sailors. Recruiting met with great success in Portland, resulting in the city furnishing 4,500 men for the war effort.

REGISTRATION CERTIFICATE.

To whom it may concern, Greetings:

No. 83

(This number must correspond with that on the Registration Card.)

THESE PRESENTS ATTEST, That in accordance with the proclamation of the President of the United States, and in compliance with law, Arthur W. Barbour (Name), Rockland (City or P. O.) Precinct 4 County of Knox, State of Maine, has submitted himself to registration and has by me been duly registered this 5th day of June, 1917.

Philip I. Rosenberg
Registrar.

8—4227

The Selective Service Act of 1917 required that all male citizens between the ages of 21 and 30 register for military service. This certificate confirmed that Arthur W. Barbour of Rockland had enrolled for service in the first nationwide registration drive on June 5, 1917. A native of Deer Isle, the 23-year-old Barbour served stateside in the Army from October 1917 to November 1918. (Harden.)

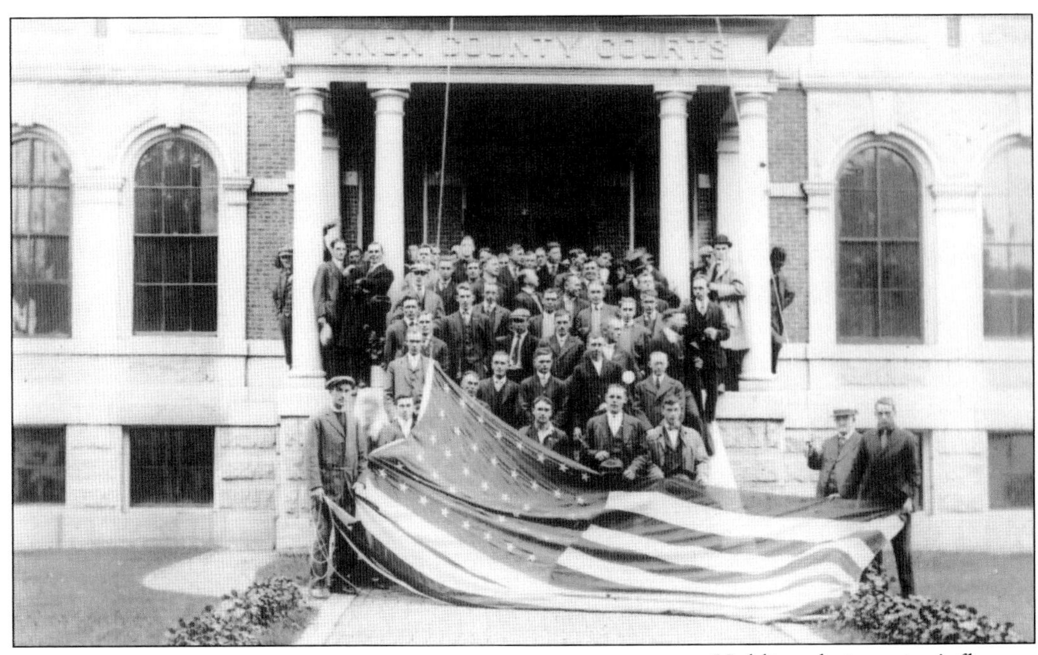

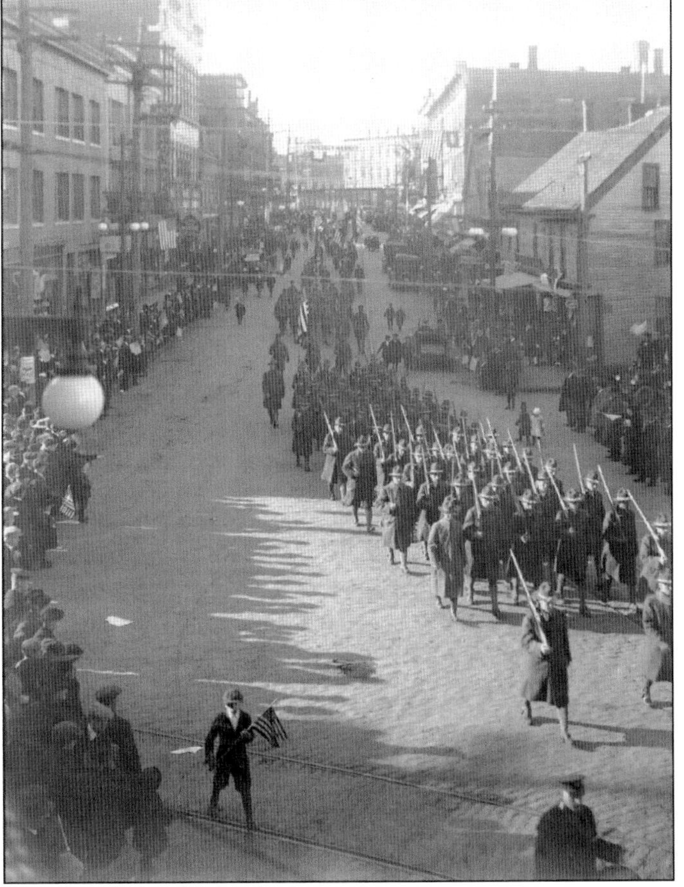

Holding their nation's flag, a group of young men from Knox County drafted to serve in the Army stand on the steps of the courthouse in Rockland. Early on the morning of September 19, 1917, these men were escorted to the railroad station by a parade through the streets of Rockland that included Civil War veterans, Naval Reservists, and cheering local residents. (Harden.)

A patriotic parade was held in Biddeford and Saco on Patriots Day, April 19, 1917. A number of civic organizations, fraternal societies, veterans, members of the Coastal Artillery Corps (CAC), and even the governor, marched in what organizer F.B. Harris of Biddeford deemed "the greatest parade ever planned for this county and I believe it is one of the largest patriotic parades ever planned for this state."

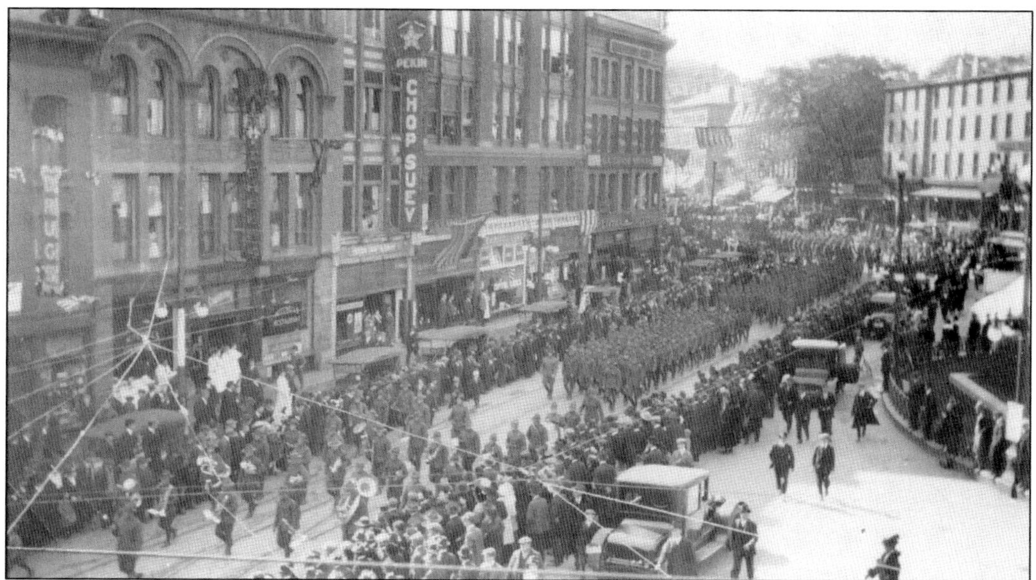

The 1st Maine Heavy Artillery Regiment parades through Portland in October 1917. A majority of the regiment, originally nicknamed the Milliken Regiment in honor of Gov. Carl E. Milliken, was eventually renamed the 56th Pioneer Infantry Regiment. The 56th arrived in France in September 1918 and remained until their return home in June 1919. While in Portland, Bishop Louis Walsh blessed the regimental colors.

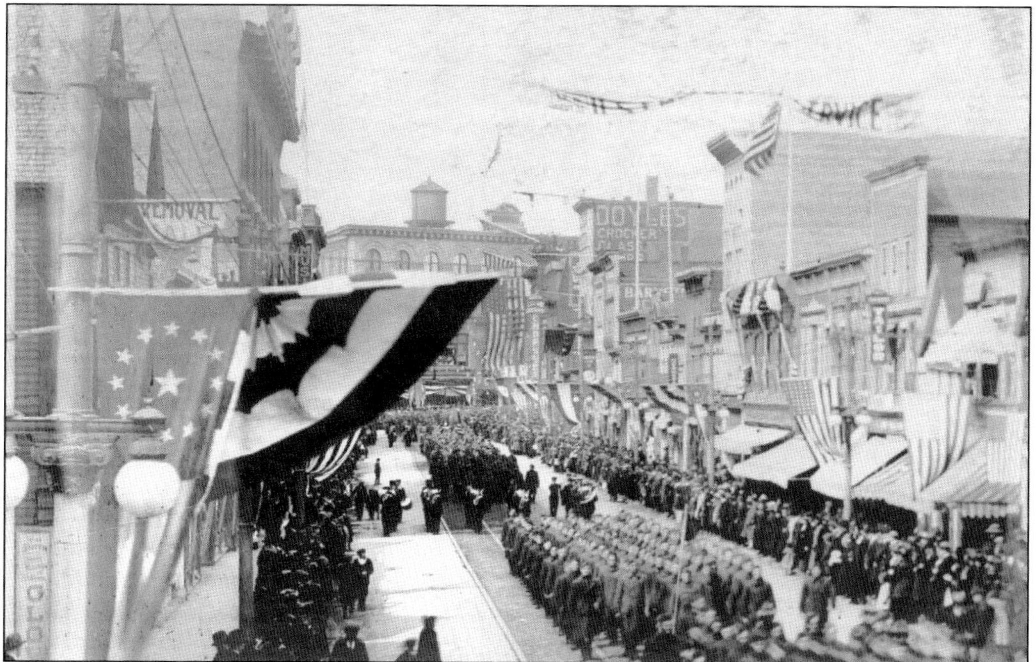

Members of the 2nd Maine's Company F, based in Dover, march through the streets of Lewiston in April 1917. The company was detailed to guard Lewiston and Auburn before eventually being sent to Camp Keyes. The soldiers were quartered at a former grammar school in Auburn. One soldier, reflecting upon the likelihood of sleeping on the hardwood floors, said "Hotel for me if the cots don't come." (LePage.)

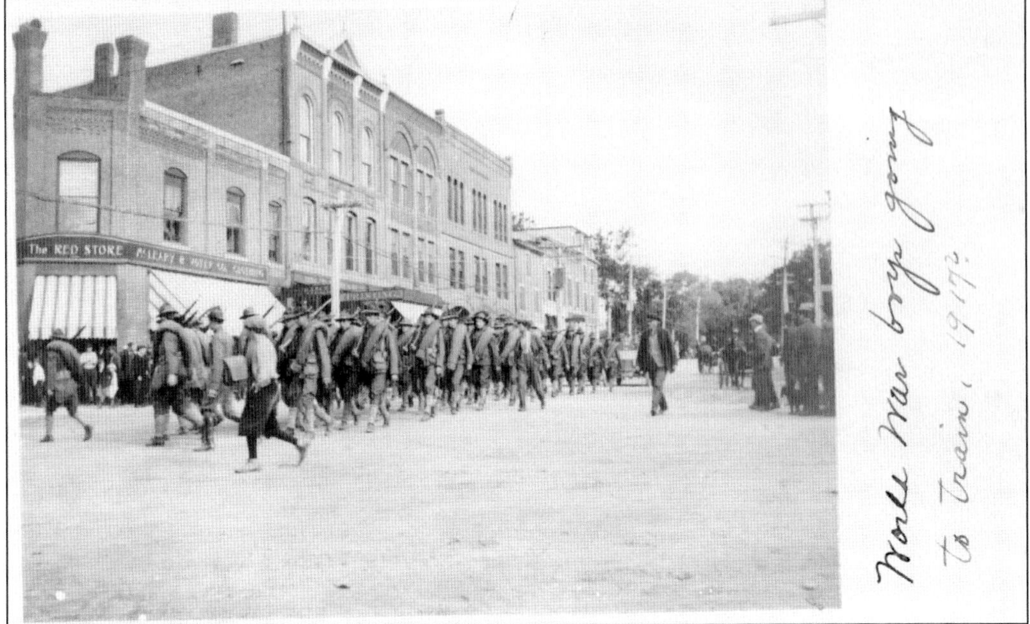

Company K of the 2nd Maine marches down Main Street in Farmington to the train station on April 30, 1917. During the days leading up to the departure, the troops drilled and even had a chance to play baseball against the high school team, winning by a score of 12-5. Local dentists also offered to provide examinations and other services at no charge to the departing troops.

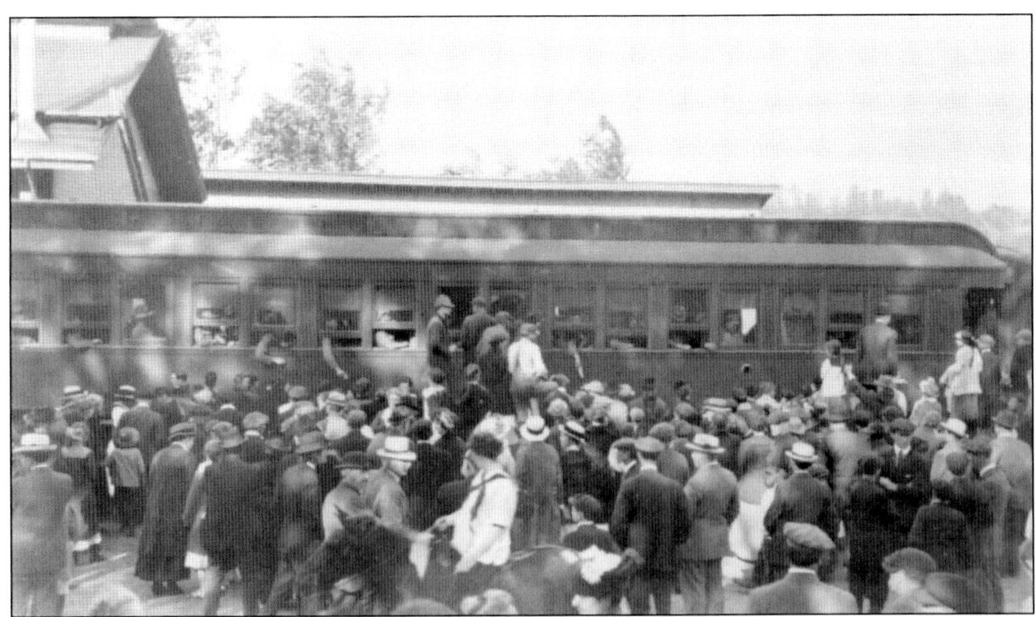

A large gathering of relatives, friends, and neighbors say goodbye to members of Company K at the Farmington train station. The *Lewiston Daily Sun* reported that "they were given rousing cheers, bugles were sounded and flags waved." The troops were being sent to Bangor for guard detail and then eventually to the state muster grounds at Camp Keyes. (MSL.)

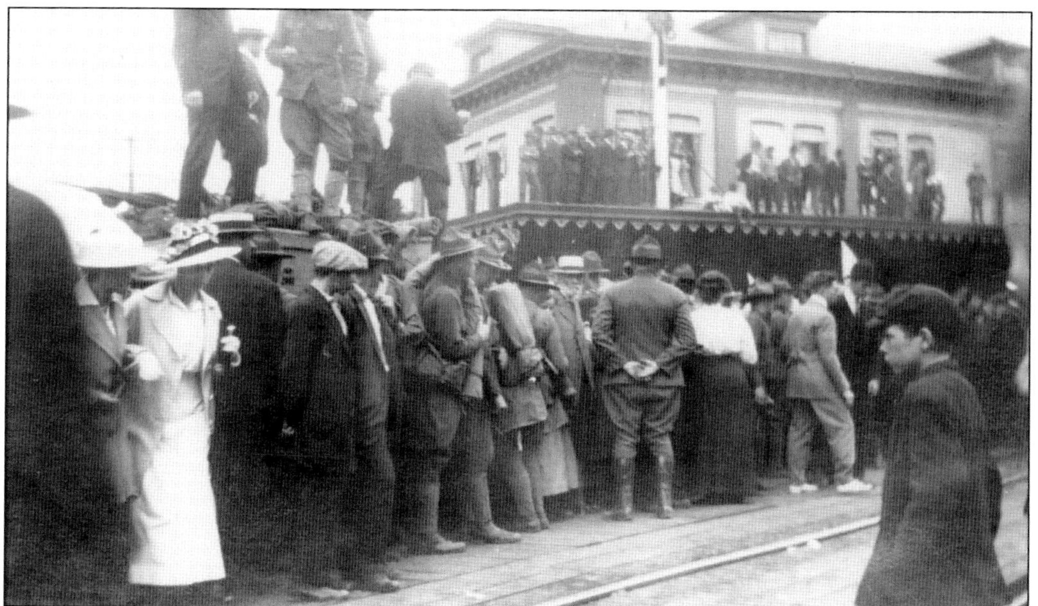

Across Maine in 1917 and 1918, crowds gathered at railroad stations whenever young men left for the war. Here, a large group stands on the platform of the Waterville station. Across the tracks was Colby College, 40 of whose students enlisted as soon as war was declared. For those who stayed, training was provided by the Colby Military Company, which was soon replaced by a unit of the Student Army Training Corps.

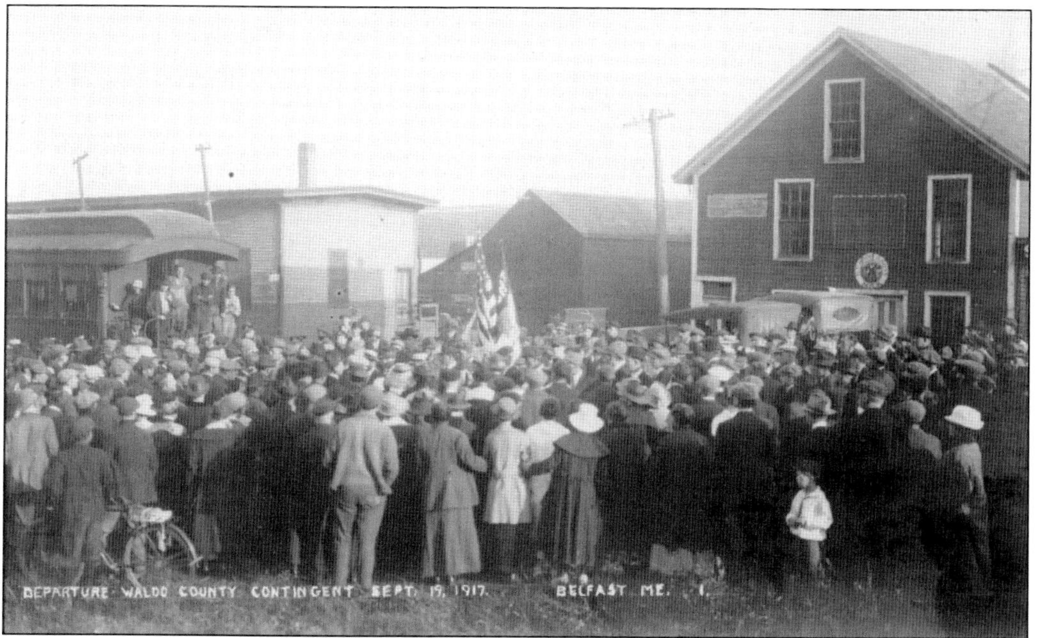

On September 19, 1917, more than 2,000 people gathered at the Belfast Railroad Station to bid farewell to the first recruits from Waldo County, who boarded a special train for Camp Devens in Massachusetts. The *Belfast Republican Journal* observed that "while men, women, and children were struggling to keep back the blinding tears, they waved flags, hands, hats, and handkerchiefs as the cars left the station."

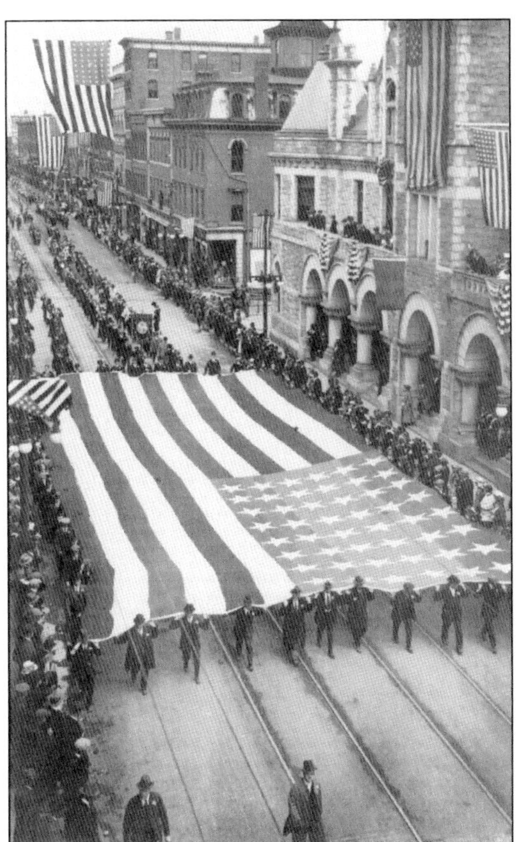

On May 8, 1917, Kennebec County held this patriotic parade on Water Street in Augusta, which was attended by thousands of area residents, some of whom carried this huge flag. Seven hundred people alone came from the adjacent community of Hallowell, including city officials, the fire department, Civil War veterans, shoe factory workers, and schoolchildren.

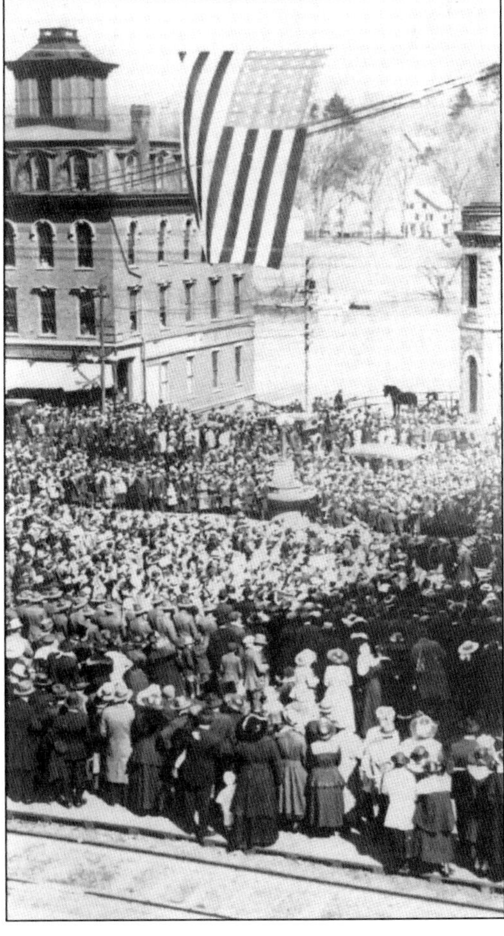

Augusta's May 8, 1917, parade attracted 10,000 participants and stretched three miles long. This huge crowd lined Water Street to witness, in the words of the *Kennebec Journal* for May 9, 1917, "sturdy lads and comely maidens marching with the flag above them, buoyant in spirit and step and knowing full well that the day might soon come when great burdens would be placed on them."

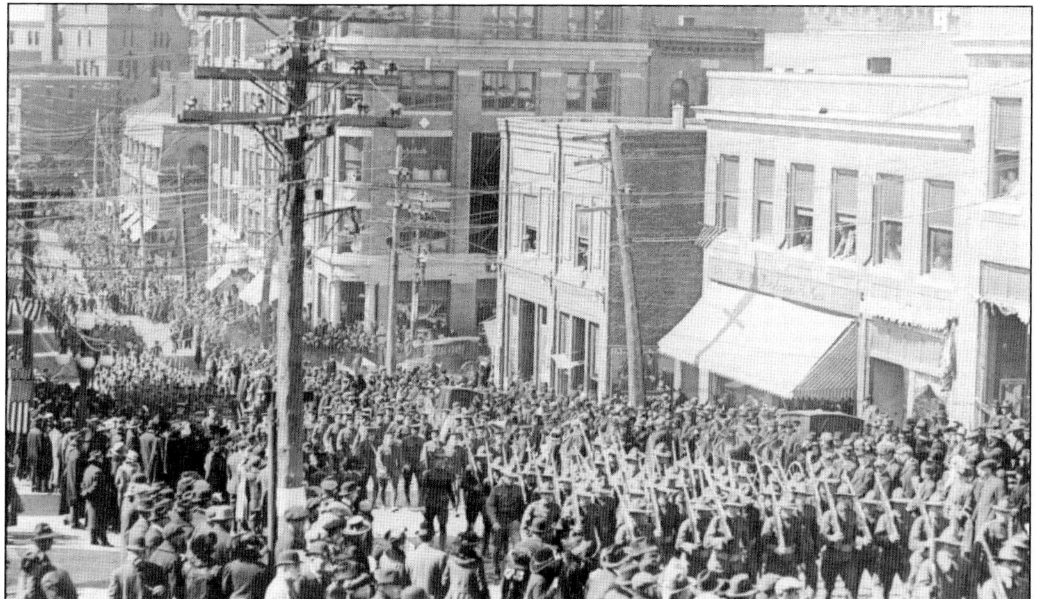

On the eve of America's entrance into the war, Bangor staged a massive parade on April 4, 1917. The procession was led by Governor Milliken and featured National Guard units from Bangor, Augusta, and Dexter. Here, guardsmen march up State Street to Broadway in what the *Bangor Daily News* for April 5, 1917, called "a patriotic demonstration on a scale of magnitude which has never been equaled in Eastern Maine."

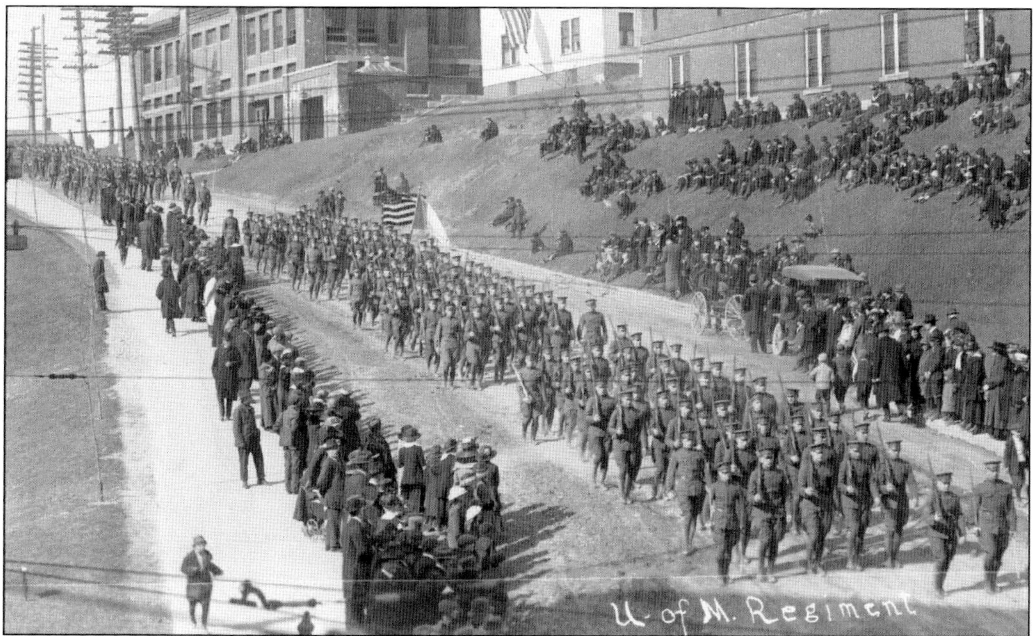

Since its founding in 1865, the University of Maine had offered military instruction through its student cadet program. As World War I approached, cadets received National Guard training and were ready to participate in Bangor's April 4, 1917, parade. Here, the university regiment marches down Park Street. The next day, the *Bangor Daily News* commented, "The splendid showing of the University of Maine was the subject of much favorable comment."

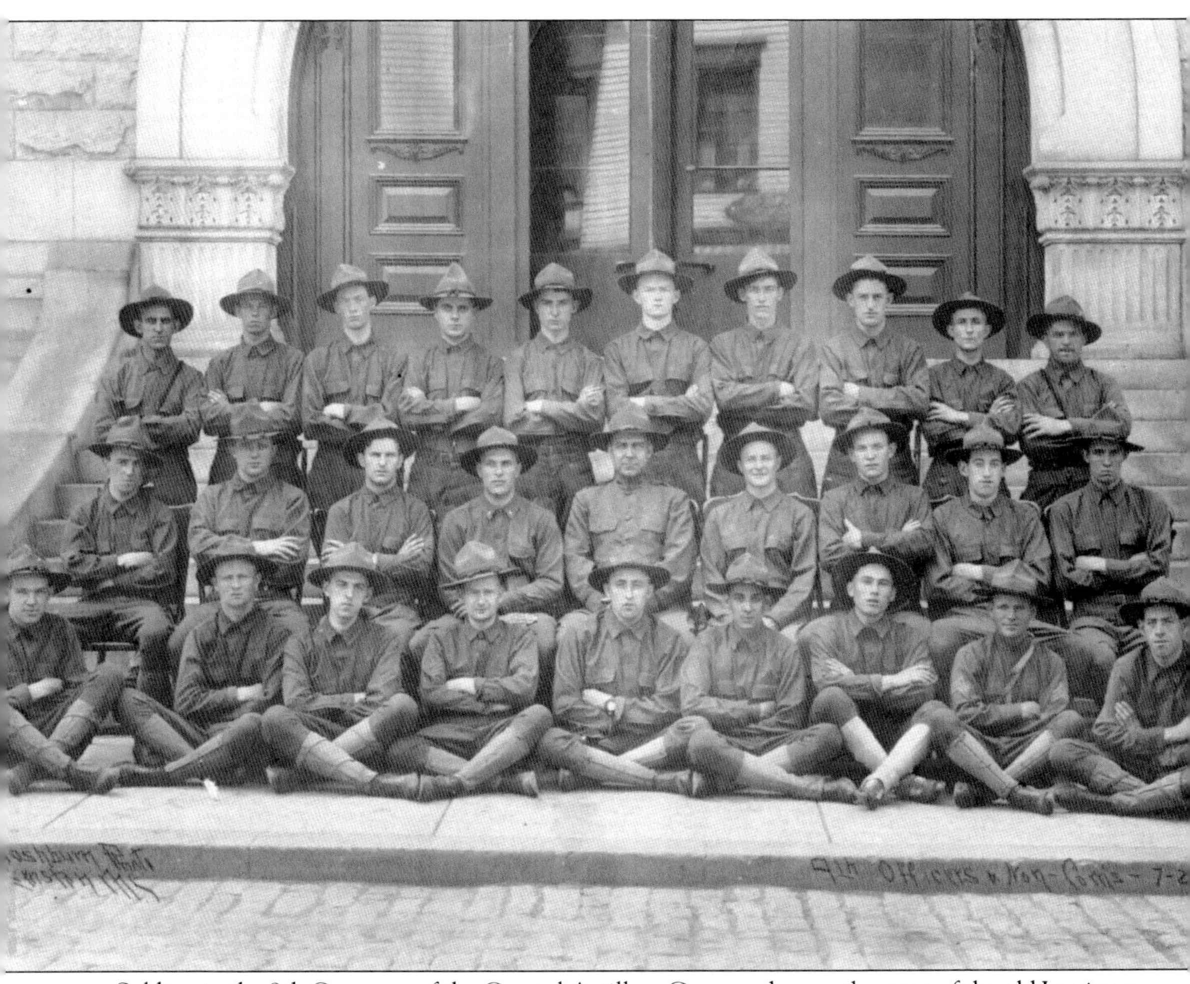

Soldiers in the 9th Company of the Coastal Artillery Corps gather on the steps of the old Lewiston Post Office on July 25, 1917. Companies throughout Lewiston and Auburn marched and drilled, with many soldiers noticeably without uniforms or their full equipment. The *Lewiston Evening Journal* appealed to the citizens of both communities, asking for residents to donate to a company mess fund that would provide such occasional extras as pie or fruit for the soldiers. Other cities throughout the state conducted similar fundraising for the units based in their communities. Two days after this photograph was taken, the company boarded a train to Portland. As the *Journal* noted, "For the first time since 1861, there departed from the city a body of young men who, in all human probability, are going straight to the battlefield, and some of whom will not return." (LePage.)

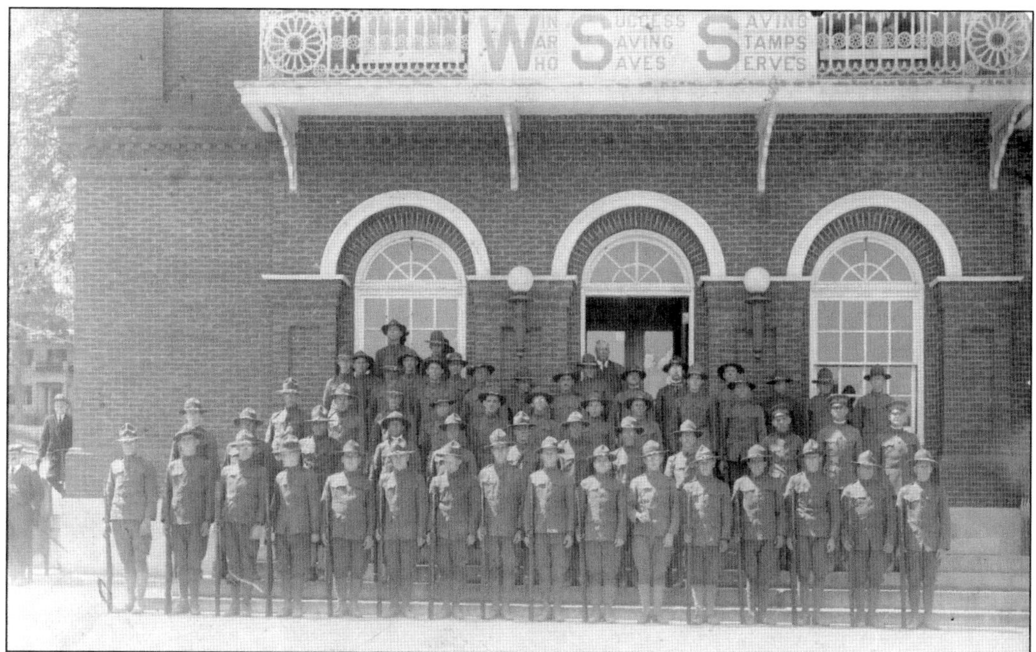

Waldo County soldiers stand proudly with their rifles in front of the US Custom House and Post Office in the center of Belfast. Above them hangs a large sign urging the public to buy War Savings Stamps to help the government to finance the war. A total of 55 Waldo County men lost their lives in the war. A bridge in Belfast was dedicated to their memory in 1921.

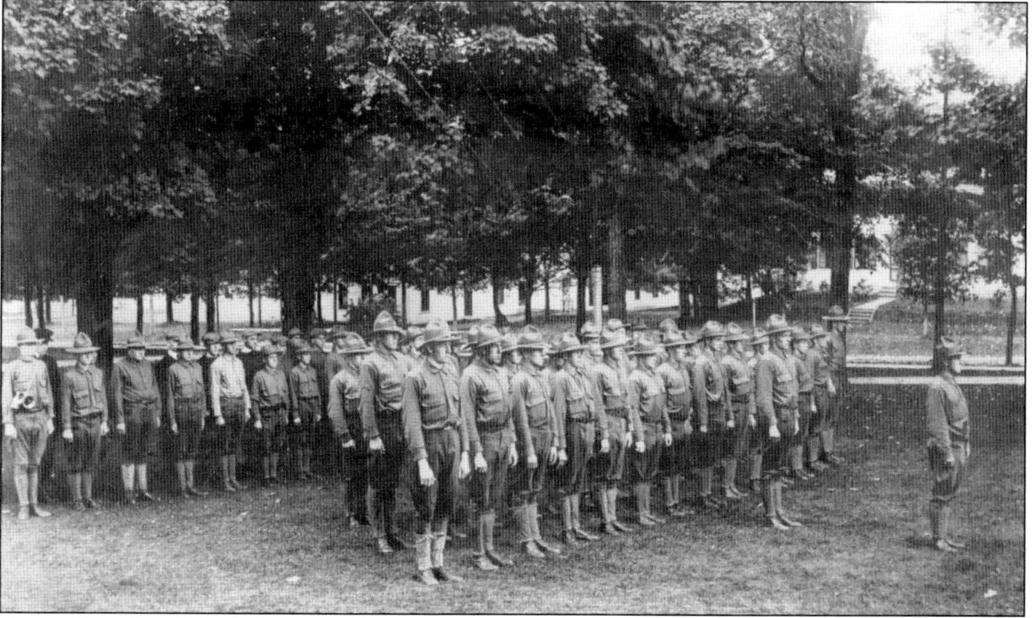

A company of cadets at Kents Hill School in Readfield stands at attention on the campus grounds. When the war broke out, students at many college preparatory and boarding schools formed volunteer cadet companies that would drill and study tactics. School administrators at some institutions allowed for credit to be given to those who participated and eventually enrolled in a unit that was called up. (LePage.)

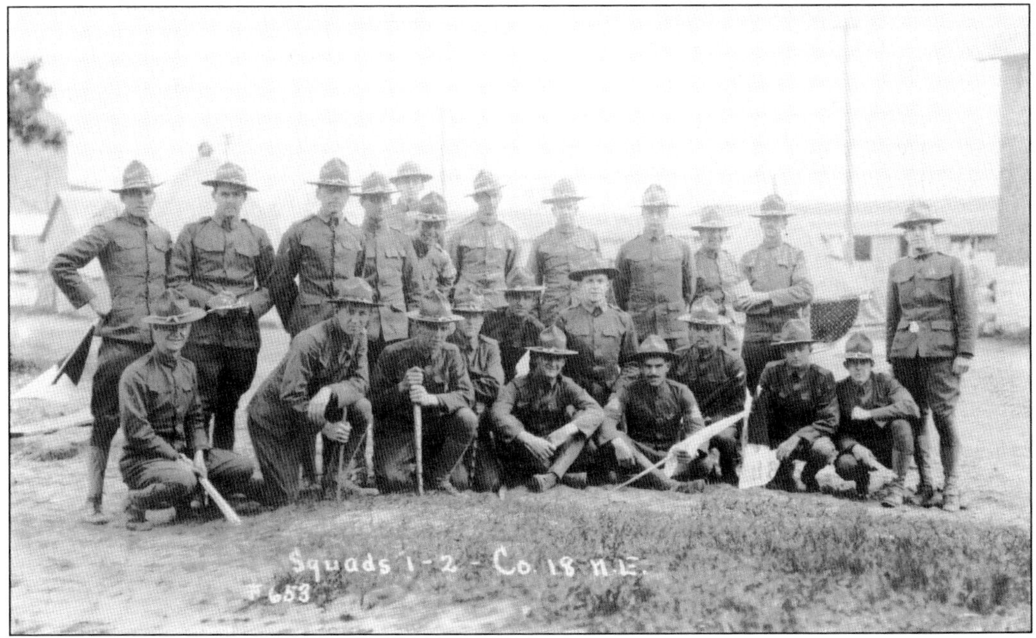

This June 1917 photograph shows a group of soldiers undergoing training at the National Army Officer Candidate School in Plattsburg, New York. One of the men pictured here is of French Canadian descent from Maine, for he wrote a message in French to Celanire Bourque of Waterville describing his Signal Corps classes.

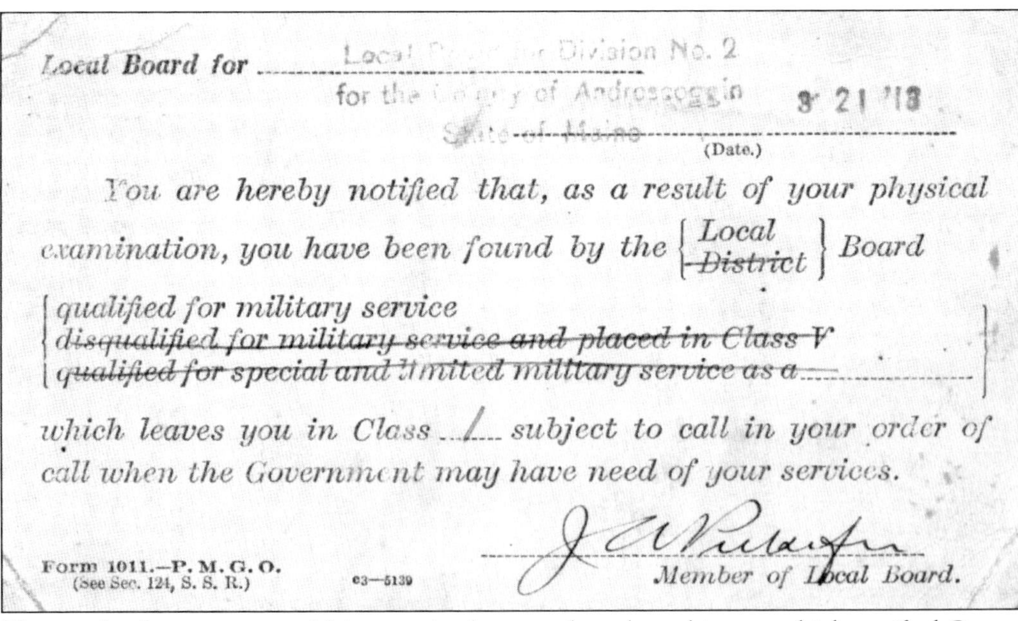

Local Board for Division No. 2 for the ... of Androscoggin ~~State of Maine~~ 8 21 '18
(Date.)

You are hereby notified that, as a result of your physical examination, you have been found by the {*Local* ~~*District*~~} *Board*

{*qualified for military service*
~~*disqualified for military service and placed in Class V*~~
~~*qualified for special and limited military service as a*~~ }

which leaves you in Class 1 *subject to call in your order of call when the Government may have need of your services.*

Form 1011.—P. M. G. O.
(See Sec. 124, S. S. R.)
63—5139

Member of Local Board.

Thousands of young men in Maine received postcards such as this one, which notified George S. Thompson of Livermore that he had passed his physical examination and was qualified for military service. Local draft boards informed recipients that "the Government may have need of your service."

Three

PARADES, RALLIES, AND CIVILIAN SUPPORT

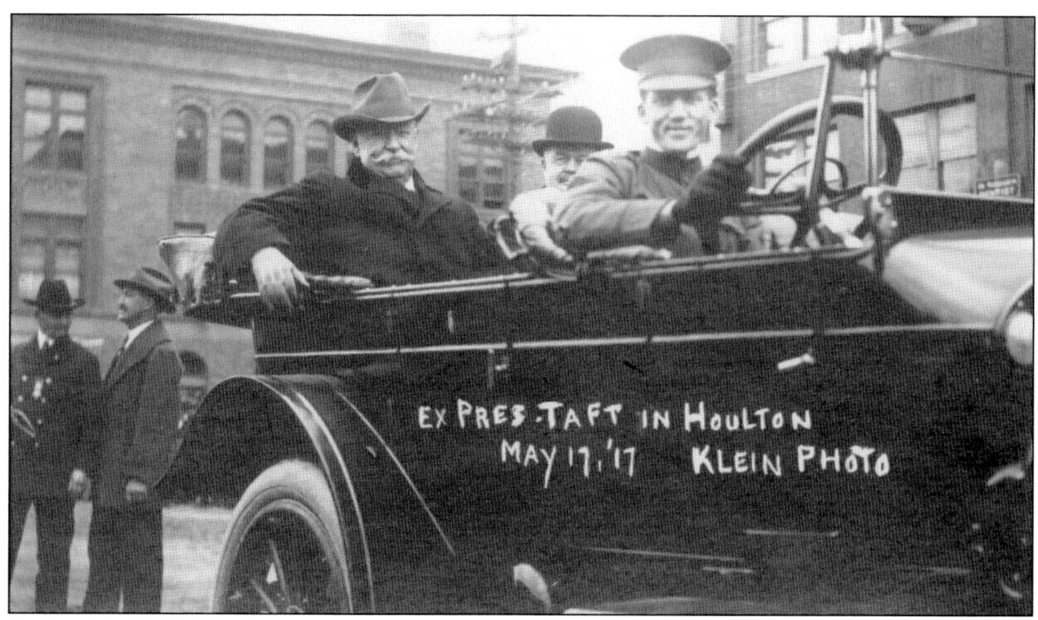

On May 17, 1917, the Bangor & Aroostook Railroad brought former president William Howard Taft to Houlton, the county seat of Maine's northern potato growing region. Touring the town in an open car, Taft urged Aroostook County farmers to support the war effort through increased food production. He delivered this message on behalf of his successor, Pres. Woodrow Wilson.

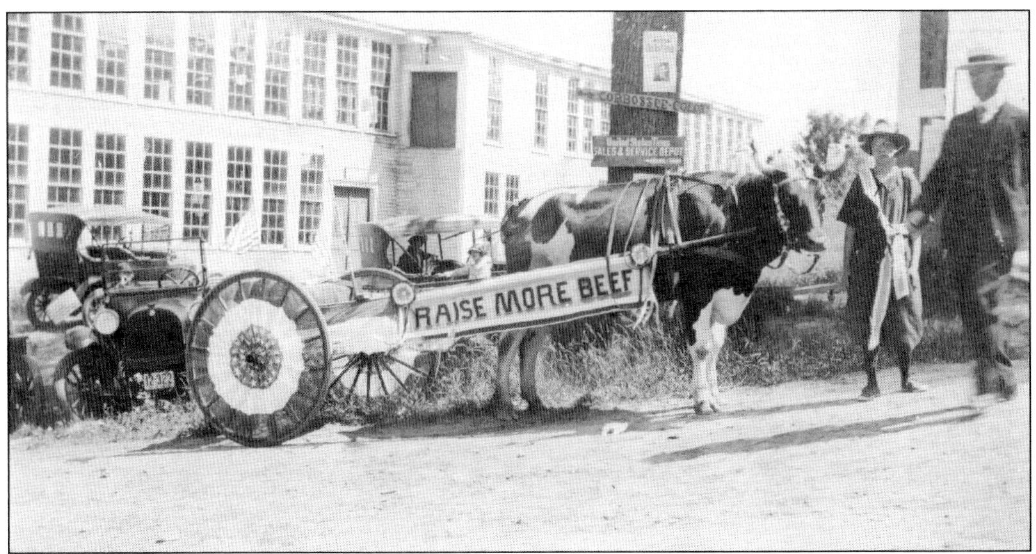

This July 4, 1918, float in Monmouth is right to the point, perhaps to the dismay of the beast of burden. Food supplies were an important consideration for the sake of the military and the home front. State, civic, and agricultural officials encouraged farmers to raise as much food as possible and even asked textile mills with spare land to make it available for agricultural production.

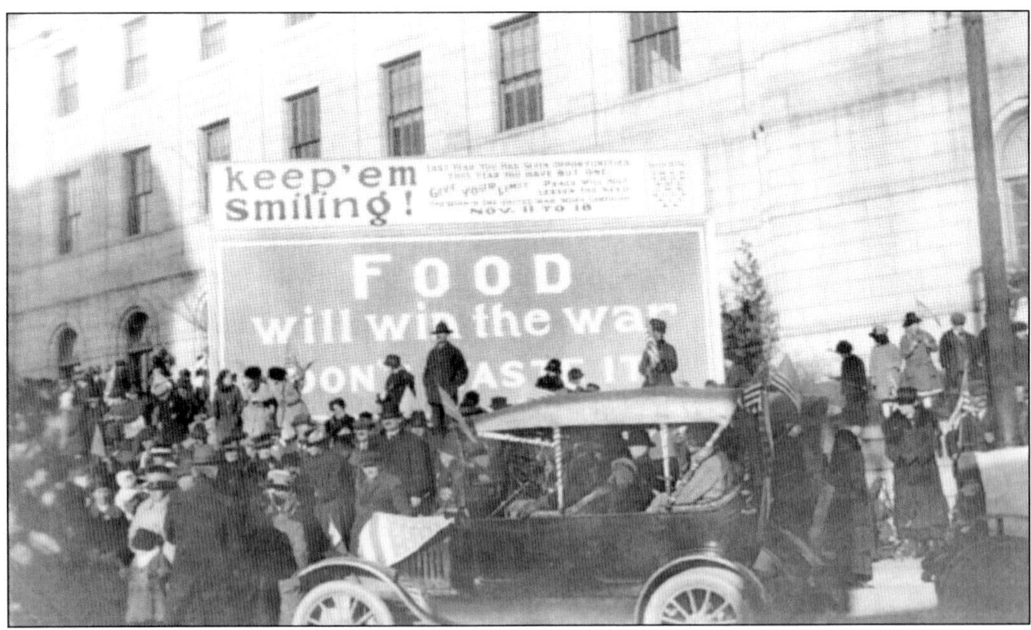

At a 1918 rally in front of the Bangor post office, a banner proclaims a familiar World War I slogan: "Food will win the war. Don't waste it." Throughout the war, the federal government conducted a highly successful campaign to engage the public to ration wheat, sugar, and meat, consume less food, and plant home Victory Gardens. At the same time, farmers were encouraged to grow more wheat and livestock. (Shaw.)

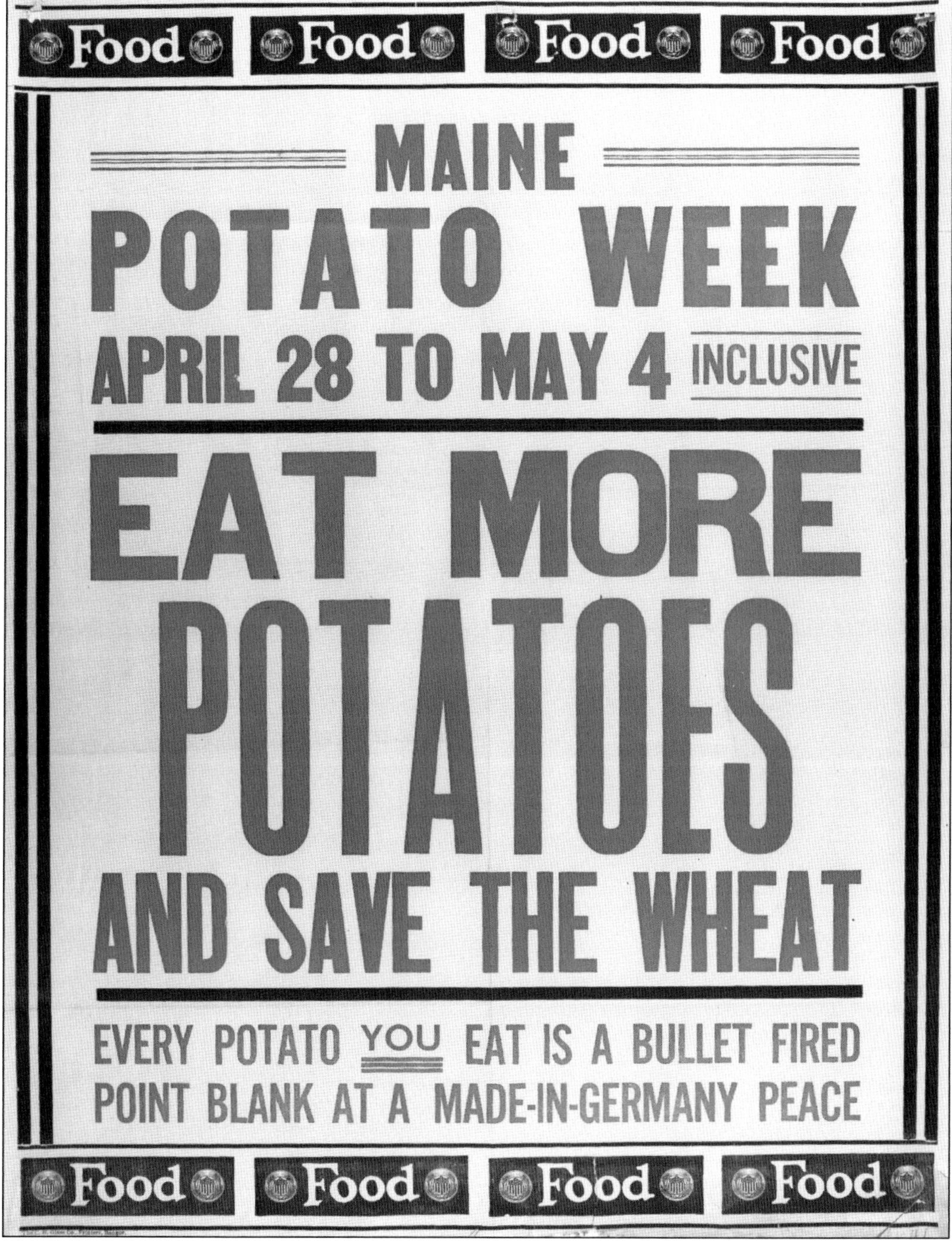

Throughout World War I, Maine looked to its largest and most northern county, Aroostook, as a major source of potatoes. In the first months of the war, Aroostook potatoes were sent to Belgium to help relieve starvation. By 1917, a total of 52,445 acres of potatoes were being grown in the county, a 27 percent increase over the previous year. Maine Potato Week was celebrated in 1918 to encourage Mainers to "eat more potatoes and save the wheat" for the troops. (MHS.)

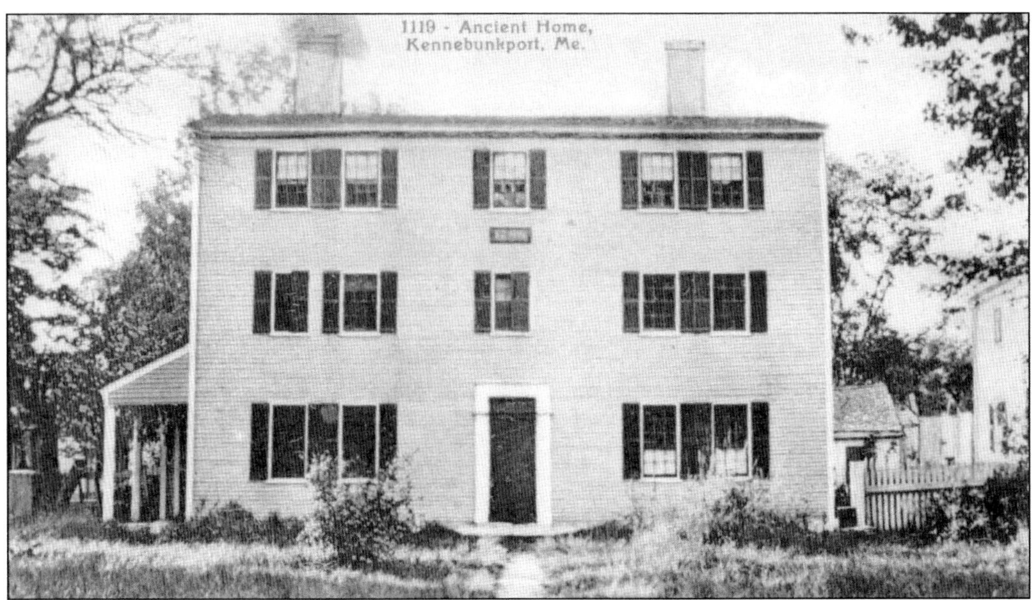

In May 1917, a Red Cross auxiliary was formed in Kennebunkport, and Ernestine Burrage was elected president. By summer, the auxiliary had grown to 130 members, and Ernestine invited the group to use her guesthouse "Tory Chimneys" as its headquarters. Local women met here on Tuesdays and Fridays to make bandages and knit socks for the troops.

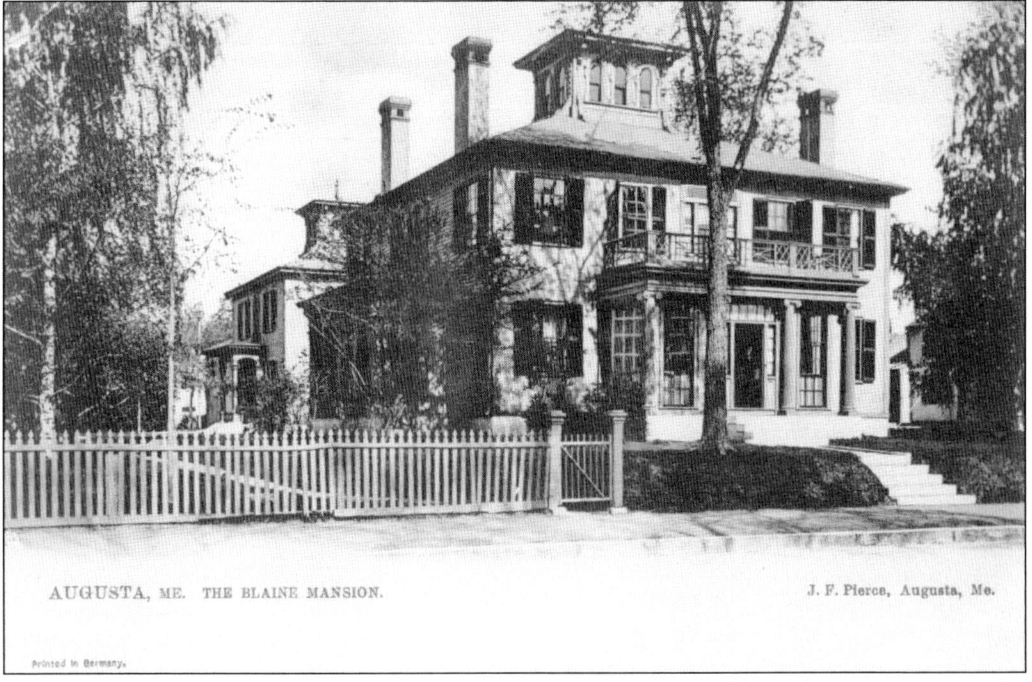

In March 1917, Maine formed the Committee of One Hundred on Public Safety to coordinate the state's war activities. That month, James G. Blaine's grandson Walker Blaine Beale offered the committee the Blaine House in Augusta for its headquarters. After Lieutenant Beale was killed in action in France in 1918, his family gave the mansion to the state in his memory to serve as the home of Maine's governors.

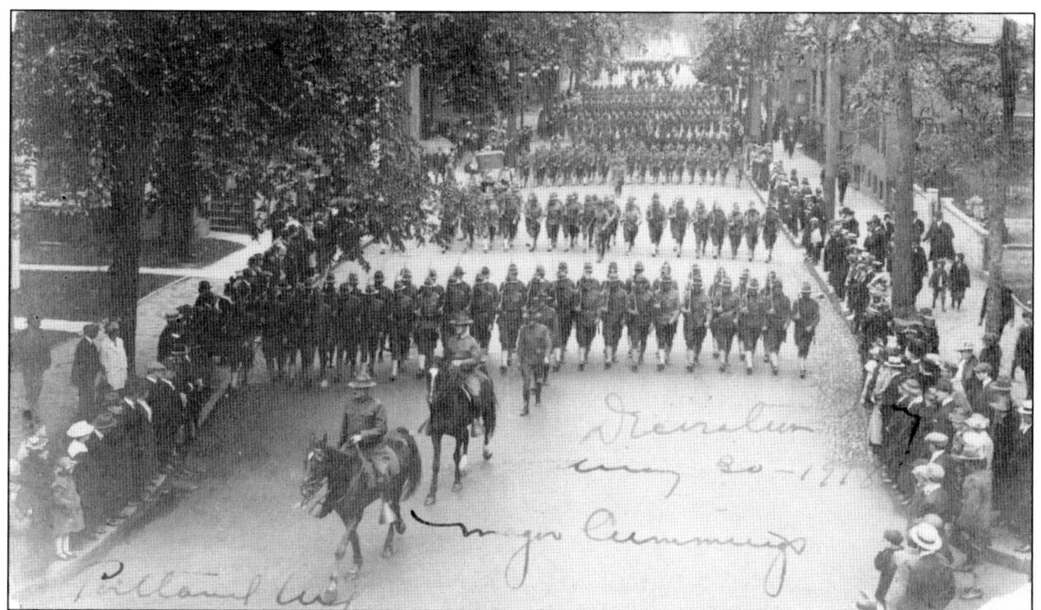

Portland observed Memorial Day, May 30, 1918, with a military parade on Cumberland Avenue. The troops in this photograph were members of the Coastal Artillery Corps that manned the city's harbor defenses. Their leader on horseback was Maj. Frank E. Cummings, a Westbrook native. The *Eastern Argus* commented, "This day is consecrated anew to thousands who have recently given their lives in the noblest cause for which America has fought."

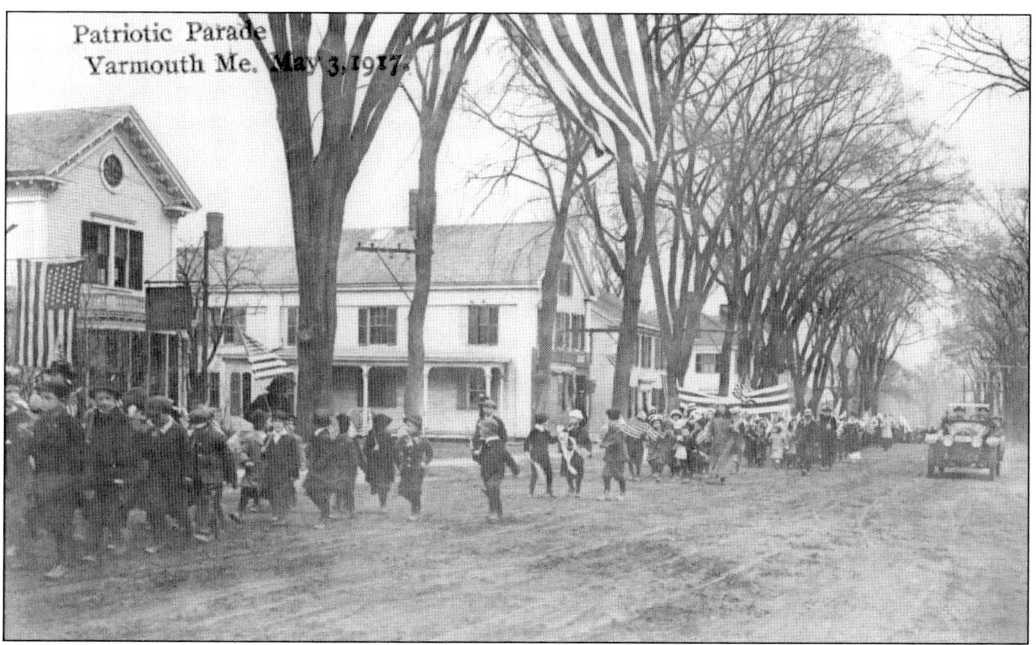

In the spring of 1917, patriotic parades were a common occurrence in small towns across Maine. On May 3, 1917, schoolchildren marched in this parade on Main Street in Yarmouth, a coastal manufacturing town of 2,000 people. Such events were inspired by Pres. Woodrow Wilson's and Gov. Carl E. Milliken's calls for broad public support for the war.

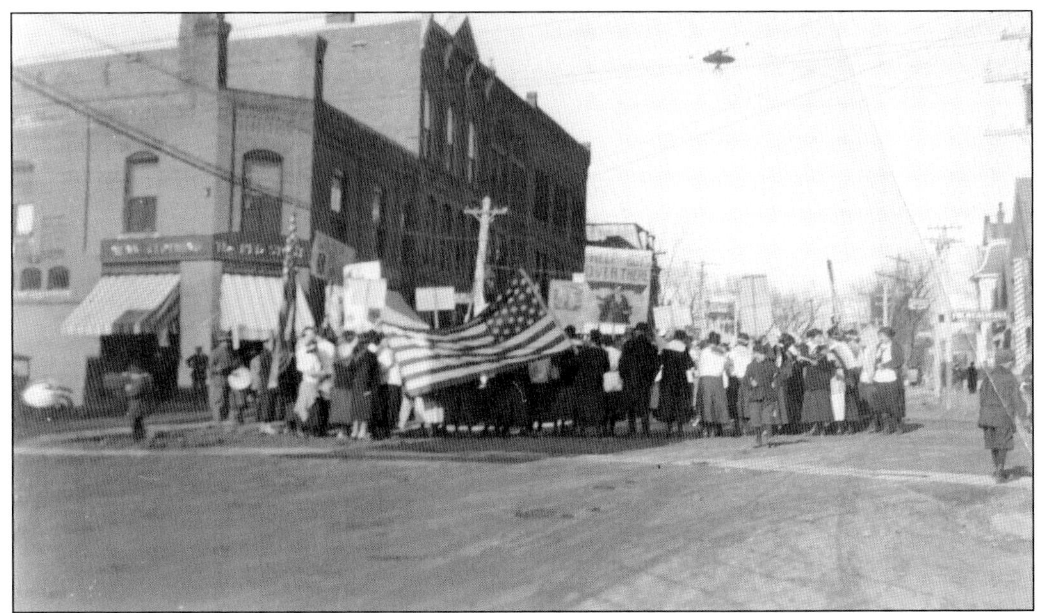

Citizens rally at the corner of Main Street and Broadway in Farmington, encouraging others to buy bonds and support the troops. A large contingency of female students from Farmington State Normal School are visible in the crowd. Students raised money at local fairs and other events for the Red Cross to send supplies overseas.

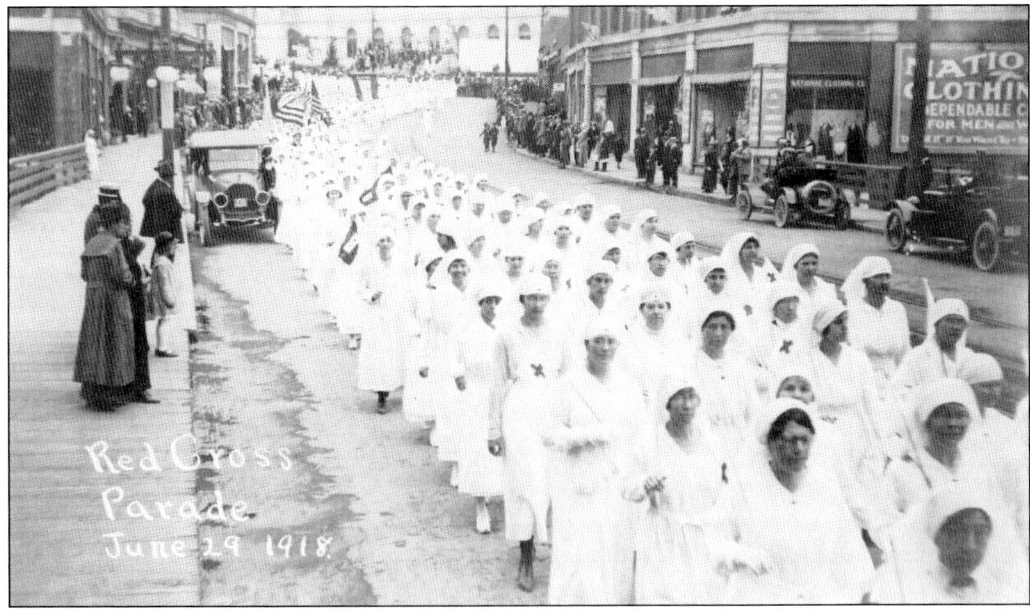

The work of the Red Cross was highlighted on June 29, 1918, when 1,200 local women paraded through the streets of Bangor in their white uniforms. Calling the event "a parade such as seldom if ever equaled," the *Bangor Daily News* reported on July 1, 1918, that the ladies marched "through crowded streets surrounded by thousands cheering them along the way."

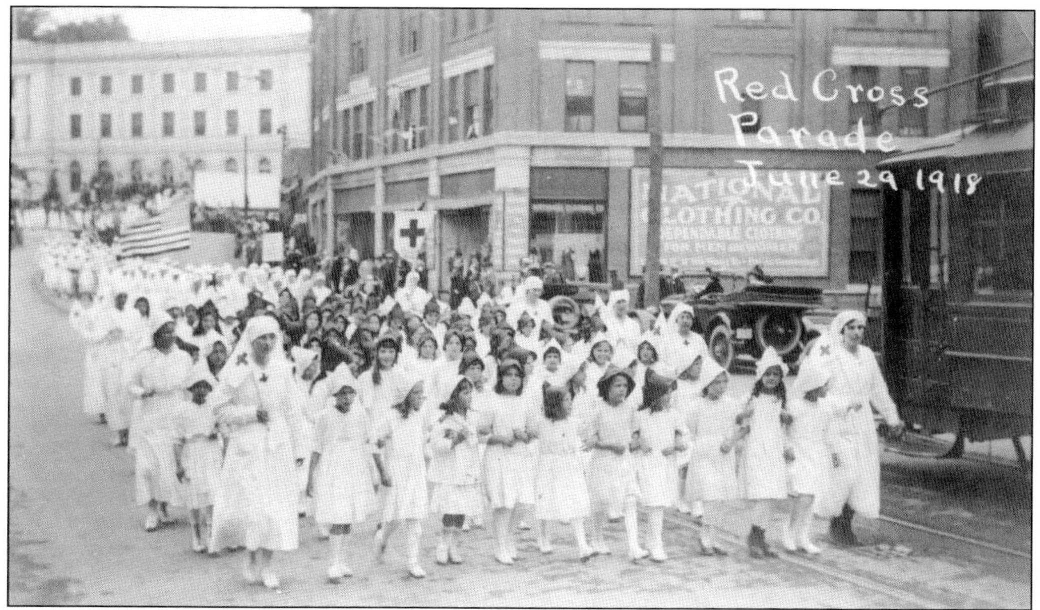

A headline in the July 1, 1918, *Bangor Daily News* declared that the "Red Cross Parade Astonished the Public by its Numbers and Superb Marching." According to the newspaper, the success of the parade was due in part to "scores of little girls all garbed like their elders in white caps and gowns." Bangor's Central Street is the setting for this photograph.

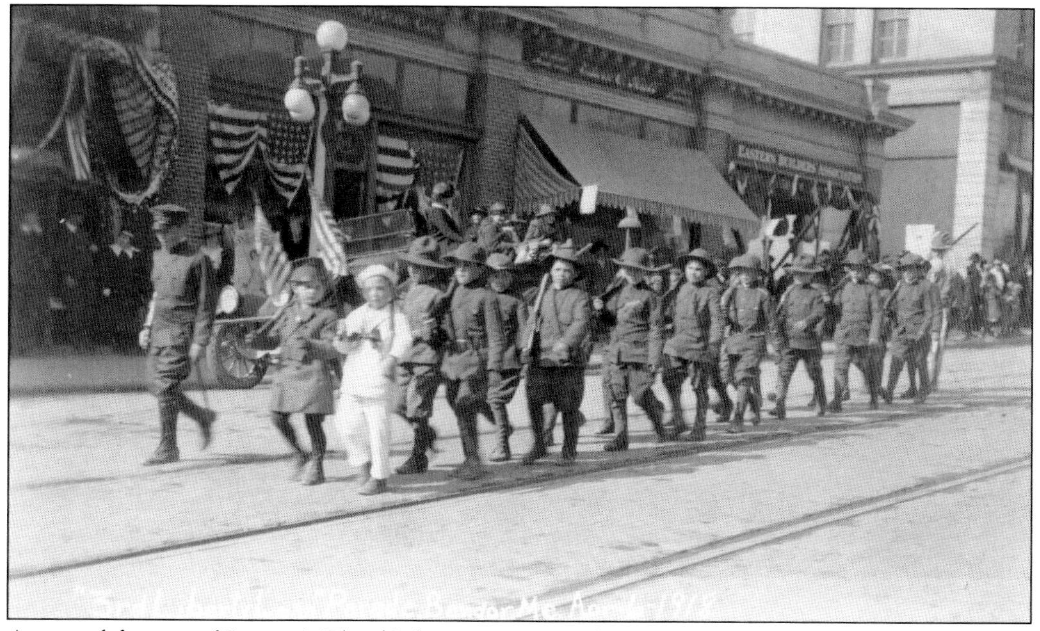

A special feature of Bangor's Third Liberty Loan parade on April 6, 1918, were the Boy Scouts who marched down Central Street in their military uniforms sporting toy rifles on their shoulders. When they marched in the June 29, 1918, Red Cross parade, they carried hoes and shovels to represent their volunteer work in Victory Gardens.

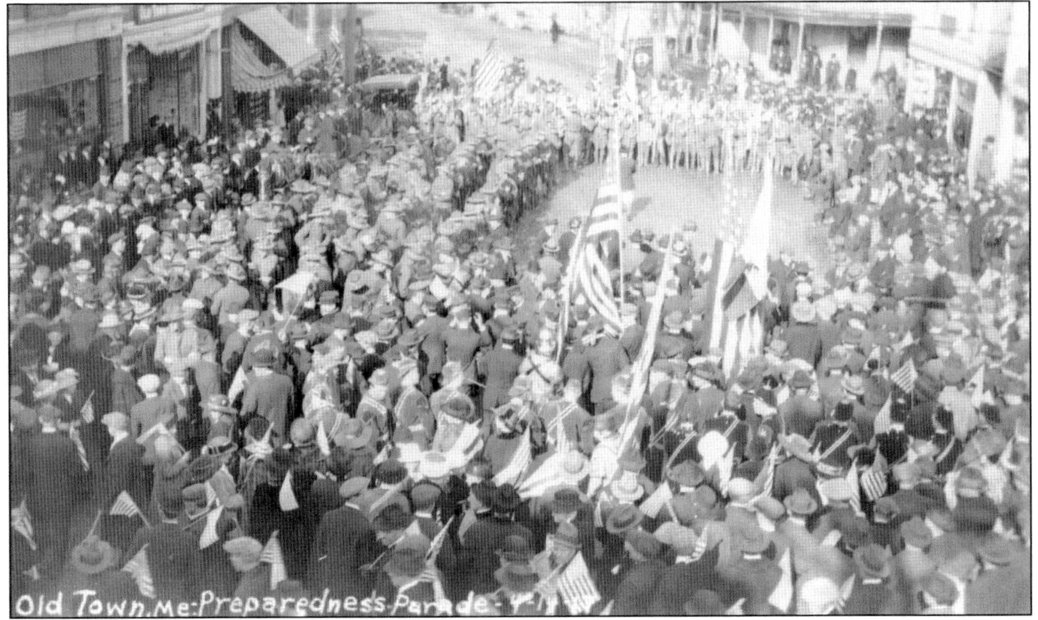

Many smaller communities staged impressive events in support of the war. As soon as war was declared, Old Town, population 6,950, started planning its April 14, 1917, preparedness parade. The day following the parade, the *Bangor Daily News* stated that "the patriotic demonstration was an unequaled success. Hundreds joined the parade, which was a mile long. When the parade started, the streets were crowded." (Libby.)

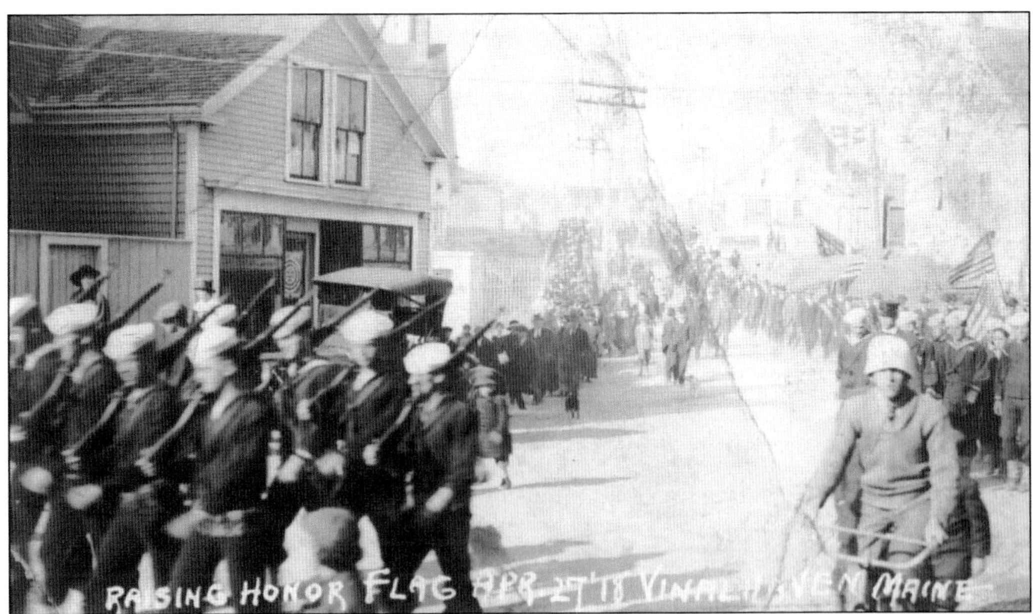

Naval reservists from the Rockland Naval Training Center march in a parade on Vinalhaven on April 27, 1918. The patriotic event was held to celebrate the town receiving an Honor Flag. Honor Flags were awarded to communities that met their quota in selling Liberty Bonds and stimulated a sense of competition among towns and cities throughout the country.

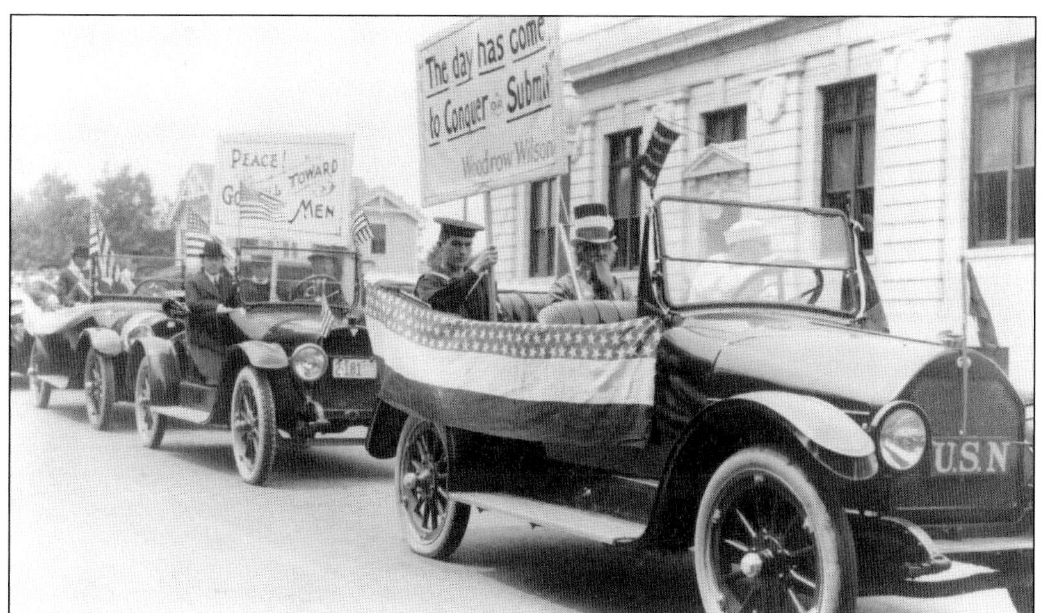

For its Fourth of July celebration in 1917, the Mount Desert resort town of Bar Harbor staged a large patriotic parade that included a line of decorated automobiles shown here passing the post office on Cottage Street. The Naval Reserve was represented by the car at the right carrying a local Uncle Sam named Joseph A. Stevens and a young sailor holding a sign declaring, "The Day has come to Conquer or Submit."

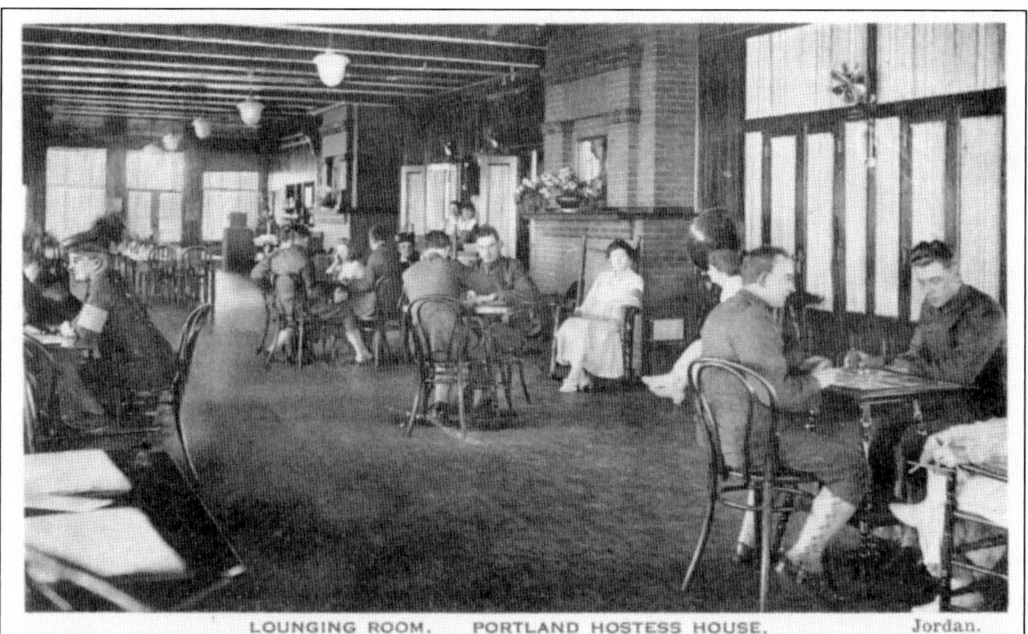

LOUNGING ROOM. PORTLAND HOSTESS HOUSE. Jordan.

During World War I, Portland Harbor was defended by five forts: Fort Williams, Fort Preble, Fort Levett, Fort Lyons, and Fort McKinley. These forts were manned by hundreds of members of the Coastal Artillery Corps. To support these soldiers, Portland opened a hostess house to provide such recreational activities as games, reading, dining, and dancing. The Portland Hostess House was a forerunner of the USO in World War II.

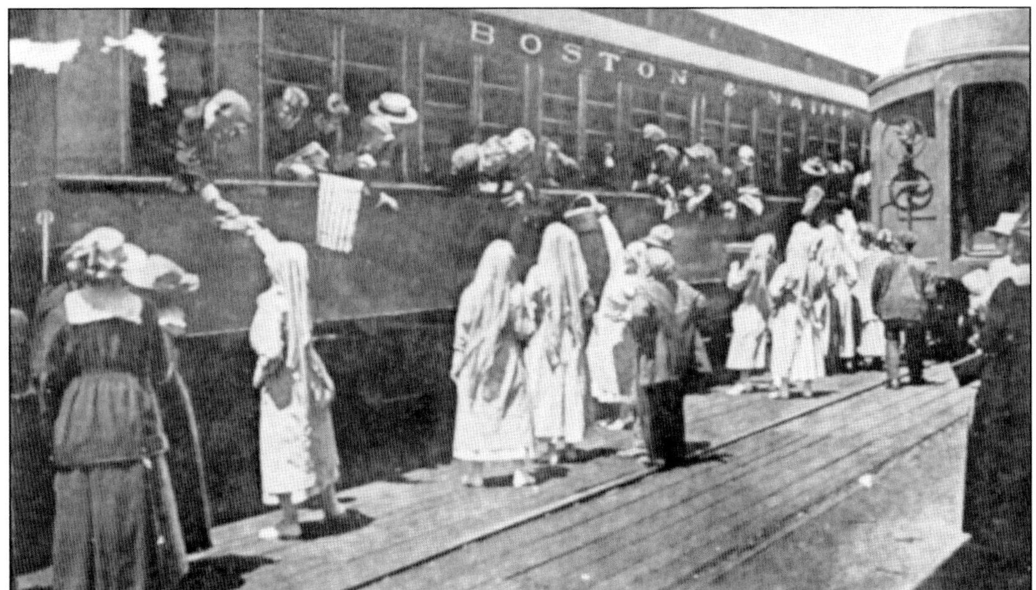

One of several activities of the Portland Chapter of the American Red Cross was to greet the troop trains stopping at Union Station. Young women in Red Cross uniforms stood on the station platform distributing sandwiches, fruit, candy, and cigarettes to the soldiers bound for training camps. During the war, Maine citizens donated $1.9 million to the Red Cross to support its military relief work.

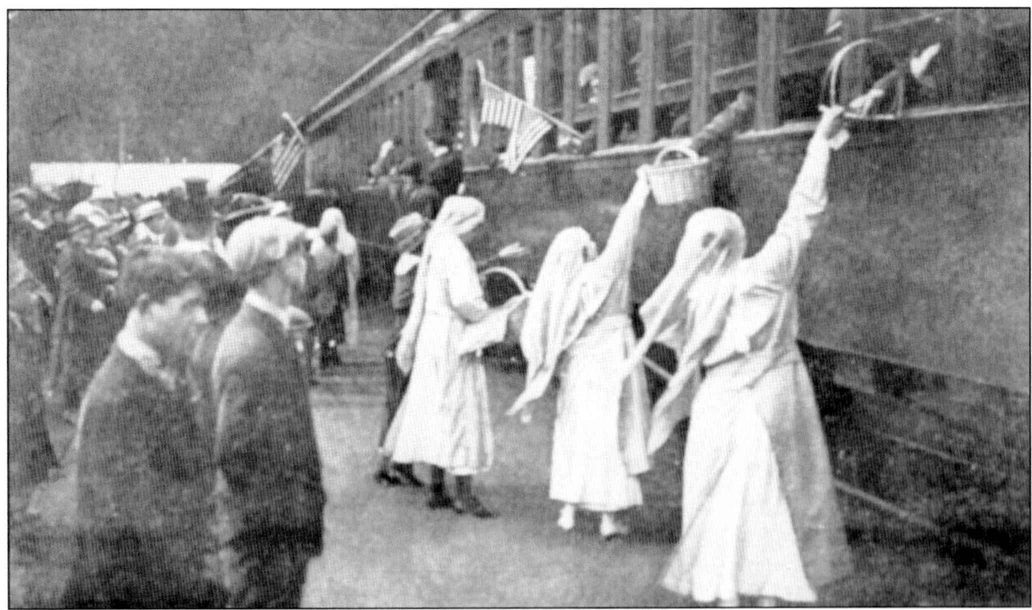

From its first meeting in February 1917, to the end of the war, the Portland Chapter of the American Red Cross grew to 30,000 members in Southern Maine. The money it received from memberships and donations sent nurses to France and purchased surgical dressings and other medical supplies for field hospitals.

Featuring blue stars in a white field with a red border, the service star flag was widely adopted in 1917 by the public and the government to symbolize those serving on active duty for their country. This postcard issued in 1918 by the First Baptist Church in Portland indicates that 65 members of the congregation were in military service.

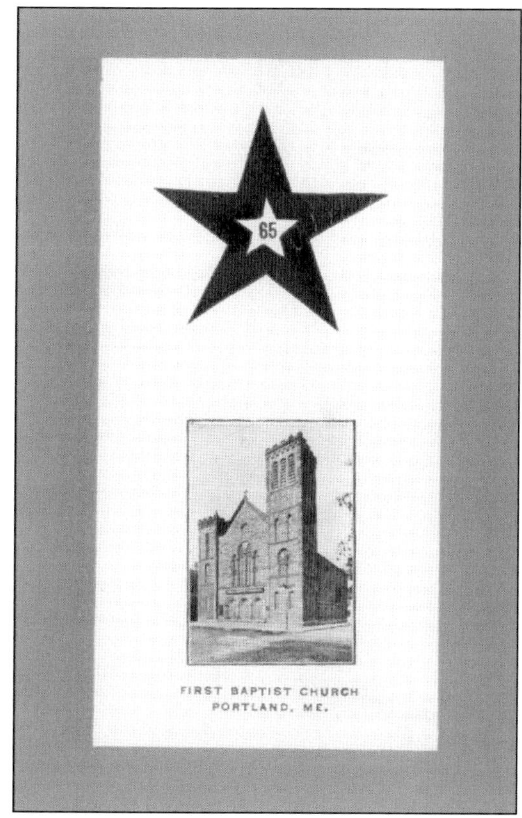

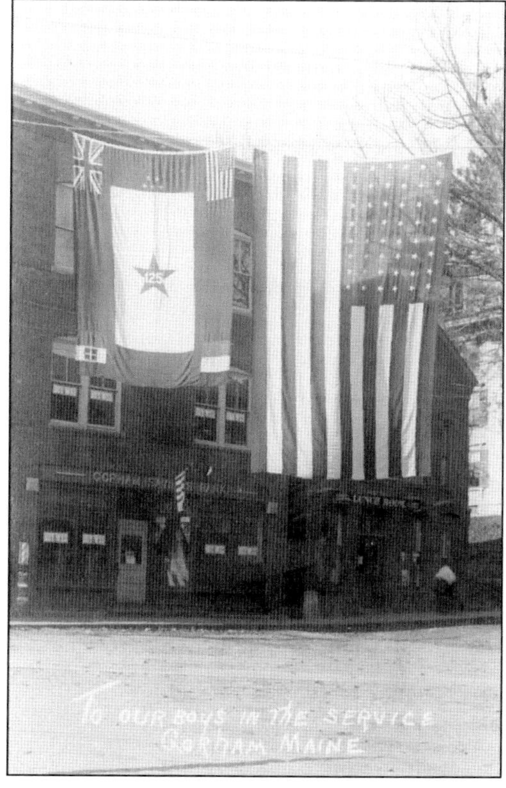

The town of Gorham proudly hung its large service star flag next to an American flag in the downtown business district. Gorham's flag displays a blue star indicating that 125 community members were on active service. Near the top are five gold stars representing servicemen who have died while on duty. The flags of America and its allies appear at the corners.

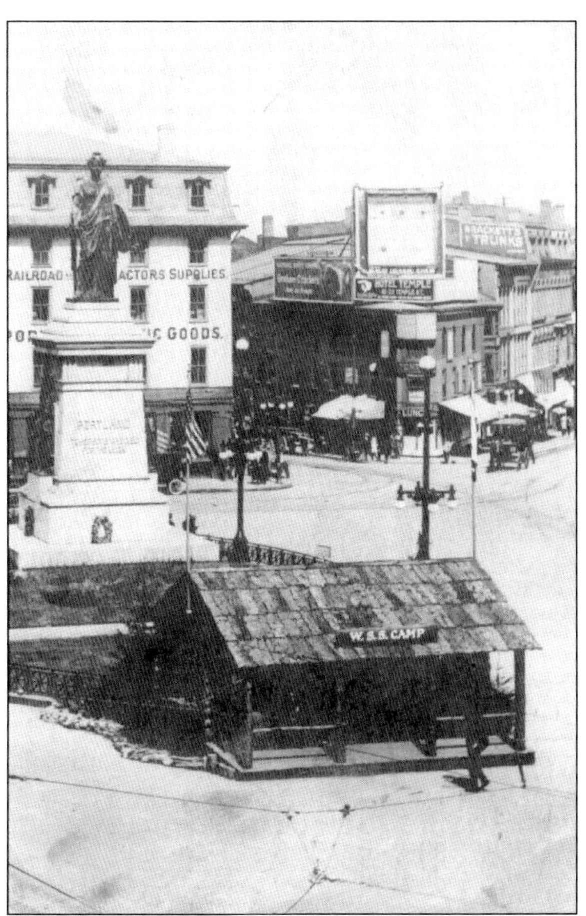

A picturesque log cabin in front of the Civil War statue in Portland's Monument Square served as the city's headquarters for the War Savings Stamp campaign that raised money to fund America's participation in World War I. So successful were bond and stamp drives across the state that by the end of the war, Mainers had purchased $118.4 million in bonds and nearly $8 million in stamps.

In September 1917, Congress authorized the sale of $2 billion in war savings stamps to help finance the war. In Maine, these stamps were aggressively marketed through banks, schools, thrift clubs, and workplaces. By the end of the conflict, Maine citizens had bought nearly $8 million in stamps, the equivalent of a $10 purchase for every man, woman, and child in the state.

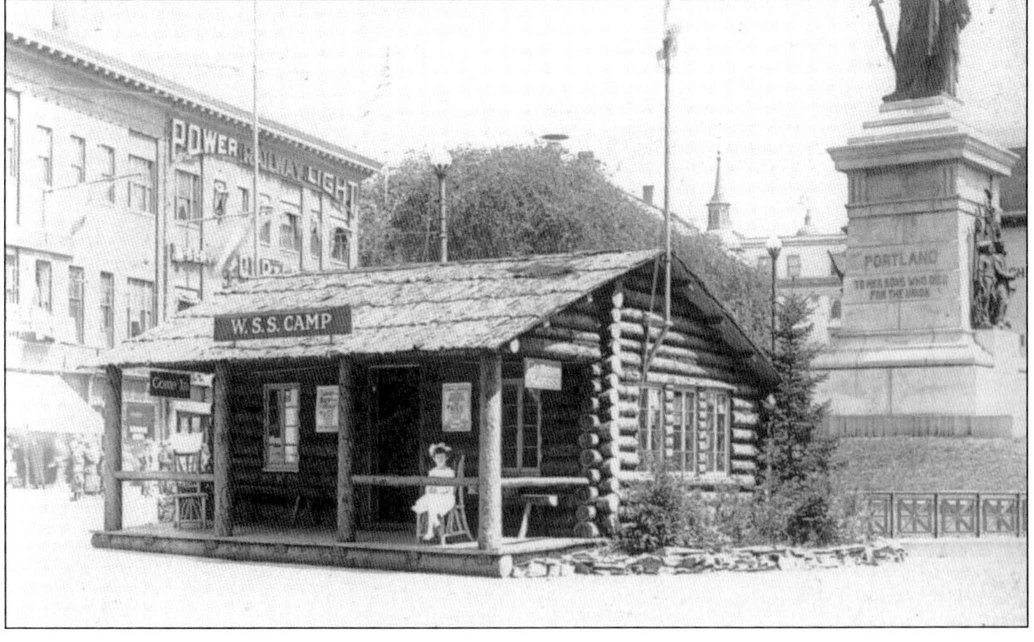

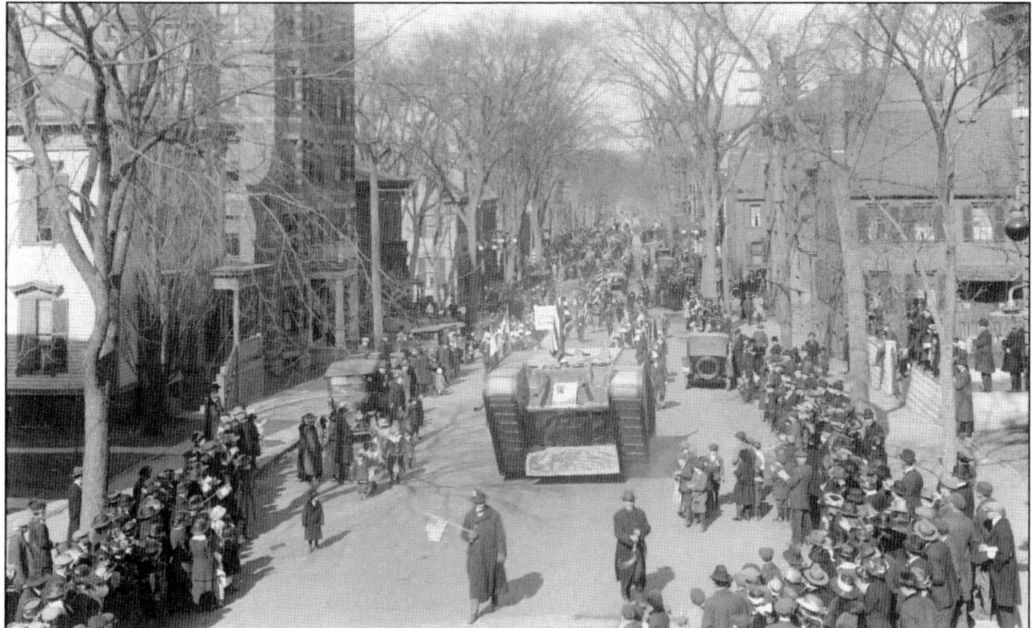

Parades such as this one on Cumberland Avenue were a popular means of promoting the sale of Liberty Bonds. The tank leading this parade displays a Liberty Loan poster on the front. During five campaigns spanning 1917 and 1918, Maine banks sold $118.4 million worth of bonds, and the state stood second to Connecticut in oversubscriptions in New England.

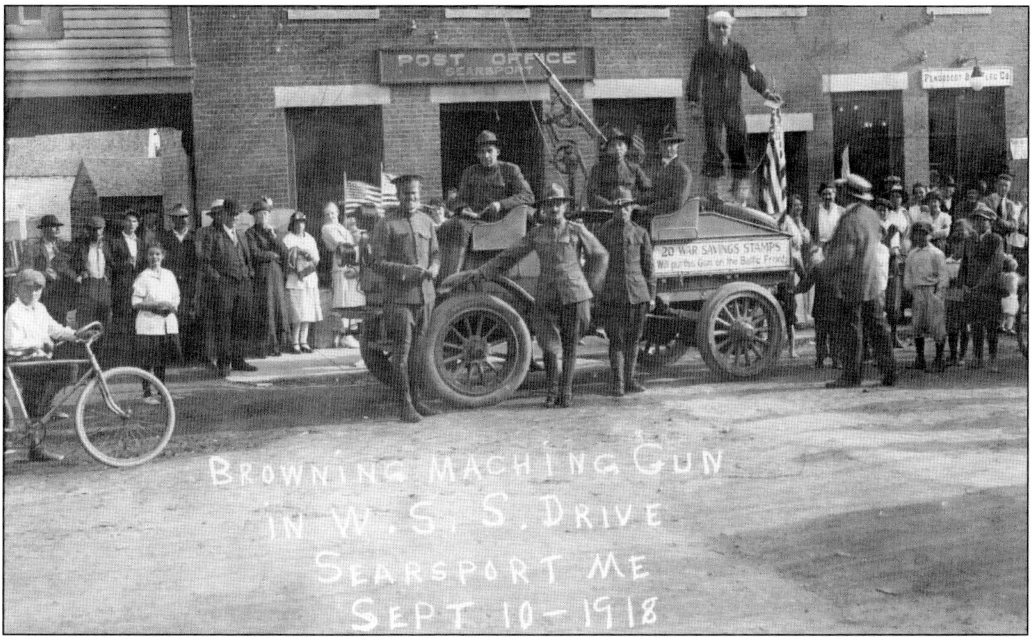

This Browning machine gun was exhibited in Searsport by soldiers from Fort Preble in South Portland in September 1918. Displays of US military equipment of all types were brought to communities throughout the country in order to raise money for the war effort. Similar traveling demonstrations of captured German "war relics" such as cannons, mortars, and machine guns were used to sell Liberty Loan bonds.

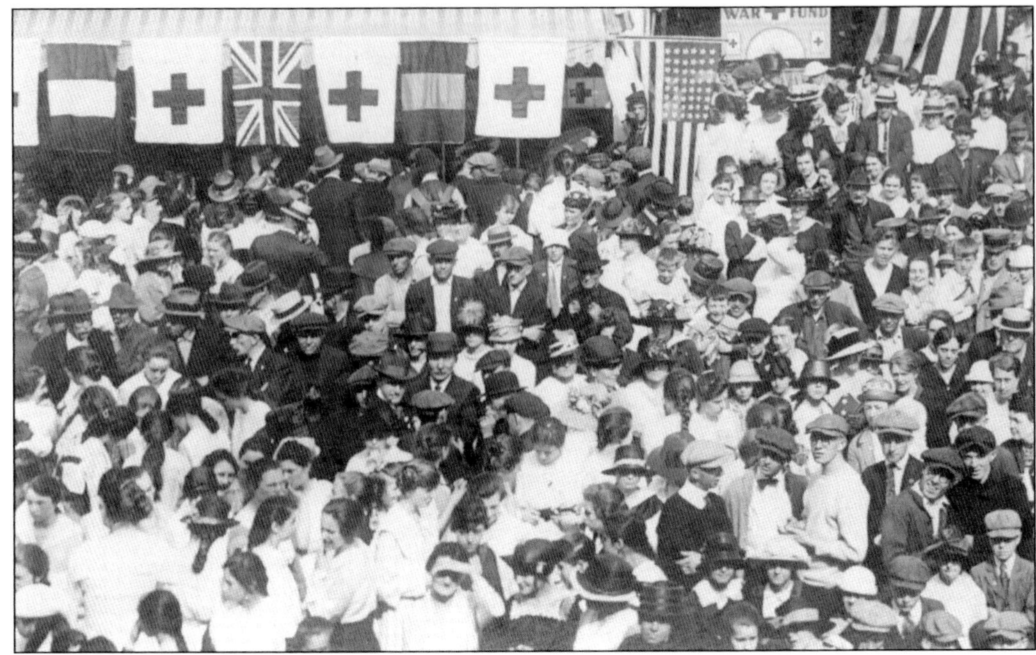

A large crowd gathered for a Red Cross rally in downtown Skowhegan in 1917. The town was home to Company E of the 2nd Maine, which became part of the 103rd Regiment of the 26th Yankee Division. Company E's captain, Roy L. Marston, who would later be promoted to lieutenant colonel, was the first National Guard officer to arrive in France in 1917 and had charge of landing the division.

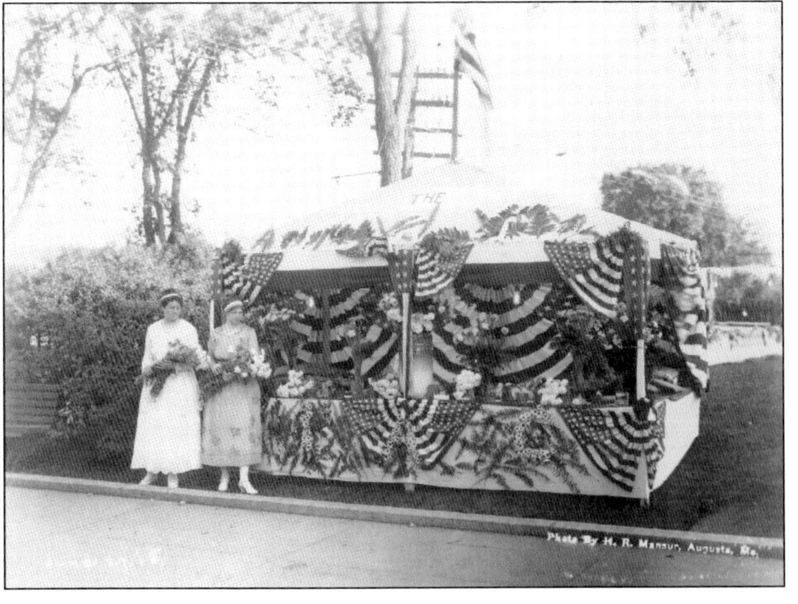

These ladies are selling flowers at a floral booth that was part of a patriotic festival held on the State House grounds in Augusta on June 27, 1918. Sponsored by State House Associates, the fair attracted more than 3,000 people who bought items that supported the purchase of surgical dressings for the troops by the American Red Cross. (MSM.)

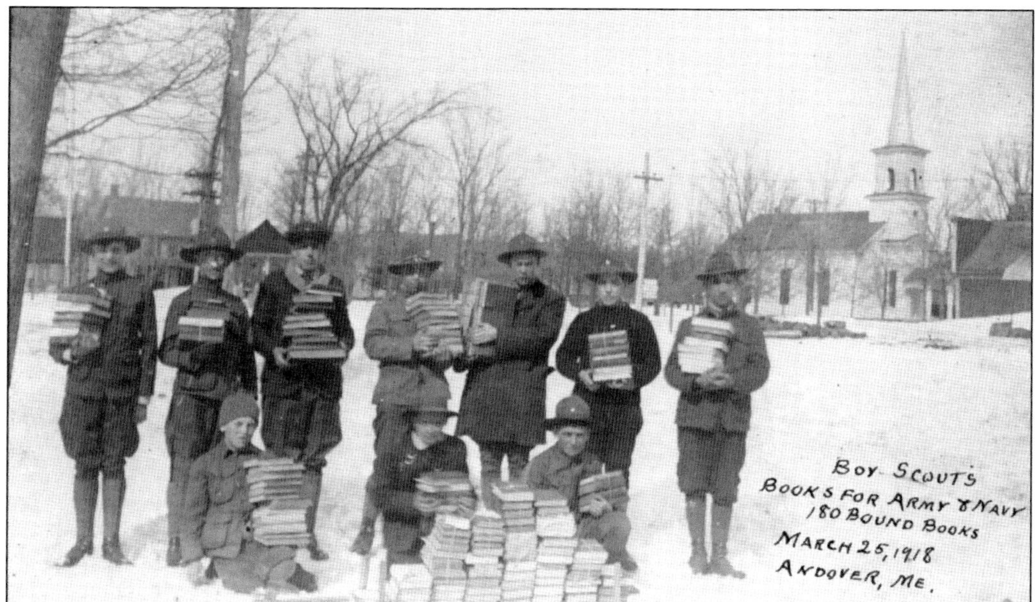

The Boy Scouts of America were a strong partner in raising money and material for the war effort. Nationally, the Scouts sold over $350 million in bonds and war savings stamps, organized coastal patrols, planted gardens, and collected aluminum and other needed materials. This troop from Andover collected 180 books, which were given to the local library and subsequently sent to sailors and soldiers abroad for their enjoyment. (Libby.)

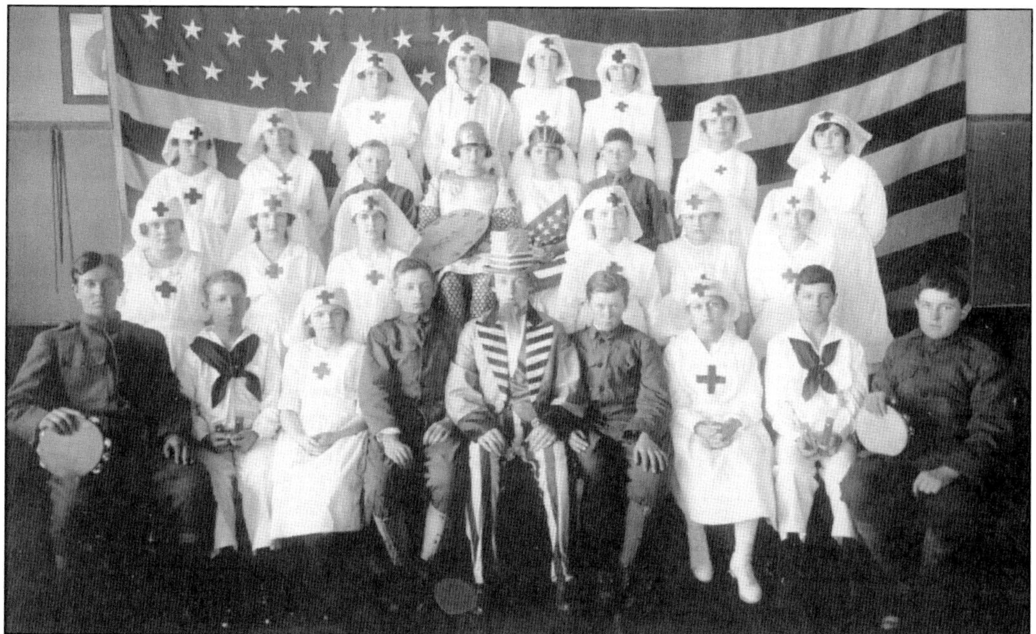

Patriotic fervor for the war extended into the classroom, as reflected by this school group in Hallowell seated in front of a large American flag. A youthful Uncle Sam is surrounded by equally young soldiers, sailors, and Red Cross girls in outfits that demonstrated their mothers' sewing skills. Known for its granite quarries and shoe factories, Hallowell sent 121 servicemen to the war. (HFL.)

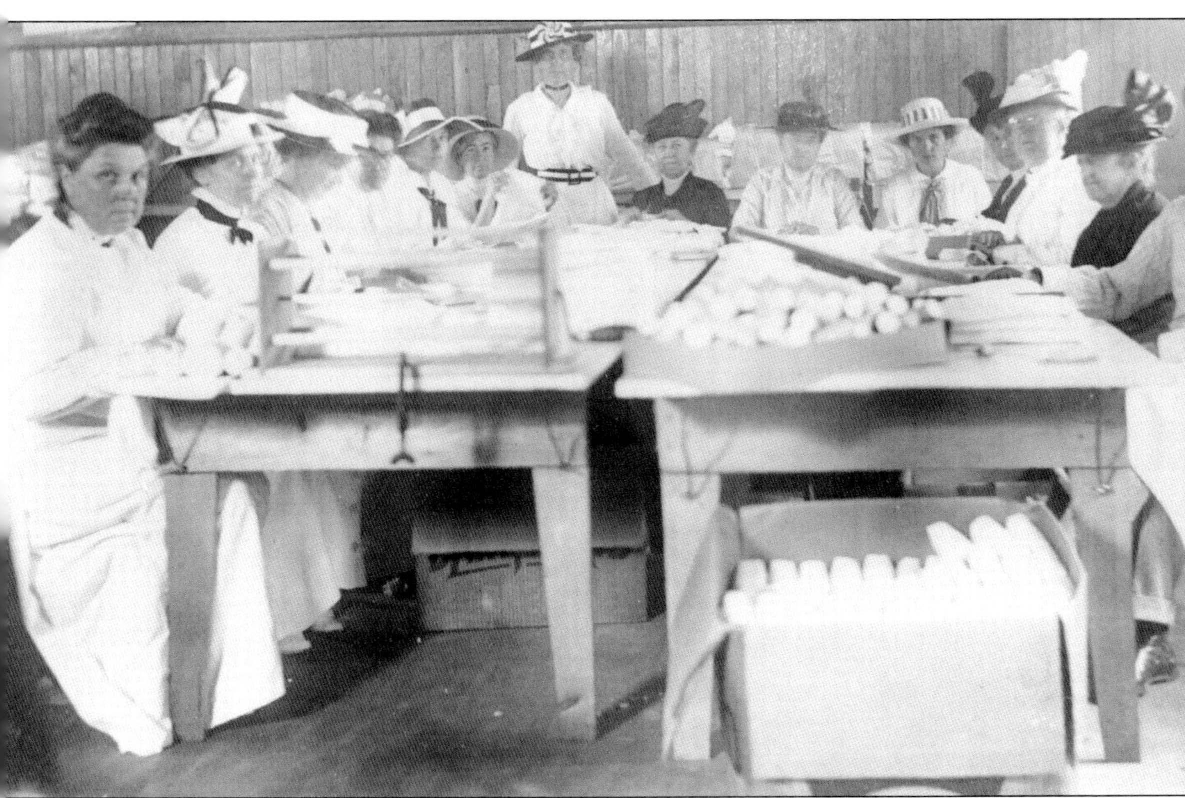

As early as 1915, Seal Harbor's summer and permanent residents were meeting at the local fire station to roll bandages and organize medical supplies for shipment to France. On this typical morning, 14 individuals from the community gathered to prepare and pack surgical dressings for French hospitals. Between October 1917 and June 1918, Seal Harbor also sent many knitted items and articles of clothing overseas.

Four

War Industries

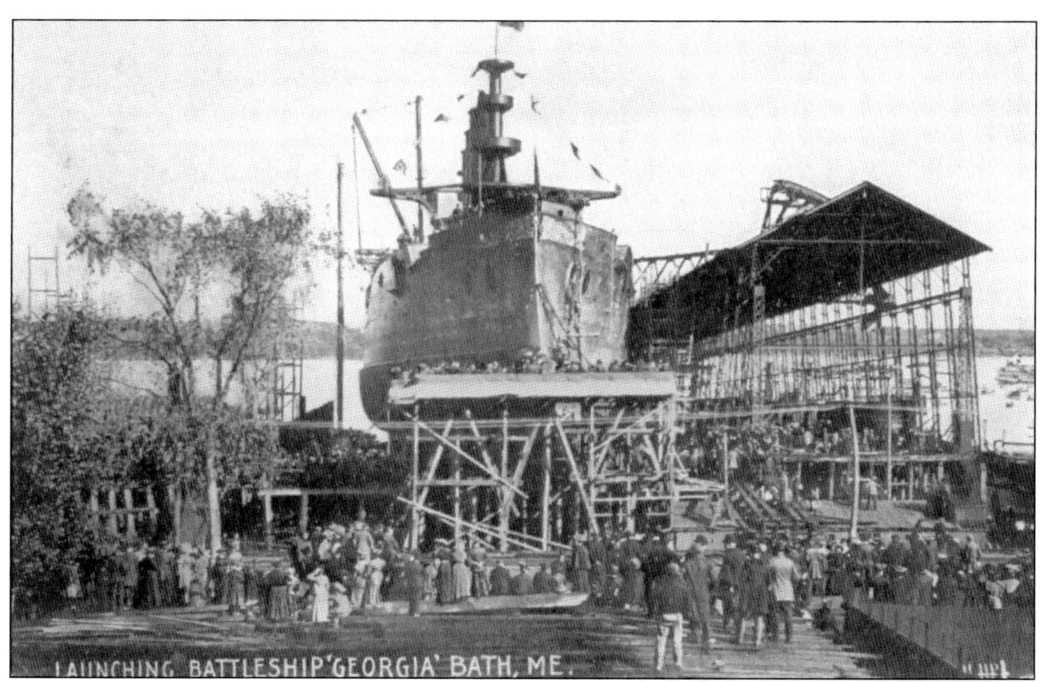

Shipbuilding is one of Maine's oldest and strongest industries, with shipyards dotting the coastline of the state. Here, the USS *Georgia* (BB-15) battleship is being launched in 1904 by Bath Iron Works (BIW), which had been building ships for the federal government since the launching of the USS *Machias* in 1891. The USS *Georgia* would see service during World War I as a training ship and convoy escort. (Libby.)

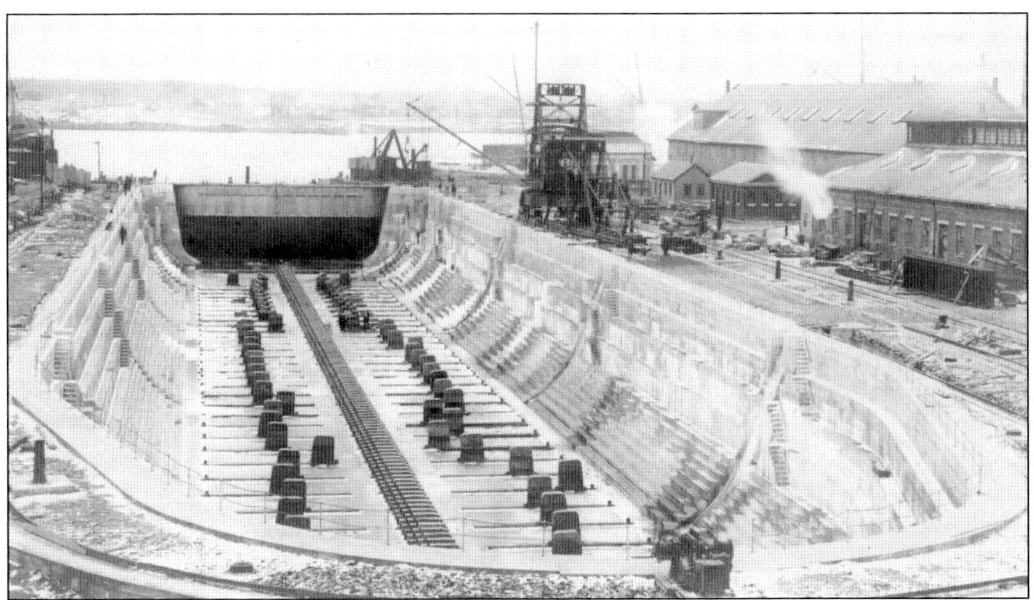

This empty dry dock at Portsmouth Naval Shipyard in Kittery is emblematic of the decline in shipbuilding in Maine before the war. After a period of stagnation, the industry saw a quick resurgence as 116 vessels were built in the year following the US entry into the war. Thirty-nine shipyards dotted the coast constructing merchant and cargo ships, patrol boats, and naval vessels, putting hundreds to work. (Libby.)

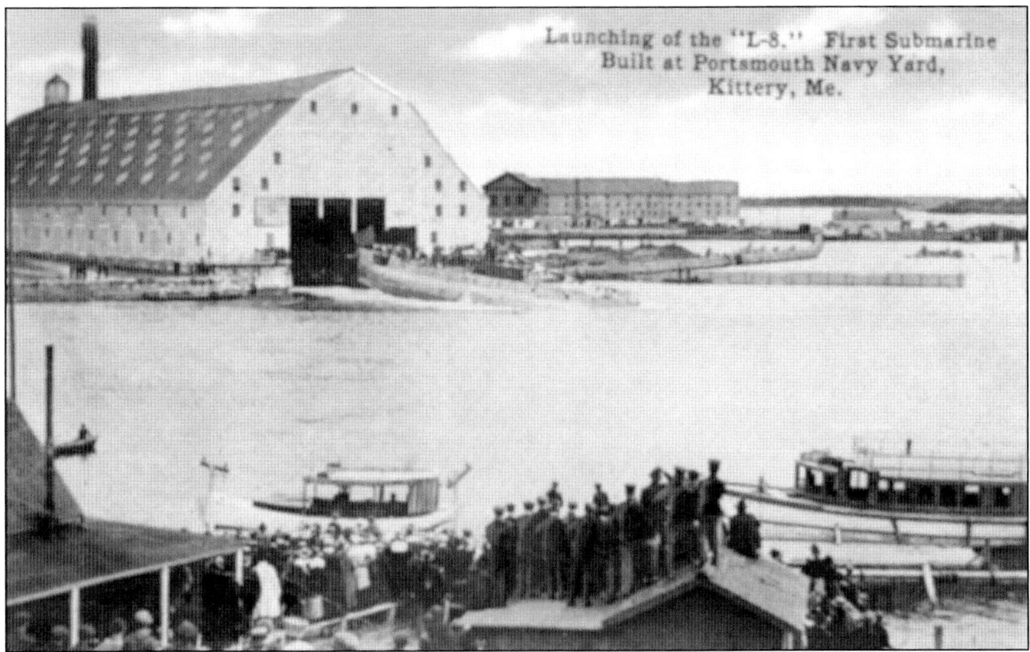

Established in 1800, the Portsmouth Naval Ship is the Navy's oldest continuously operated shipyard. On April 23, 1917, the USS *L-8* (SS-48) submarine was launched, the first submarine to be built there. Only a few individuals were admitted to attend, although crowds lined the riverbank to see the event. After its shakedown, the vessel was scheduled to sail for Europe, but the war ended before it would be used.

During World War I, Maine's shipyards received government contracts to construct a variety of vessels. In April 1918, this invitation announced the Portland Ship Ceiling Company's launching of the *Andra*, a 2,550-ton wooden transport steamer built for the Emergency Fleet Corporation. The *Andra* was the first of three such ships to be constructed in 1918 in the Russell Shipyard at the foot of Portland's Eastern Promenade.

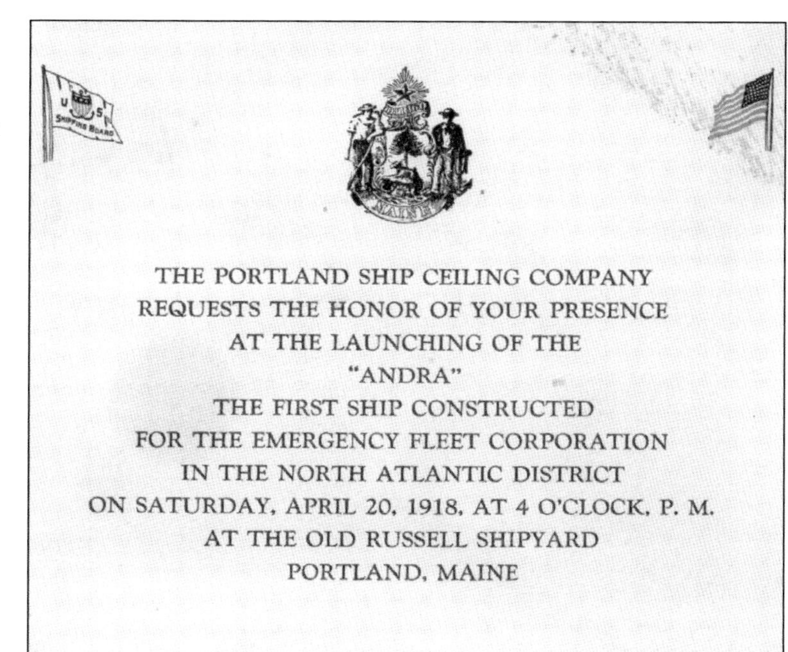

THE PORTLAND SHIP CEILING COMPANY
REQUESTS THE HONOR OF YOUR PRESENCE
AT THE LAUNCHING OF THE
"ANDRA"
THE FIRST SHIP CONSTRUCTED
FOR THE EMERGENCY FLEET CORPORATION
IN THE NORTH ATLANTIC DISTRICT
ON SATURDAY, APRIL 20, 1918, AT 4 O'CLOCK, P. M.
AT THE OLD RUSSELL SHIPYARD
PORTLAND, MAINE

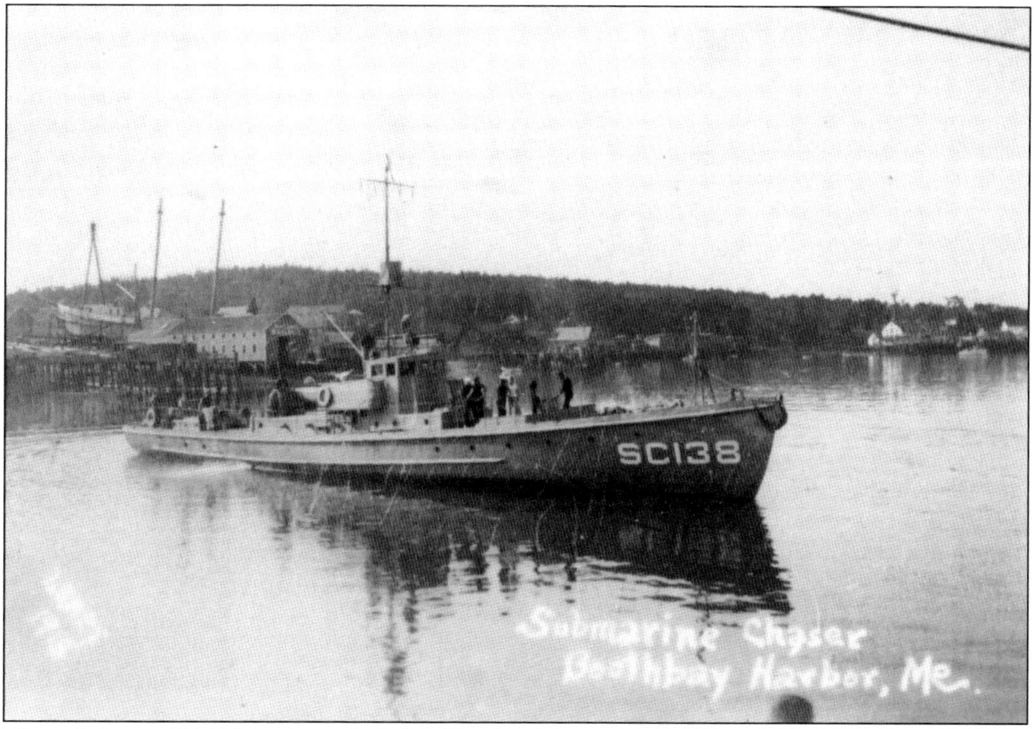

The subchaser *SC-138*, built at Hodgdon Brothers in East Boothbay and commissioned in 1918, was assigned to the Boothbay Naval Station to assist in patrolling the coast. Hodgdon's shipyard built one more of these subchasers, the *SC-137*, which was sent to Europe. Subchasers were built specifically to hunt, chase, and attack enemy submarines and were armed with depth charges, deck guns, and machine guns. (Thompson.)

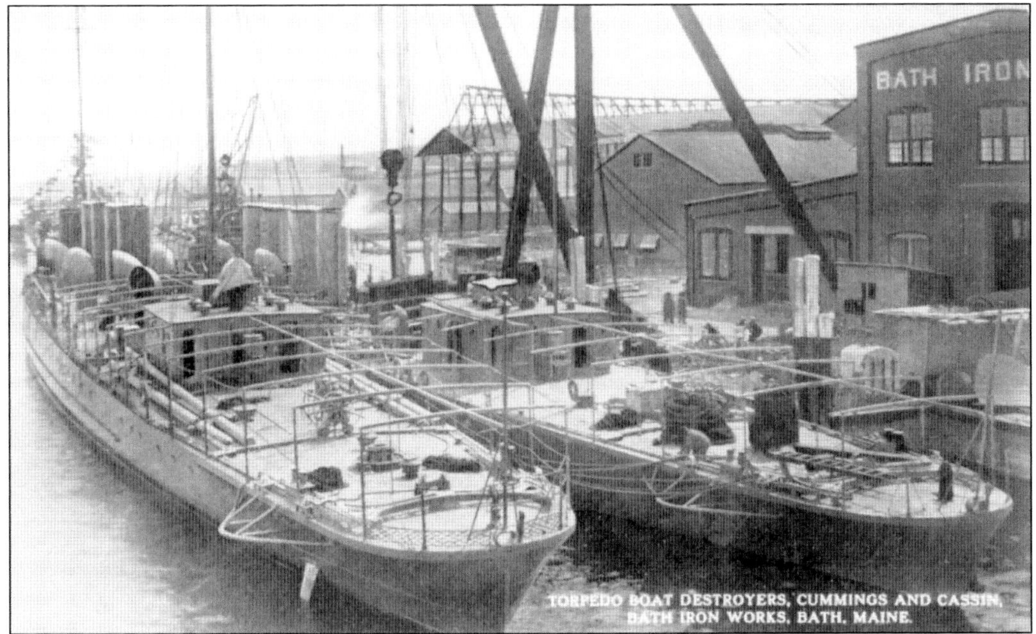

In 1913, Bath Iron Works (BIW) launched the "torpedo boat" destroyers, the USS *Cassin* (DD-43) and the USS *Cummings* (DD-44). They were larger than previous destroyer class ships and were the first to carry 50 caliber guns. In 1918, the *Cassin* was struck by a torpedo with the loss of a sailor. Following the war, both were transferred to the Coast Guard and used to discourage the smuggling of alcohol during Prohibition. (Libby.)

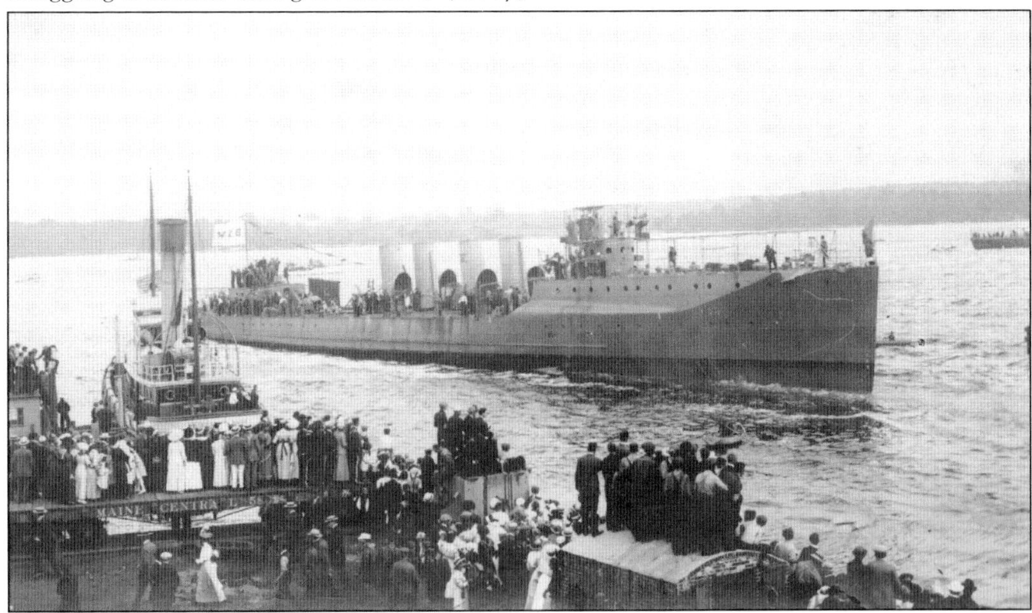

An unidentified four-stack destroyer is launched at the Bath Iron Works. Destroyers were constructed to help defend larger ships in a fleet against attacks by smaller, faster vessels including submarines. During the years leading up to and immediately following the war, BIW built Caldwell-, Clemson-, Sampson-, O'Brien-, Paulding-, Tucker-, and Wickes-class destroyers for the Navy, some of which eventually saw service in World War II. (Libby.)

Bath thrived as a wartime shipbuilding center, attracting many workers and their families. To meet the need for housing, the federal government built two projects in 1918, a neighborhood of brick houses in the city's north end and another of wooden houses on Lincoln Street. The Lincoln Street development consisted of 74 attractive Colonial Revival–style dwellings for employees of the Bath Iron Works and the Hyde Windlass Company.

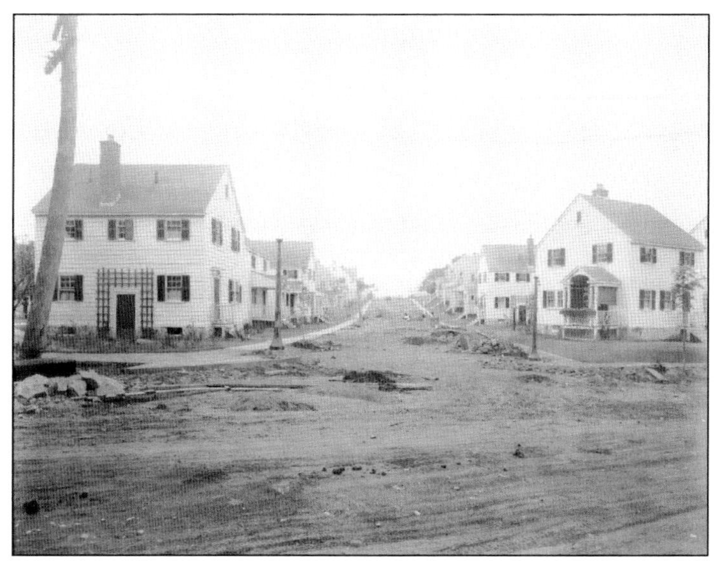

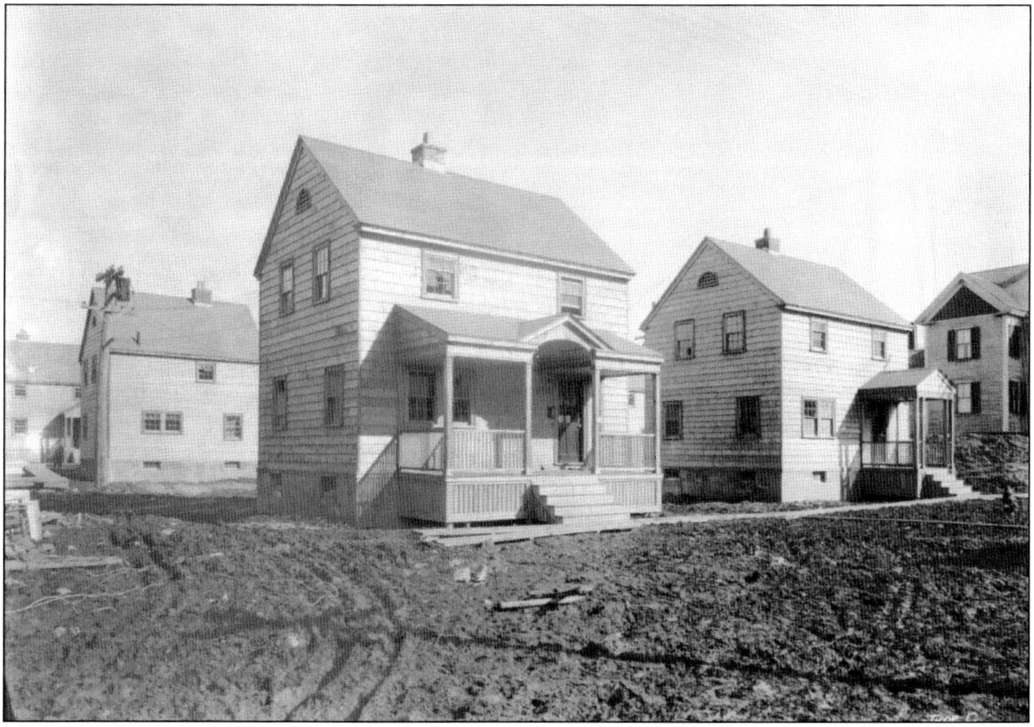

Bath's Lincoln Street development featured four different models of homes to create "a well ordered and charming New England village of attractive houses," according to the January 1919 *Architectural Record*. The architects were Parker, Thomas, and Rice of Boston. After the war, the US Housing Corporation of the Department of Labor sold the houses to their occupants, and the development became one of Bath's residential neighborhoods.

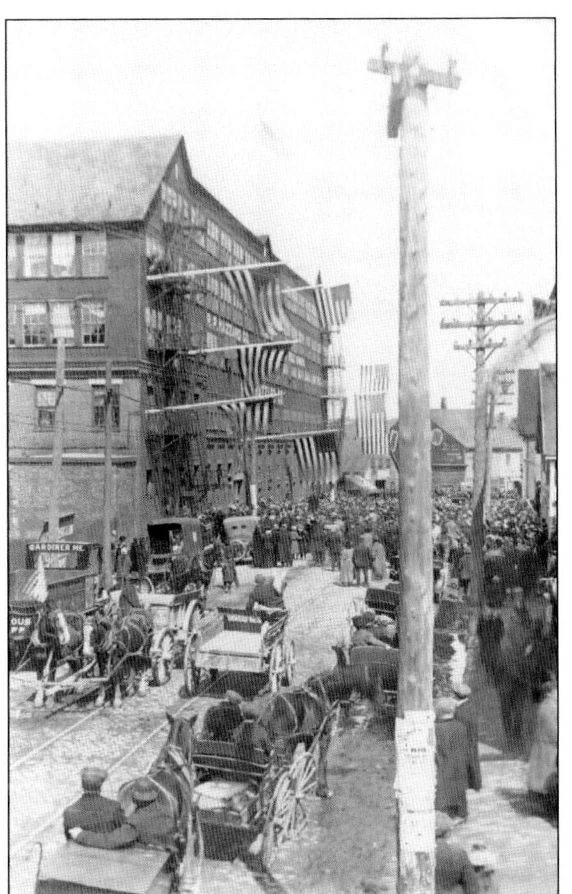

In 1906, Robert P. Hazzard started what would become the R.P. Hazzard Company Shoe Factory on Water Street in Gardiner, shown here decorated with American flags for Memorial Day 1916. With America's entrance into World War I less than a year away, Maine shoe factories were already receiving large orders from the British and French armies.

In October 1914, the Hazzard Shoe Company in Gardiner sent Maine's first freight car of army boots to New York for shipment to Europe. This order was followed by one for 100,000 pairs of shoes from the British army and another 80,000 pairs from the French army. R.P. Hazzard reported in 1915 that "recent orders received are for more than double the full capacity of the shop."

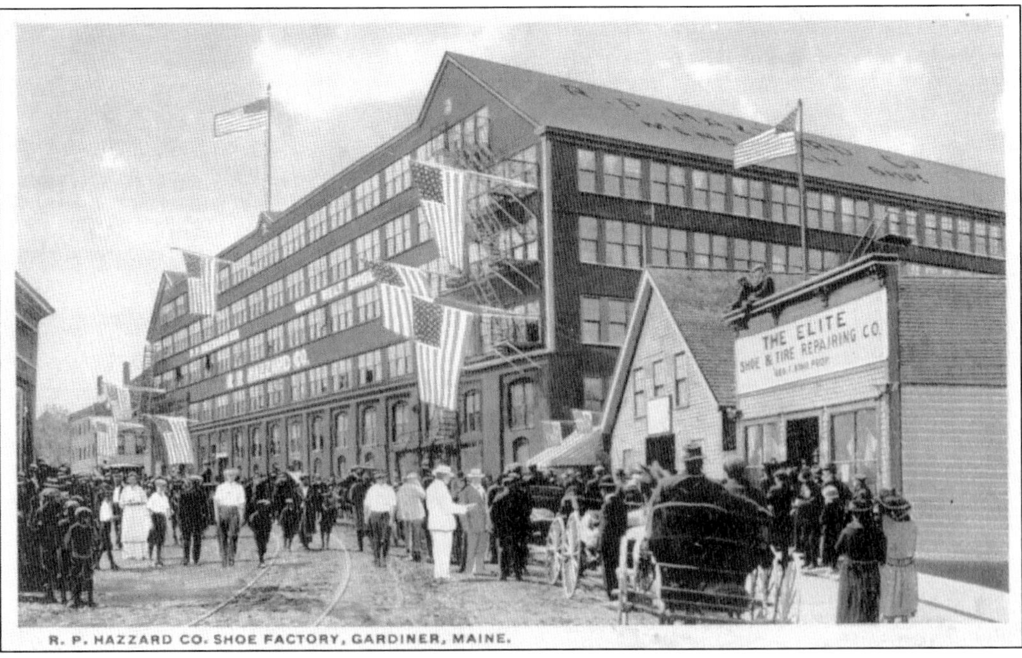

R. P. HAZZARD CO. SHOE FACTORY, GARDINER, MAINE.

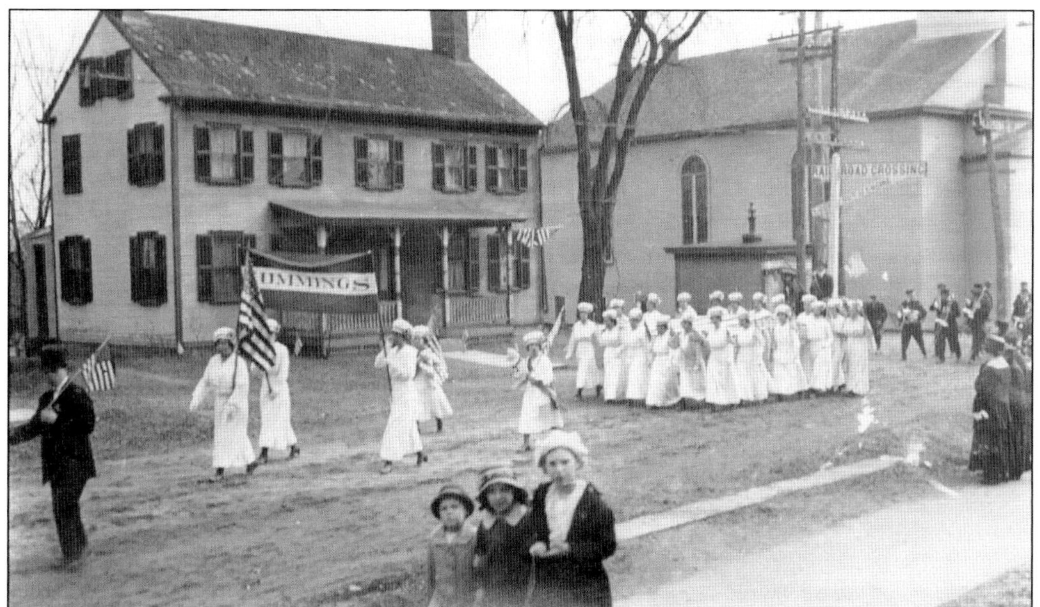

The York County Manufacturing town of South Berwick held a patriotic parade in May 1917. Prominently featured in this real-photo postcard is a group of female employees from the Cummings Shoe Factory, a company engaged in war production. On May 7, 1917, Allie C. Pray of South Berwick wrote on this card to Carrie Shea in North Berwick, "Am sending you a picture of the stitch room help."

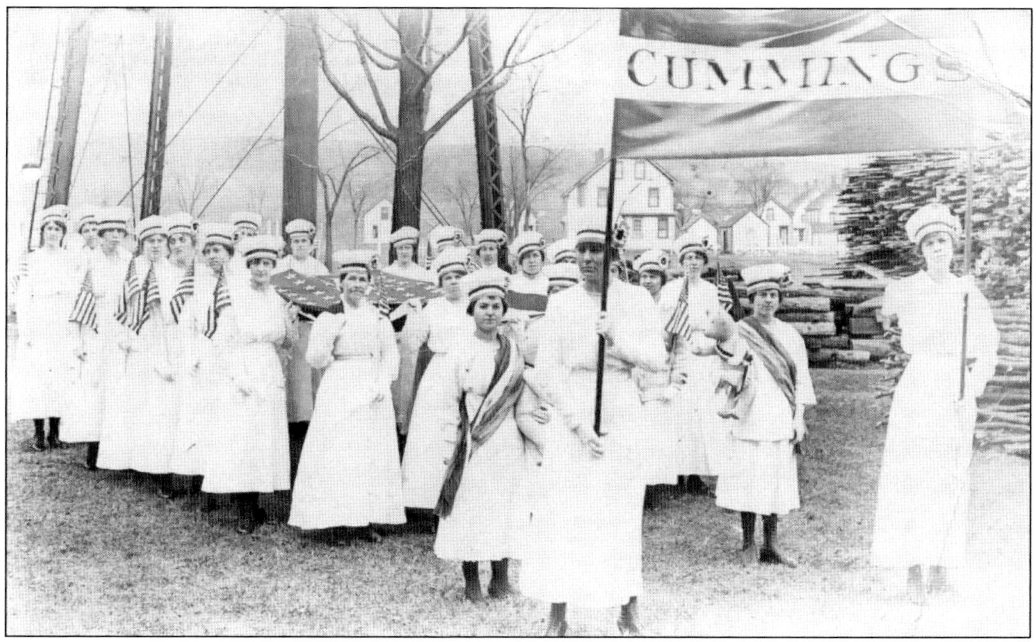

While women had worked in Maine's shoe industry since the 19th century, the world war created new job opportunities for them as men entered the armed forces in large numbers. As employees of the Cummings Shoe Factory in South Berwick in 1917, these costumed ladies proudly carry both an American flag and their company's banner. Maine shoes outfitted the armies of the United States, Britain, France, Italy, and Serbia.

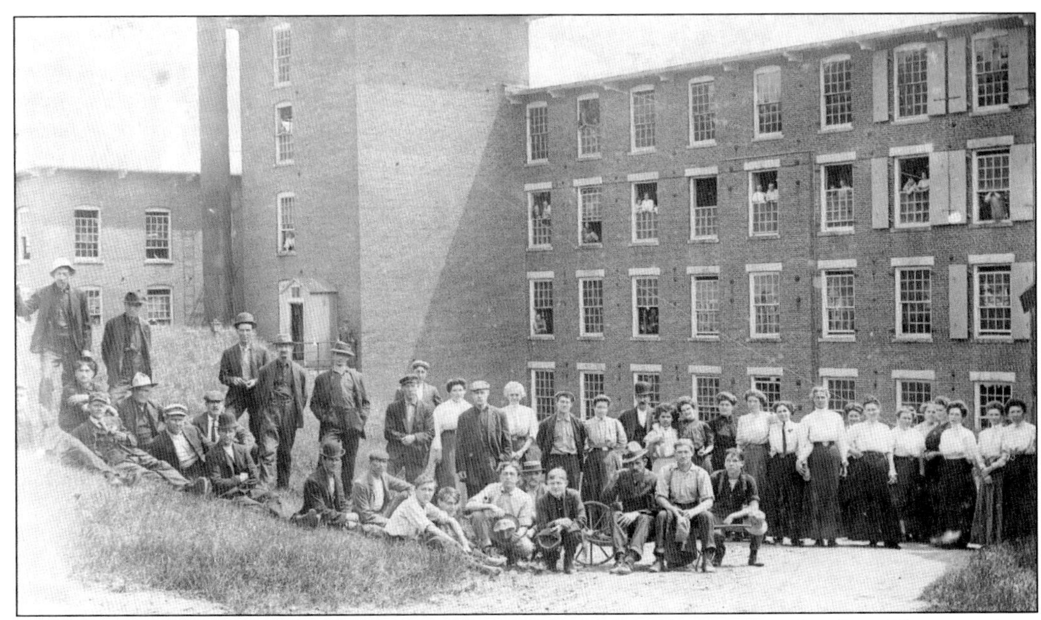

Between 1914 and 1918, Maine's textile mills were flooded with war-related orders. These workers at the American Woolen Company mill in Dover-Foxcroft produced material to make overcoats for the Russian army. Other American Woolen Company mills at Hartland, Pittsfield, and Skowhegan manufactured army blankets and woolen cloth for uniforms.

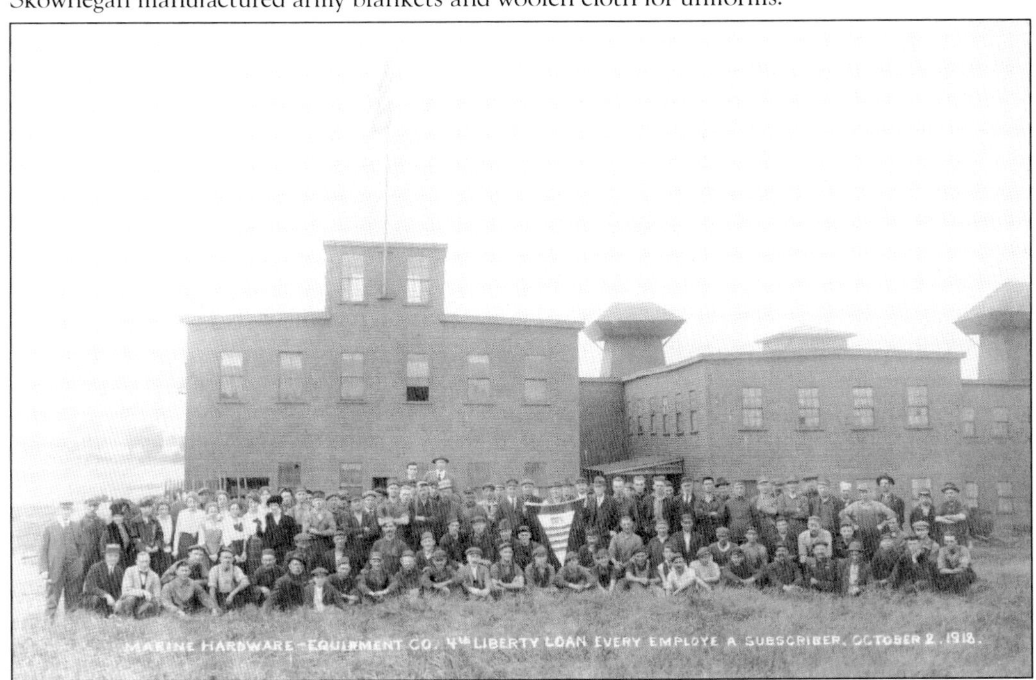

Liberty Loan and War Savings Stamp campaigns sought support in workplaces across Maine. Established in 1904, the Marine Hardware-Equipment Company was a foundry located on the South Portland waterfront to service adjacent shipyards and dry docks. On October 2, 1918, the employees posed in front of the company for a photograph to commemorate their 100 percent participation in the Fourth Liberty Loan.

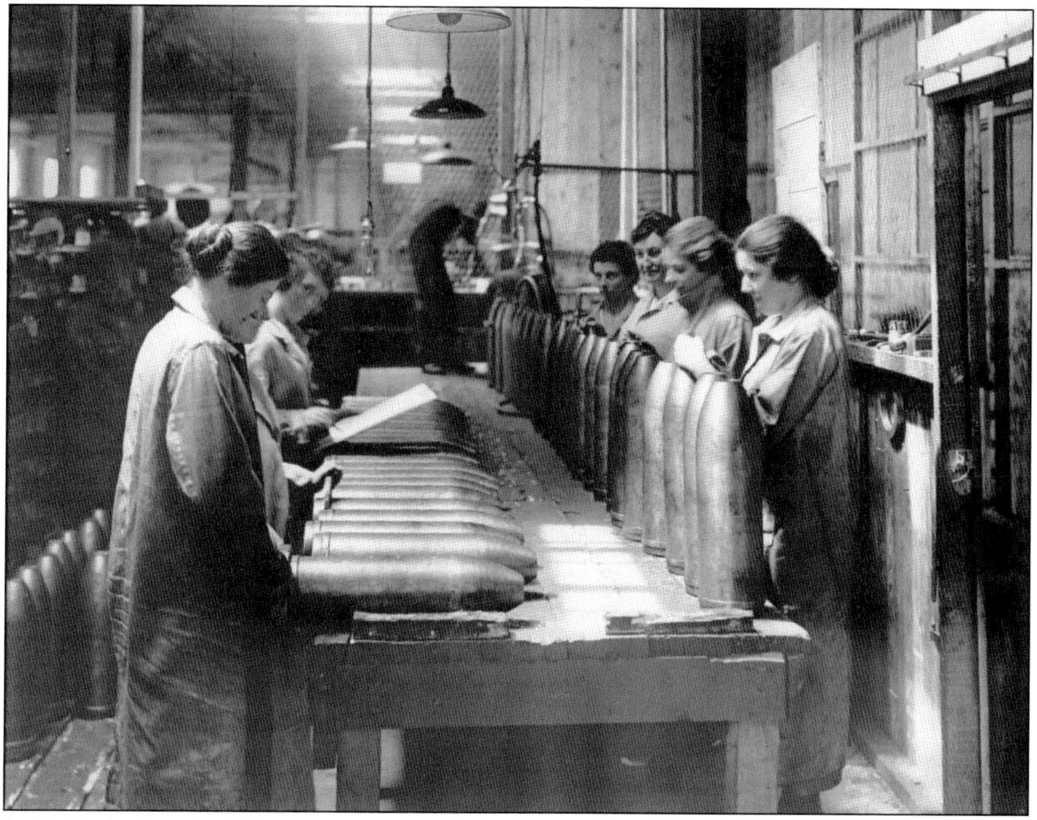

In 1846, the Portland Company was established to produce locomotives and related equipment as railroads proliferated the countryside. By the late 19th century, the company had begun to diversify its production to include pulp digesters for paper mills, marine engines, industrial machinery and when war broke out in Europe, munitions. As a result of a "shell crisis" in England in early 1915, US munitions makers received contracts for the production of artillery shells and other ammunition. As manufacturing facilities lost men to the military, there was an increased demand for women to work as machinists, riveters, and inspectors. In these photographs, female workers inspect brass artillery shells to ensure they meet specifications and then crate them for shipment. The shells were then transferred to another facility where they would be armed and eventually sent overseas for use. (Both, MHS.)

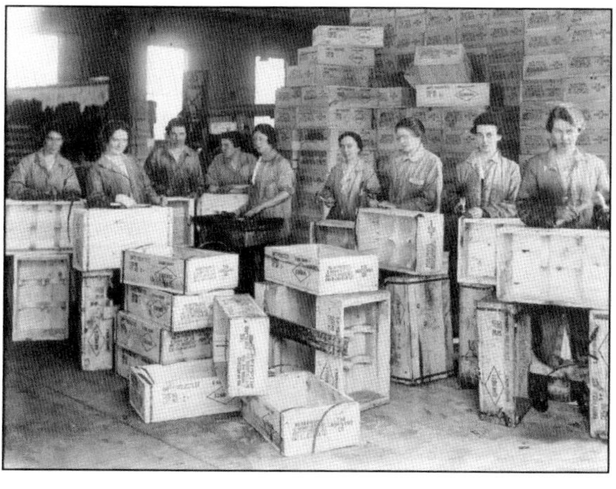

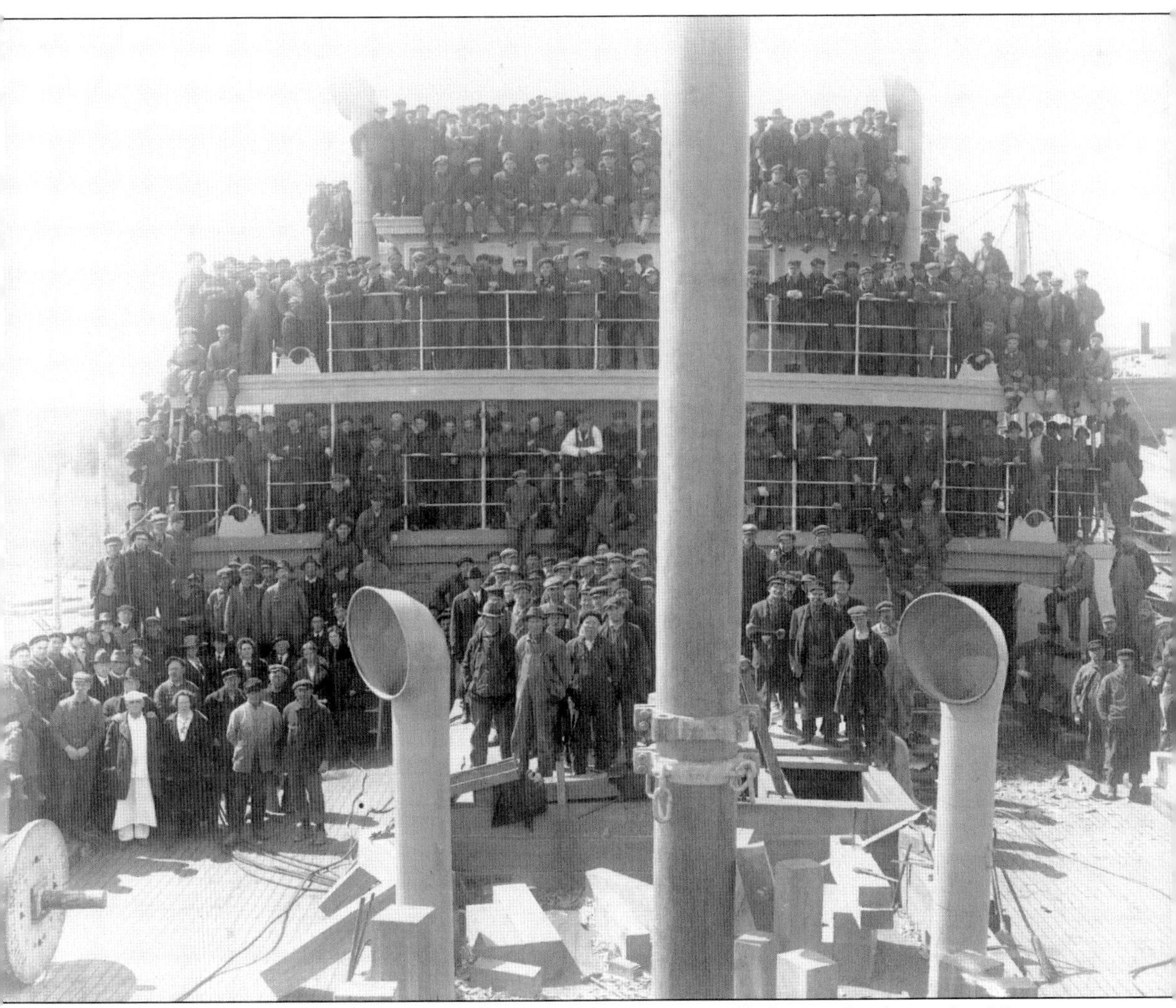

As a result of World War I and postwar commerce, small shipyards along the Maine coast received contracts to build wooden cargo ships. Here, the crew that constructed the Ferris steamer *Waukomis* at Sandy Point, Stockton Springs, gathered on the deck for a photograph before her launching in April 1919. At 3,500 tons, the *Waukomis* was the largest vessel ever launched on the Penobscot River.

Five

Coastal Defenses

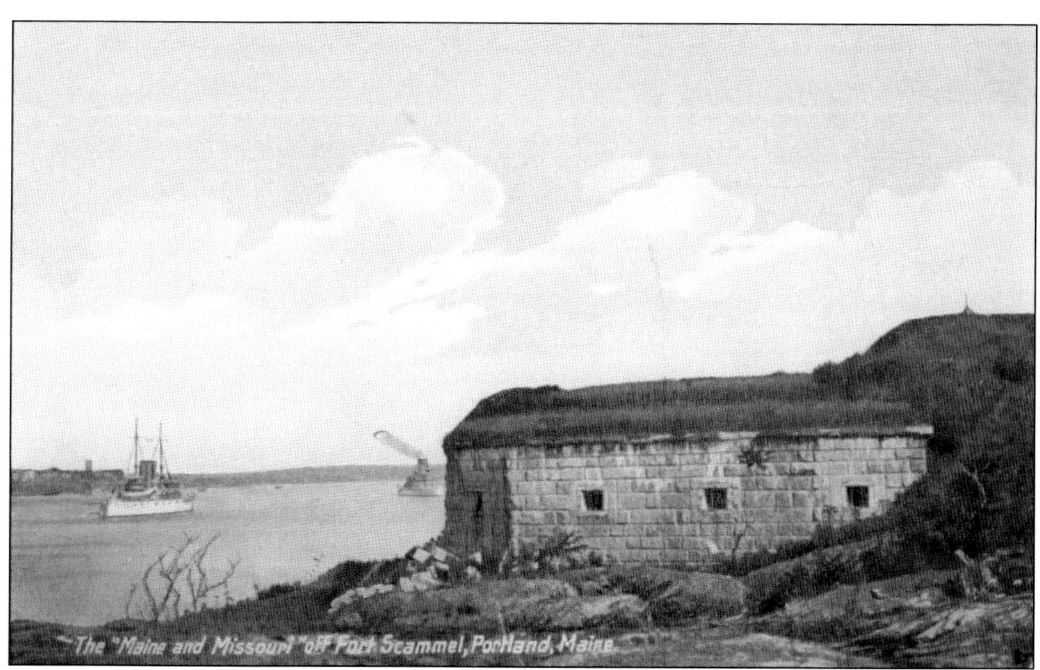

Maine has experienced a number of coastal attacks—in particular, attacks at Portland Harbor during the Revolutionary War, the Penobscot during the War of 1812, and even a raid by Confederates during the Civil War. During World War I, German submarines threatened merchant vessels and passenger ships. This is an image of Fort Scammel in Portland Harbor, which was established in 1808.

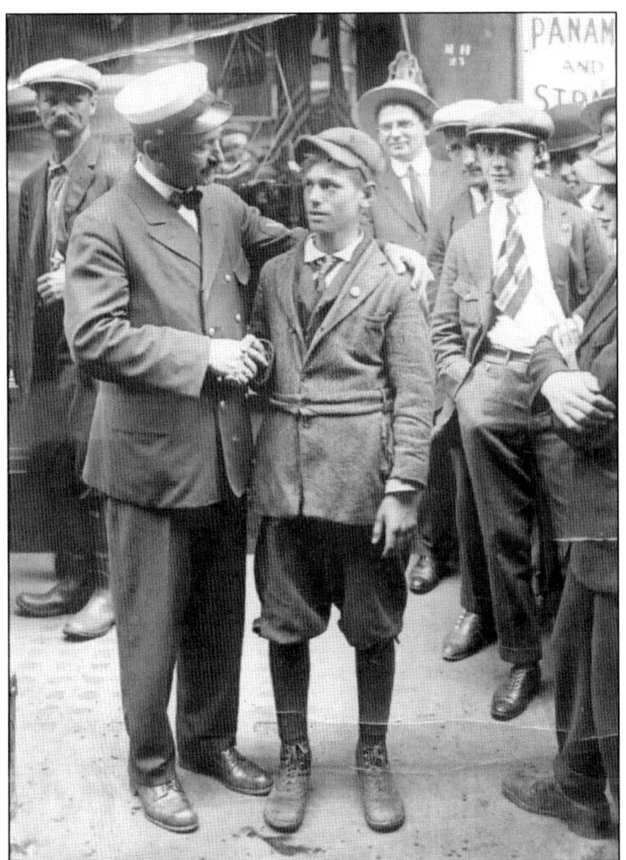

On July 22, 1918, the *Robert and Richard*, a fishing schooner, was sunk by a German submarine near Cape Porpoise. The crew was ordered onto dories, and the schooner was sent below. One German officer said he was familiar with the coast because he had owned a summer home in Maine since 1896. Here, 14-year-old Charles Grover, one of the crew members, stands safely at port in Boston. (Libby.)

Coastal defenses in Maine were particularly focused on Portland Harbor, the Kennebec River, and the Portsmouth and Kittery region during the 20th century. Organized in 1901, the Coastal Artillery Corps (CAC) had several installations in Portland harbor, including Fort Williams in Cape Elizabeth. These disappearing guns were the typical armaments of the larger gun batteries at coastal forts. By 1917, the fort had five different batteries with various gun emplacements.

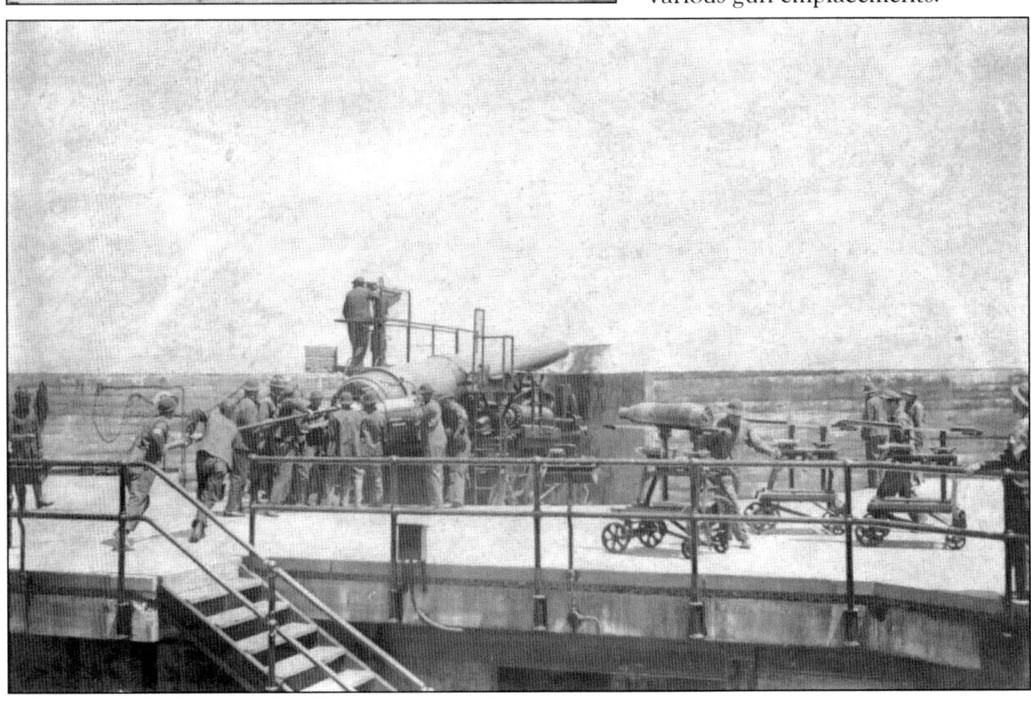

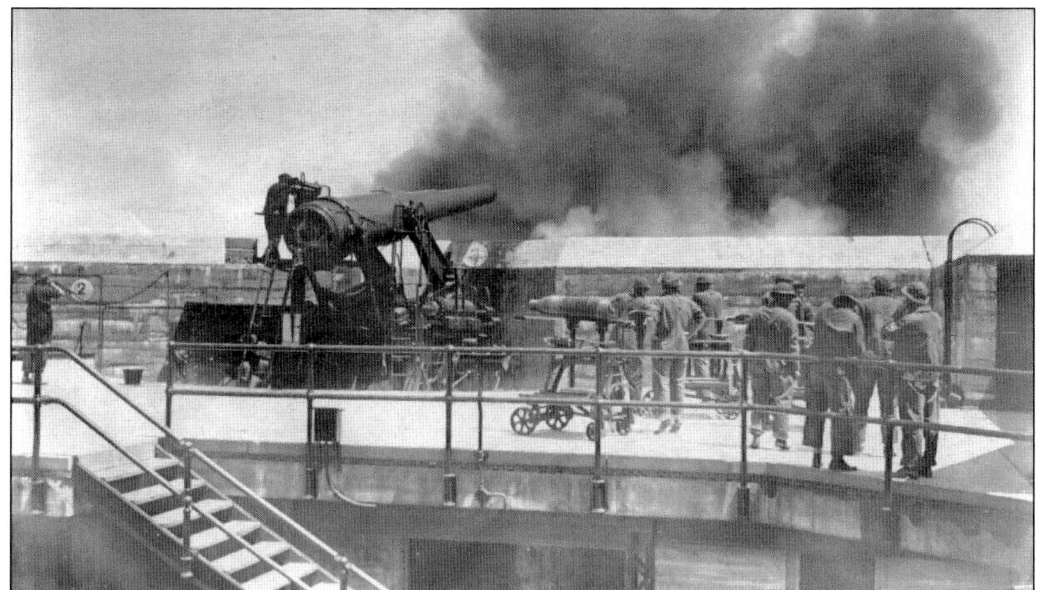

A gun detachment for a 12-inch disappearing carriage gun consisted of a gun chief, a gunner, a rangekeeper, and 18 privates. Each had various roles ranging from identifying the target to determining thickness of armor and ability to penetrate the armor, manning and inspecting the breech, loading and unloading the shell, changing the elevation of the gun, firing, and correcting the trajectory if necessary.

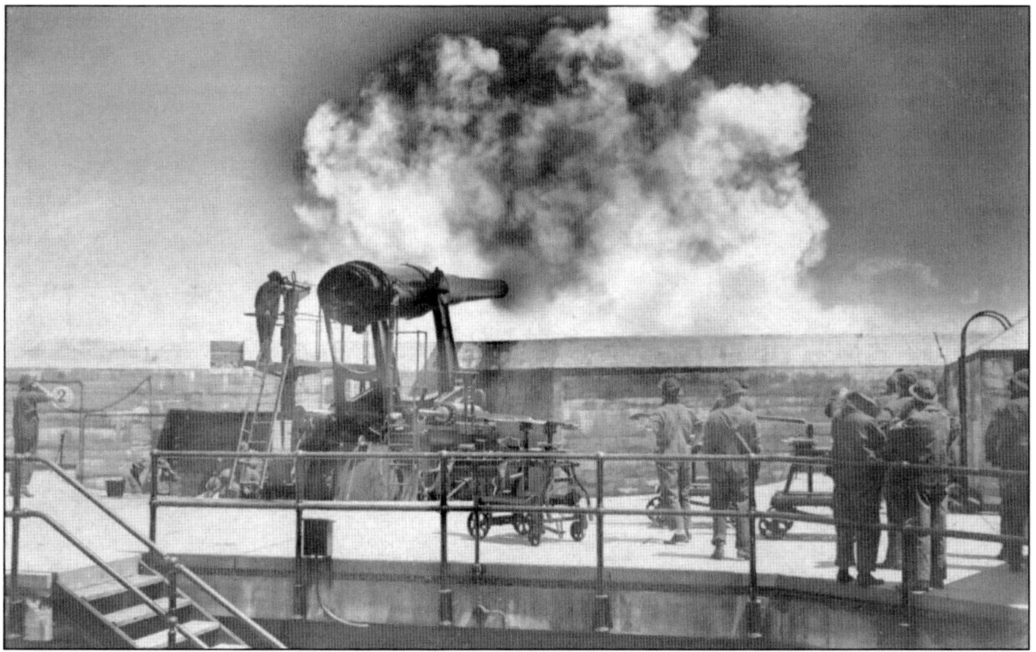

In 1917, the Maine artillery corps companies were federalized and reorganized. Some of the companies were transferred to the 103rd Field Artillery; others to the 101st Engineer and 72nd and 73rd Coastal Artillery. Most of the men were combined into the 54th Coastal Artillery Corps, which was sent to France in March 1918. Several companies remained in Portland to serve in the defense of the harbor.

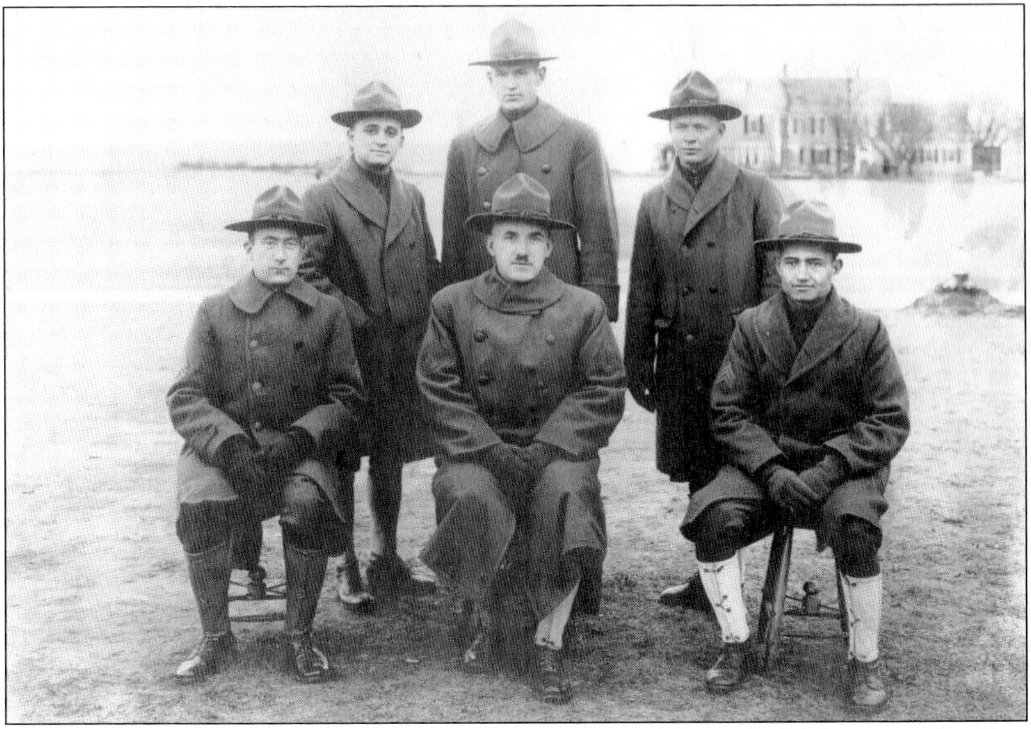

This image of noncommissioned officers is of Battery A of the 29th CAC stationed at Fort Williams. Enlisted men could see quick promotions in the years leading up to and immediately following the war as the CAC ranks swelled. Examinations for promotion covered topics such as servicing the artillery piece, identifying ships by their silhouette, and how to properly store projectiles. (MHS.)

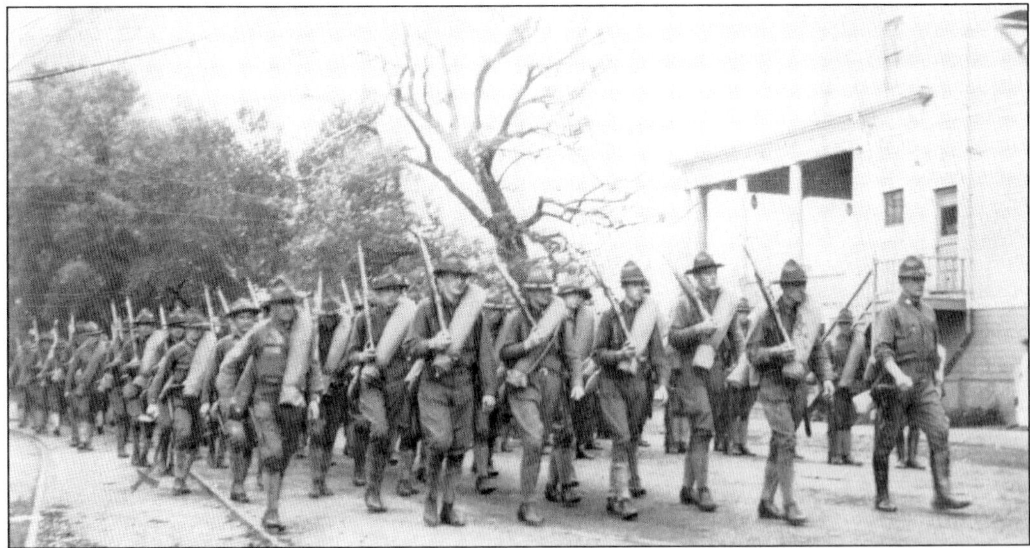

In August 1917, shortly after his arrival at Fort Williams, Pvt. Walter Towle of the 9th Company sent this postcard to friends in Old Orchard Beach: "We are having a great time, the Army life for me. This is a part of our company. The X is me." Towle served in several campaigns in France and returned to Maine safely in 1919.

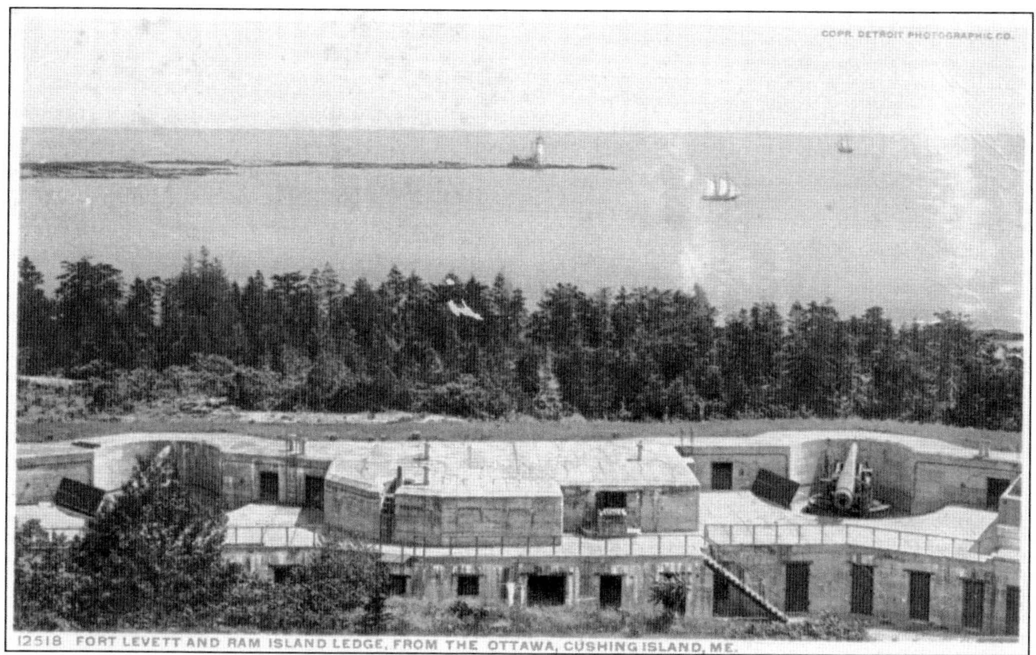

Fort Levett in Portland was built on Cushing Island in 1898 to assist in the protection of Portland Harbor. This view of the fort was taken from near the Ottawa House, a hotel adjacent to the installation. There were several batteries, including Battery Foote with a 12-inch gun. On the horizon is Ram Island Ledge Light.

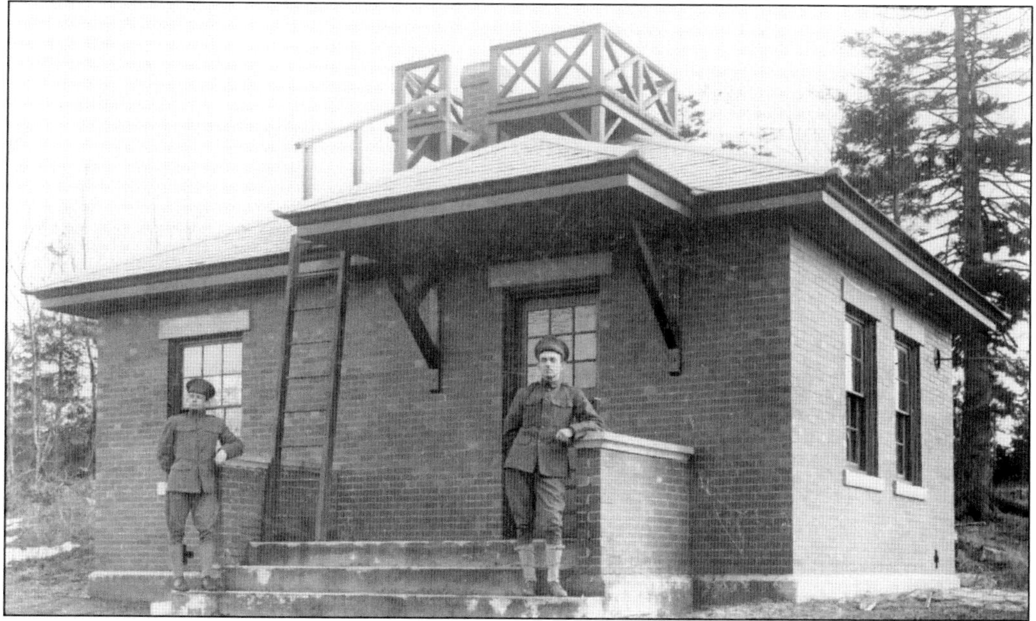

The US Navy had numerous wireless installations on the Atlantic coast by the beginning of the war, including this one at Fort Levett. Wireless signals could transmit from 25 to 100 miles and would transfer signals up and down the seaboard. After the entry into the war, the government ordered many nonmilitary stations to cease operations to keep them from interfering with naval operations.

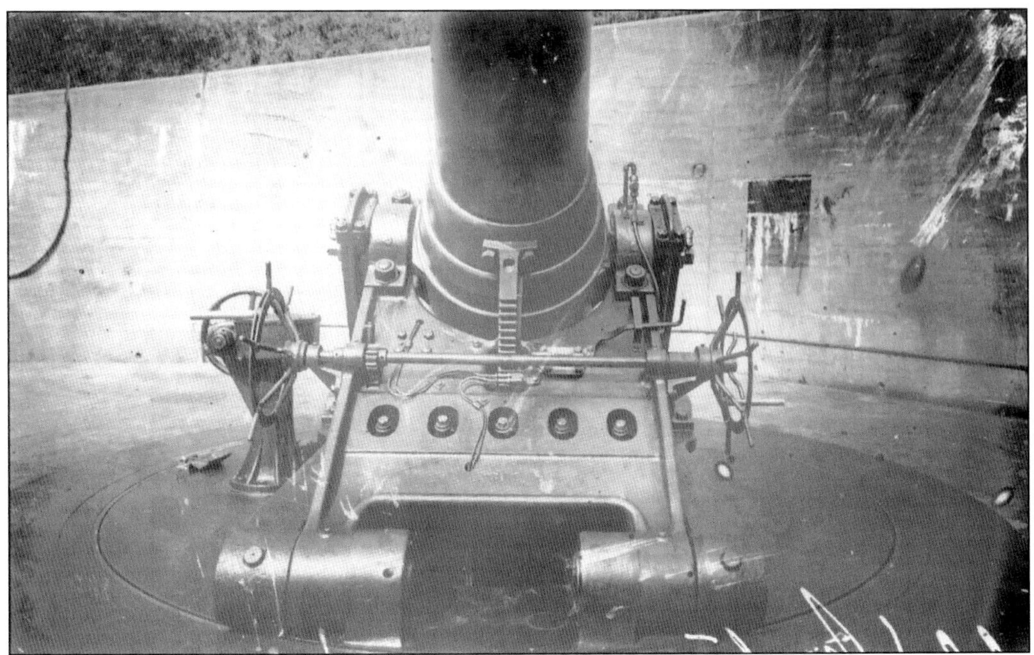

An enlisted man from Fort McKinley, on Great Diamond Island, who sent this postcard of a 12-inch mortar to a friend, wrote, "This is the kind of gun I am on now." Fort McKinley had nine batteries that had various artillery guns, including 12- and 8-inch disappearing guns and 3-inch masking parapet guns. Fort McKinley was served by a sub-post, Fort Lyon, on Cow Island. (Thompson.)

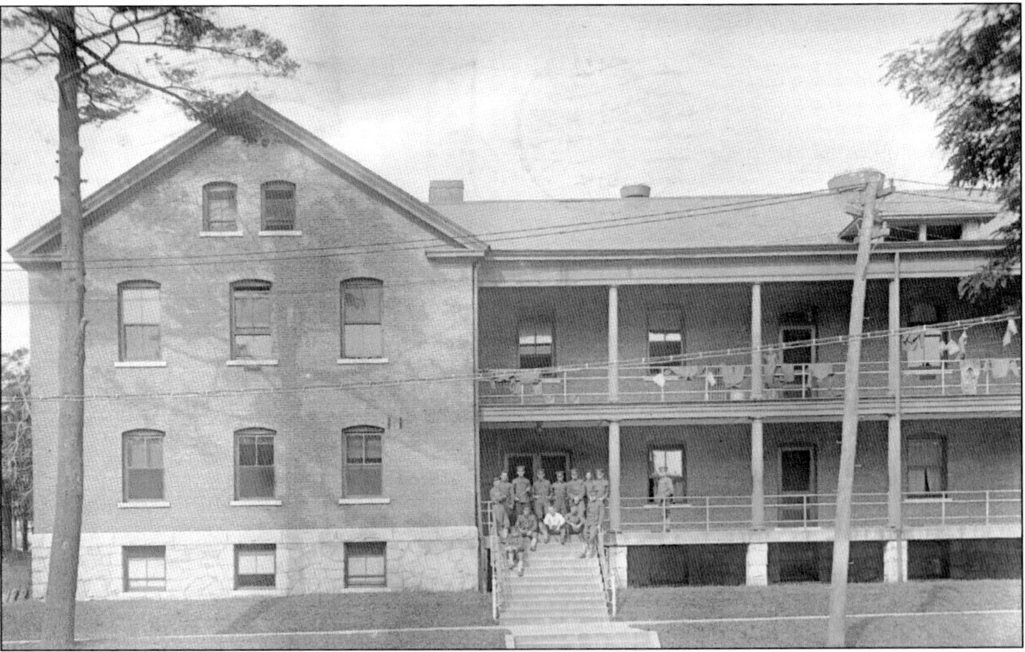

This is of one of several barracks for enlisted men at Fort McKinley. Barracks at Coastal Artillery Corps installations were constructed on one side of the parade grounds, while officers' quarters were on the opposite. The layout of these installations is in stark contrast to those built before the Civil War, where the men were housed within the fort walls.

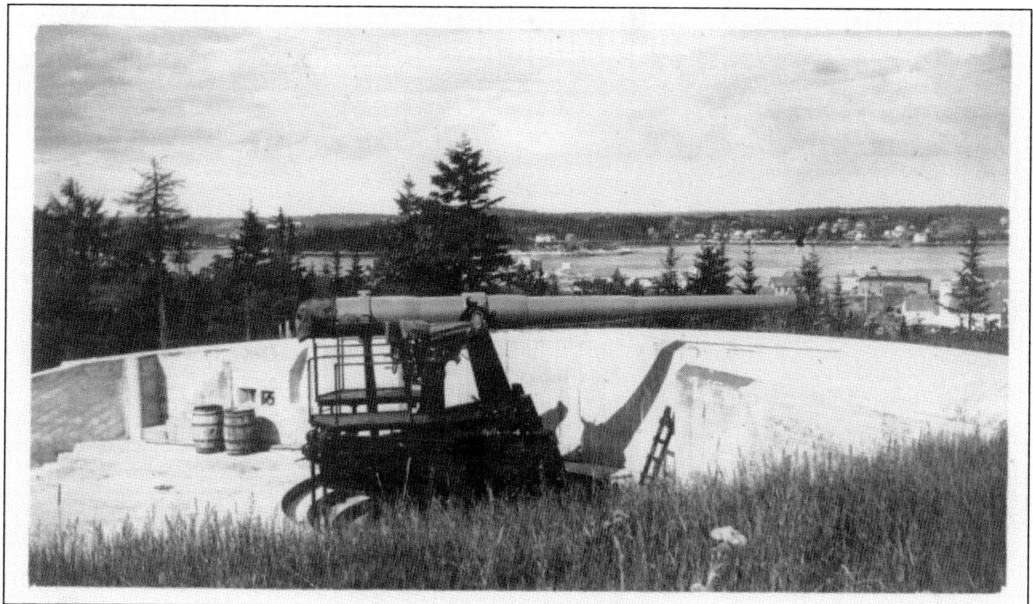

This is a six-inch disappearing gun at Battery John Hardman, which was one of three batteries at Fort Baldwin in Phippsburg. Fort Baldwin was constructed a few years prior to the war and served as the main installation for the Coast Defense of the Kennebec, which protected the Kennebec River. Eventually, the six-inch gun was removed to be sent to France to be used in the field. (Thompson.)

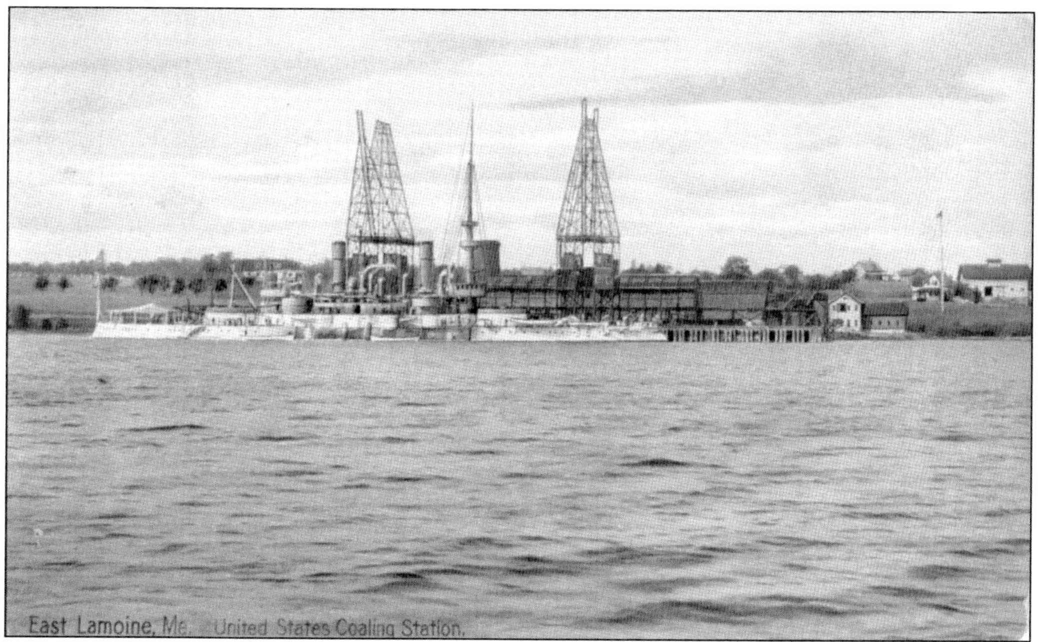

The Lamoine Coaling Station on Frenchman's Bay was a refueling station for the North Atlantic Fleet beginning in 1902. It was used for almost a decade, but it became dispensable as ships became less reliant on coal. As the United States prepared for war, the station became a storage facility for naval munitions. Following the war, the station was deactivated and the land given to the state. (Libby.)

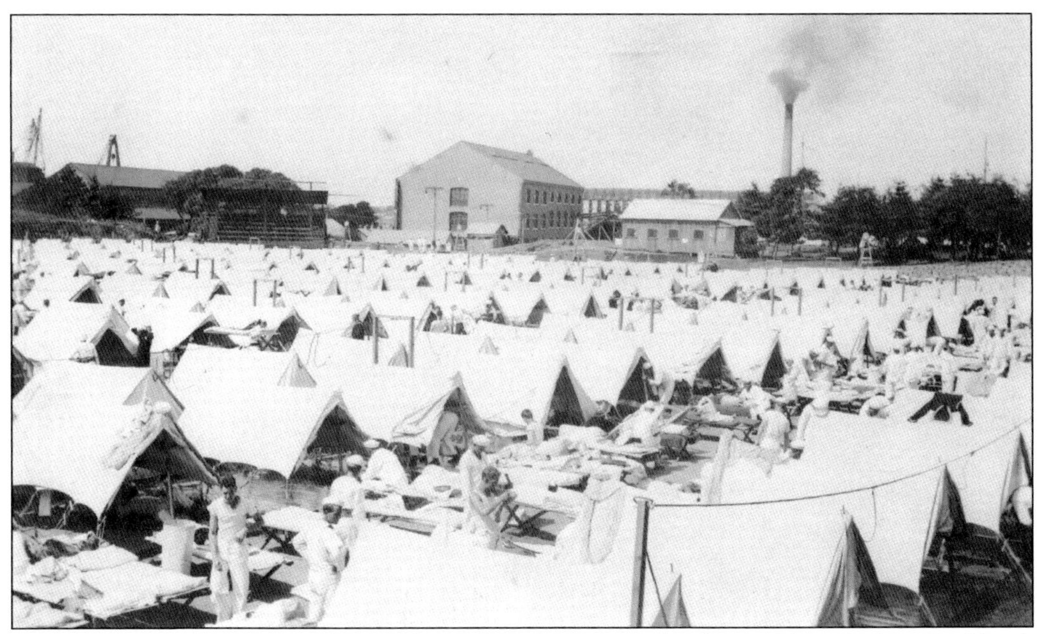

There were naval training and coastal patrol facilities at Portland, Boothbay Harbor, Rockland, Bar Harbor, Machias, and this one at Kittery. The Naval Reserve had only been in existence since 1915 and was a draw for men from coastal communities in Maine. The inscription by this sailor says, "Getting ready for Captains inspection at 9:30am at Saturday USN Training camp August 25, 1917."

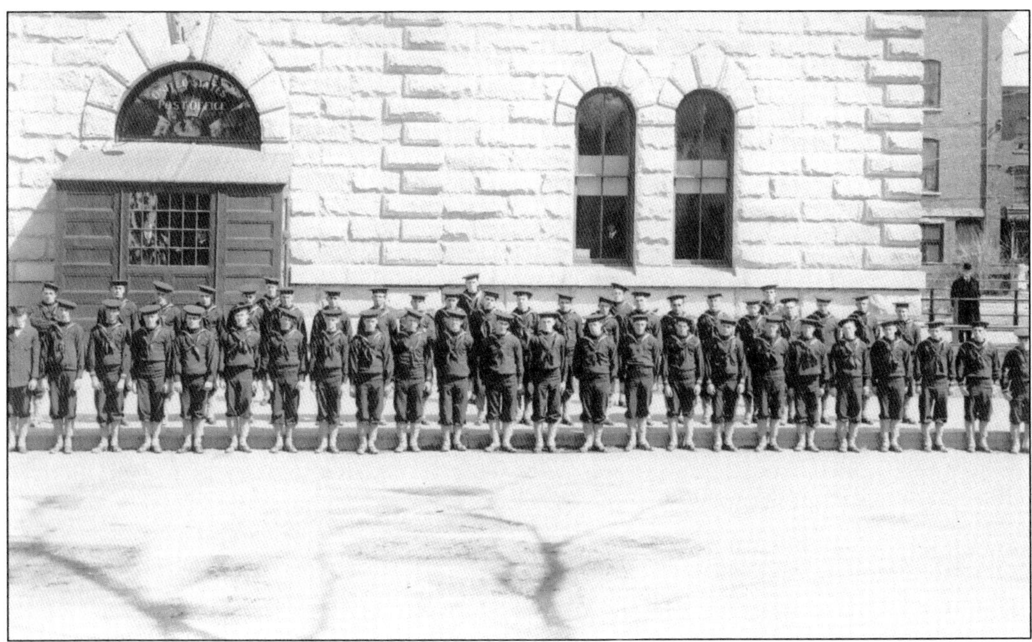

These enlisted men, sometimes referred to as bluejackets, stand at attention in front of the former Rockland post office. Upon the declaration of war, three divisions of Maine Naval Reserves were sent to Boston Naval Yard. Rockland served as an induction center for new recruits in mid-coast Maine throughout the war and was also the site of a Naval Reserve division. (Libby.)

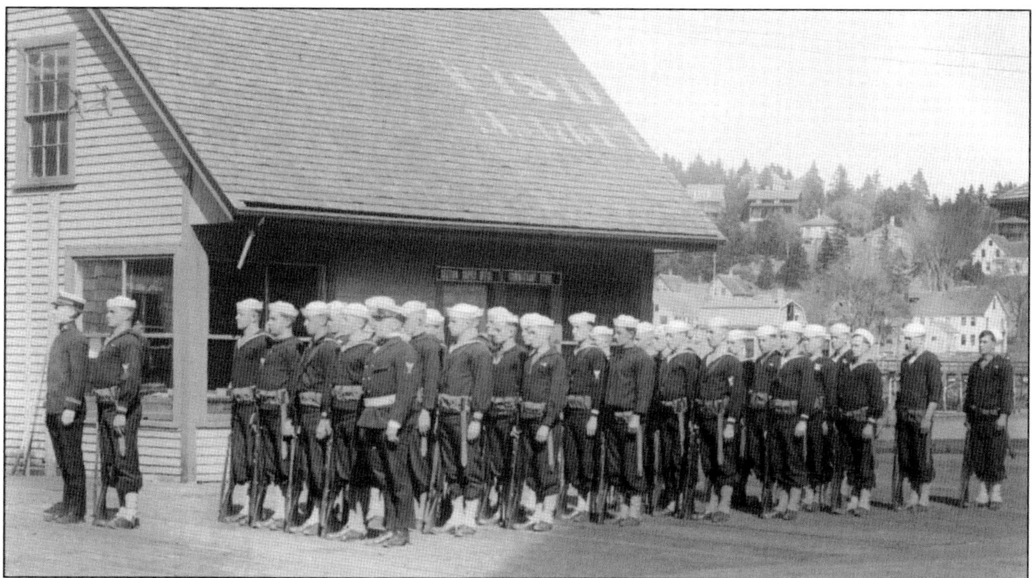

Sailors readied for drill in front of the supply office and commissary at Boothbay Harbor. The installation at Boothbay Harbor was strategically located for the protection of the surrounding shipbuilding industries. Coastal patrol stations would monitor listening stations or respond to reports by aircraft, patrol boats, or vessels at sea. If, for example, an enemy submarine was reported, subchasers would hunt, chase, and attack the sub. (Thompson.)

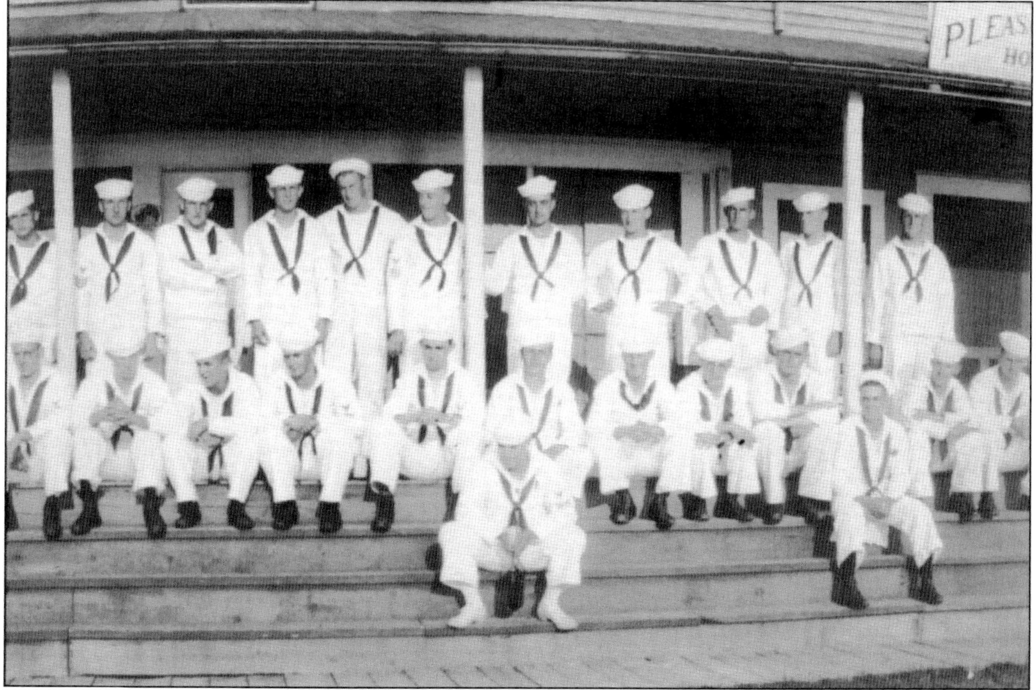

Sailors assemble in front of the Pleasant View House during an outing in East Boothbay in July 1918. While most naval concerns were related to the protection of supply lines to Europe, the Navy, as it promoted in its recruitment efforts, served as the first line of defense for protection against possible invasion or sabotage. (Thompson.)

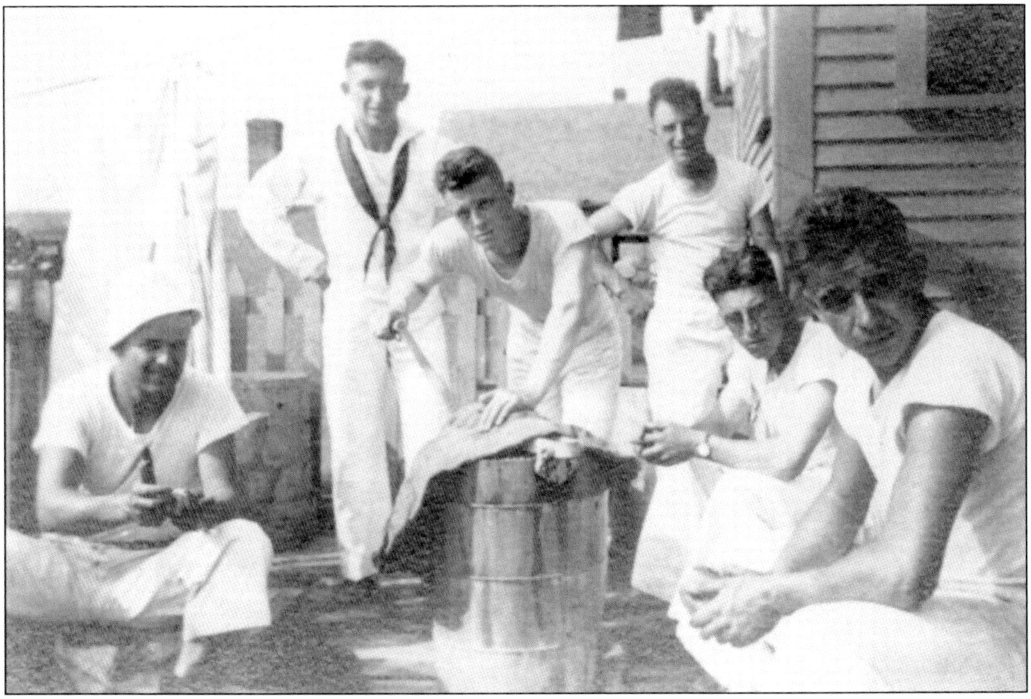

Here, a group of sailors gather to socialize while preparing some of the day's food. The approximately 100 men stationed at Boothbay Harbor were a part of the community-at-large and gave exhibition drills, participated in parades, held theatrical performances, played baseball with local groups, and assisted with events and causes during their short time in the region. (Thompson.)

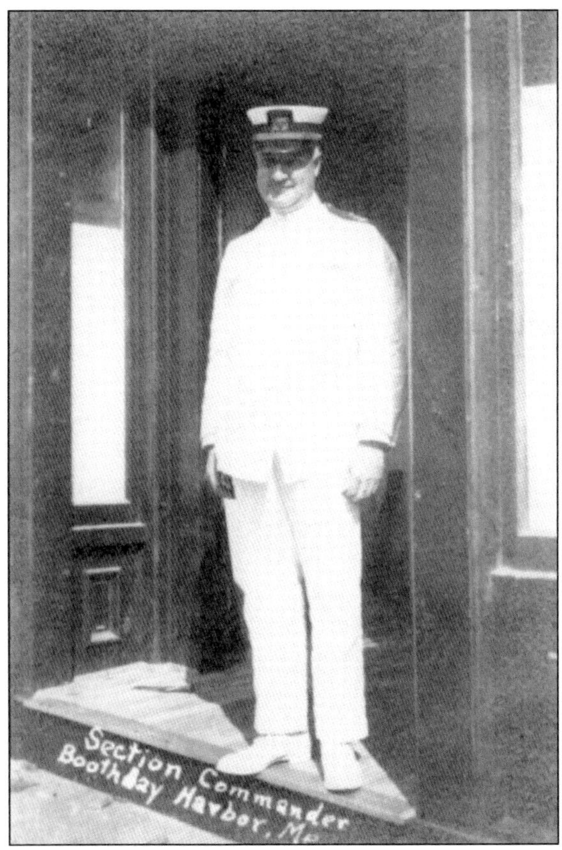

Lt. (jg) Arthur Stetson of Bath served in Boothbay as section commander of the Bath Section. Stetson was a recruiter in the Boston Naval District when war was declared. He was assigned to serve as the aide to the commander of the Bath Section and later took command. Various boats, many of which were obtained through the generosity of private citizens, were used by the post to patrol the waters. (Thompson.)

Six

Over There

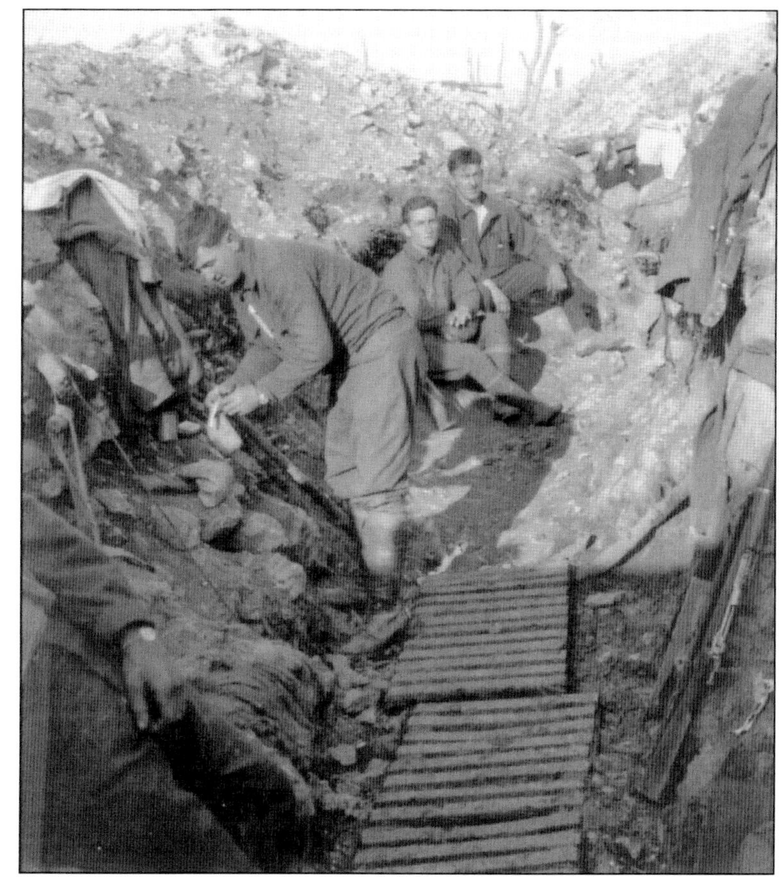

Members of the 103rd Regiment are shown in the trenches in France in 1918. The 103rd was in the 52nd Infantry Brigade of the 26th Division, also known as the Yankee Division, which was composed of National Guard units throughout New England. The 26th Division spent more time on the line than any other division and was the first complete division to be transported to France. (MANG.)

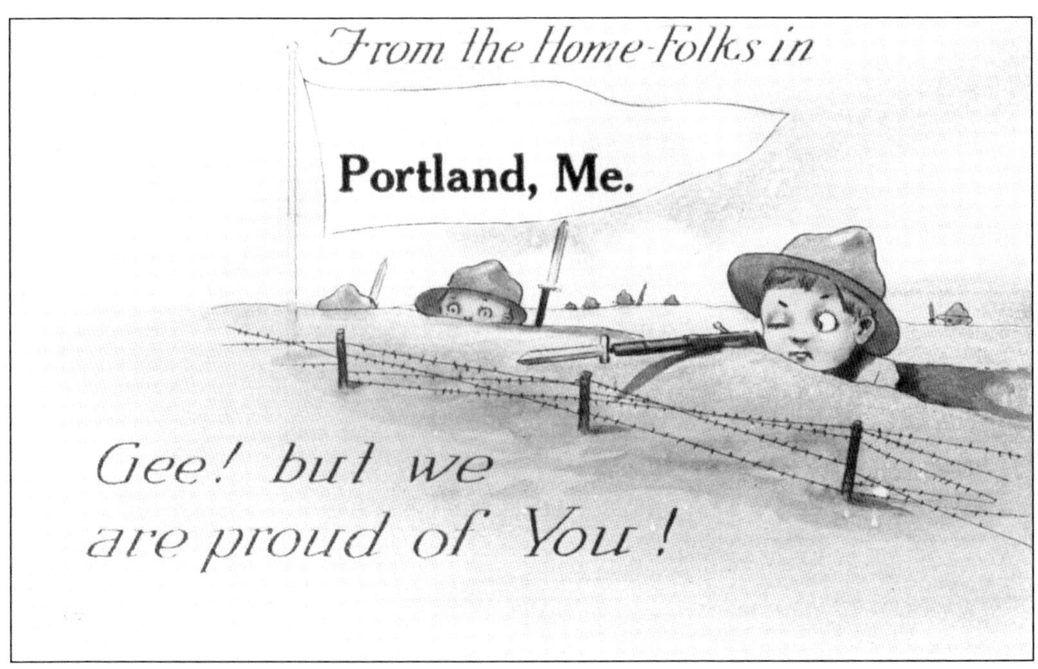

Postcards were one of the more popular and convenient means of communicating with the troops abroad. Cards with patriotic themes were common, while real-photo postcards were sent by soldiers and sailors of themselves, their unit, ship, or even the French countryside following the destruction levied by opposing forces. In one year during the war, the US Post Office transmitted over 30 million letters and postcards to military forces.

THE SHIP ON WHICH I SAILED HAS ARRIVED SAFELY OVERSEAS.

Name (Ensign) Walter Dickey

Organization U.S.N.R.F.

American Expeditionary Forces.

Best Wishes to all.

A common way of letting families know that their loved one was safe was this arrival postal card. Such cards deliberately left out sensitive details such as unit designation and the serviceman's location, information that might benefit the enemy. This card was sent by Ens. Walter Dickey of East Northport, who served in the Navy through the war and beyond.

Although used in previous conflicts, barbed wire was frequently deployed in World War I due to the reliance on trench warfare. Its widespread use for defensive purposes included the ability to halt advancement on trenches and to funnel enemy soldiers into areas where they could be captured or killed. Here, soldiers from the 103rd Regiment place barbed wire near the Chemin-des-Dames, France, in 1918. (MANG.)

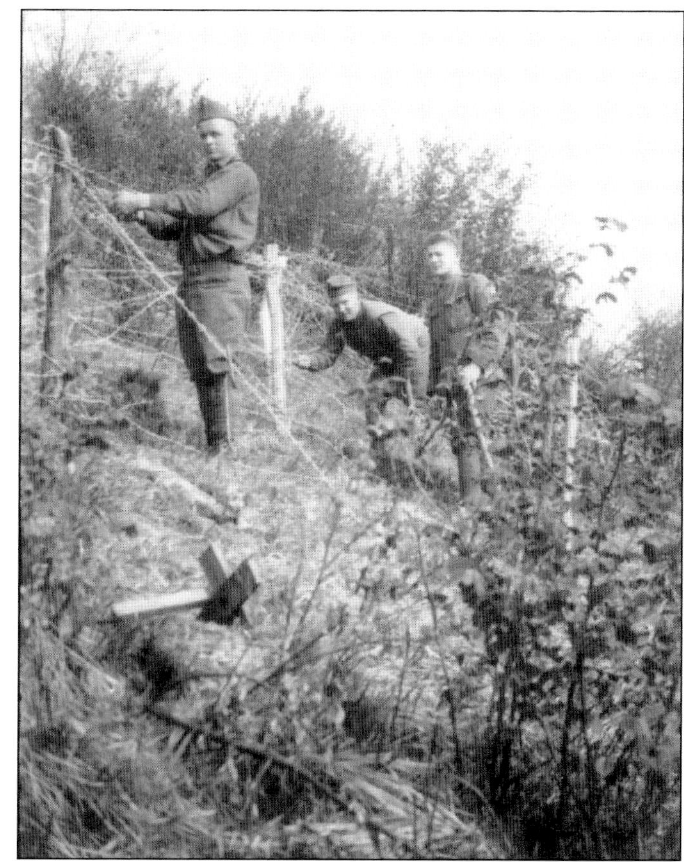

Here soldiers of the 103rd Regiment rest on a roadside in the spring or early summer of 1918. During that time period, the 103rd was engaged in fighting in La Reine and Boucq, also known as the Toul Sector, where the Yankee Division became the first American troops to engage in battle without the assistance of French infantry. (MANG.)

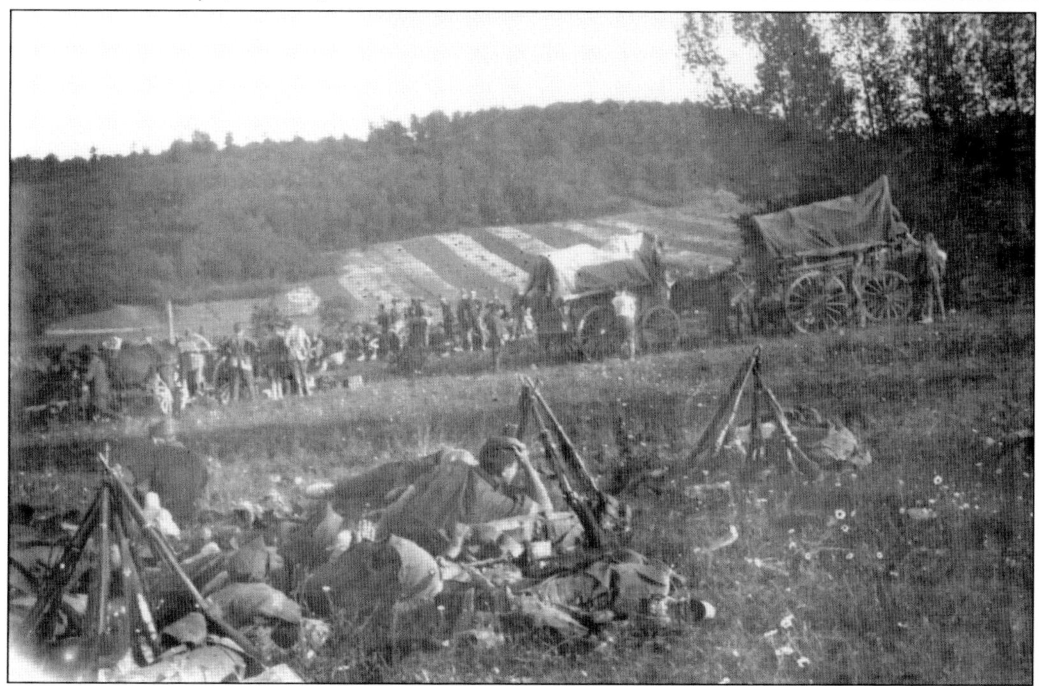

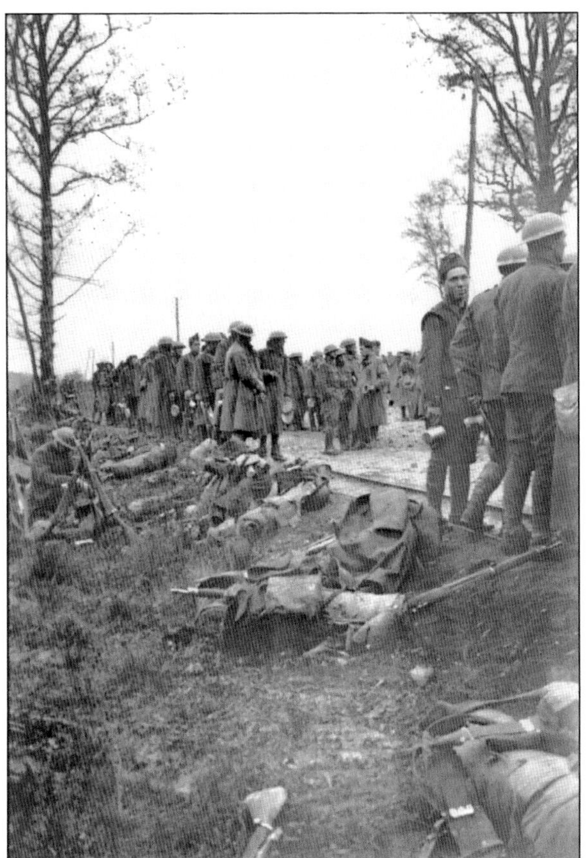

These soldiers from the 103rd Regiment are waiting in line for chow. Each soldier was equipped with a M-1910 haversack that included a mess kit. The standard-issue mess kit consisted of a canteen, cup, meat can, knife, fork, and spoon. Soldiers were issued various rations—reserve, trench, and emergency—which were to be used depending on the circumstances the soldier found himself in. (MANG.)

This group of men from Company F of the 103rd Regiment takes a rare moment to pose for the camera. Three men from the company, Pvt. Elmer H. Lindie, Pvt. Lester Palmer, and Cpl. Harry M. Nightingale received the Distinguished Service Cross, which is second only to the Medal of Honor. Nightingale was mortally wounded as he led his squad forward to attack a machine gun nest. (MANG.)

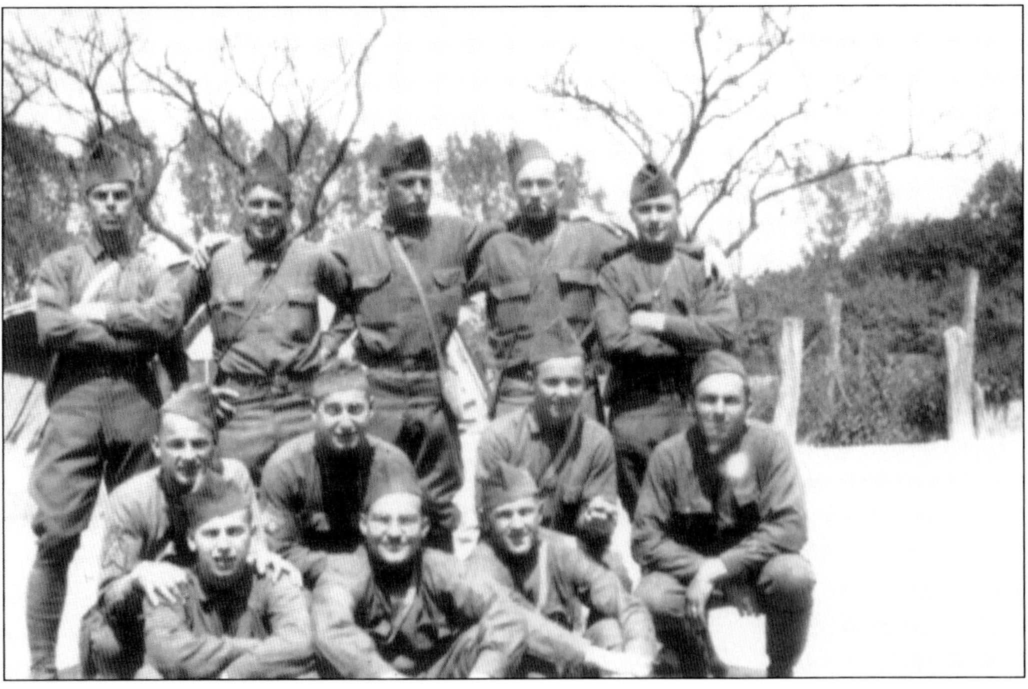

Joseph Bridges of Waterville enlisted in Company H, 2nd Maine in April 1914 and participated in the 1916 expedition to the Mexican border. When the regiment was federalized, he was assigned to Company F and was wounded in action on May 22, 1918, in the Toul Sector. In March 1919, he accepted a commission and was appointed second lieutenant, serving in that capacity until his discharge. (MANG.)

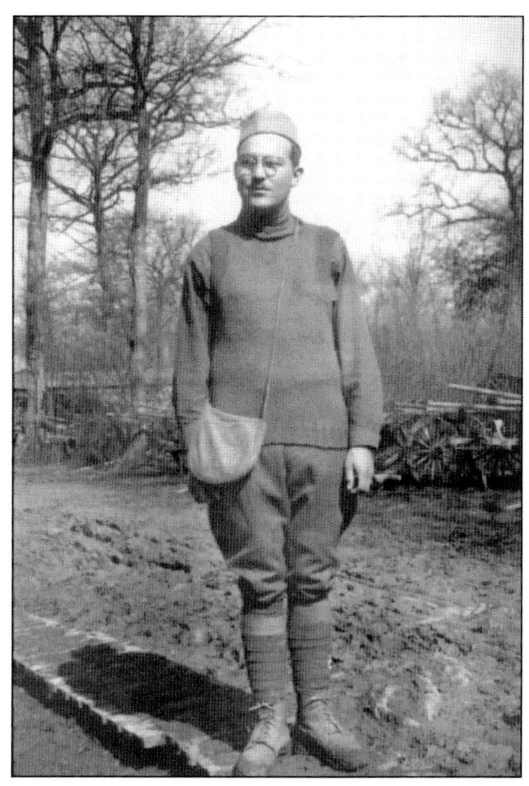

Here, Mary G. Porter greets a French official in 1918. Porter and her lifelong friend, Molly Dewson, both of whom summered in Castine, served in the American Red Cross from 1917 to 1919. During their time in France, they worked with refugees—in particular, infants and children. The Red Cross established canteens, provided soldiers with stationery to write home, and served as nurses in hospitals. (CHS.)

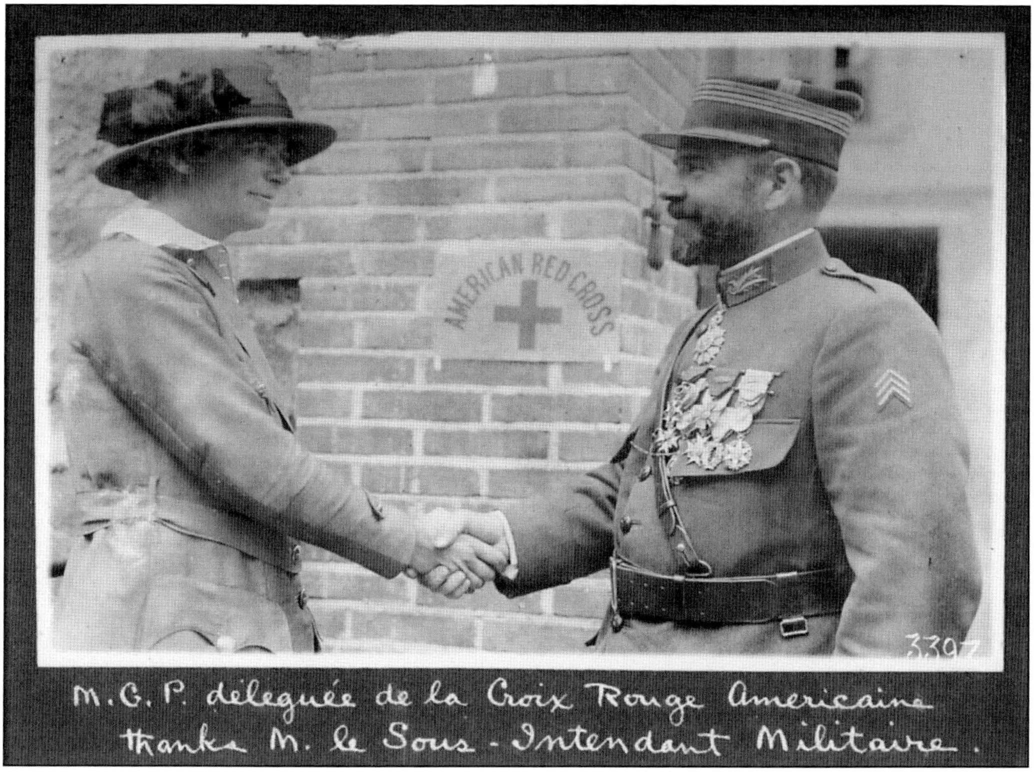

M.G.P. déleguée de la Croix Rouge Americaine thanks M. le Sous-Intendant Militaire.

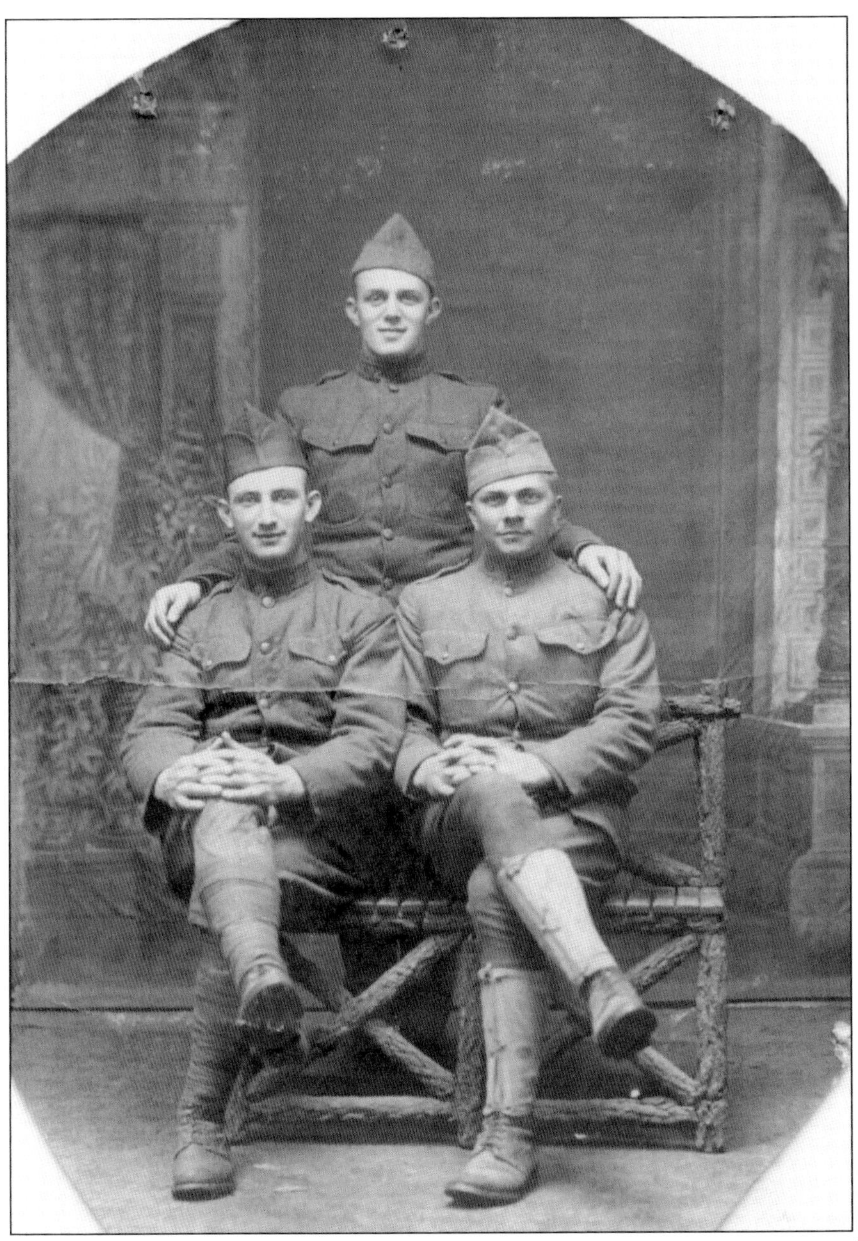

Amos E. Bodge, seated at left with two unidentified soldiers, was born in Monson and was an apprentice machinist for the Fay and Scott Machine Shop and Foundry in Dexter when he enlisted in the Regular Army in December 1917. He was assigned to the 2nd Company, 2nd Regiment Motor Mechanical of the Army Air Corps. Training mechanics for the Air Service was difficult even for those with a mechanical background, because they would be working on European engines. In order to efficiently train mechanics to work on airplanes, the United States partnered with the French, British, and Italians. Several weeks of training were offered, and they were sent to the airfields or to factories to help assemble aircraft. Bodge went overseas in March 1918, and was promoted to corporal, followed by sergeant. He was engaged in the Aisne Offensive in May and June 1918 and was honorably discharged in June 1919. He later moved to Connecticut and was employed as a toolmaker. (Gauthier.)

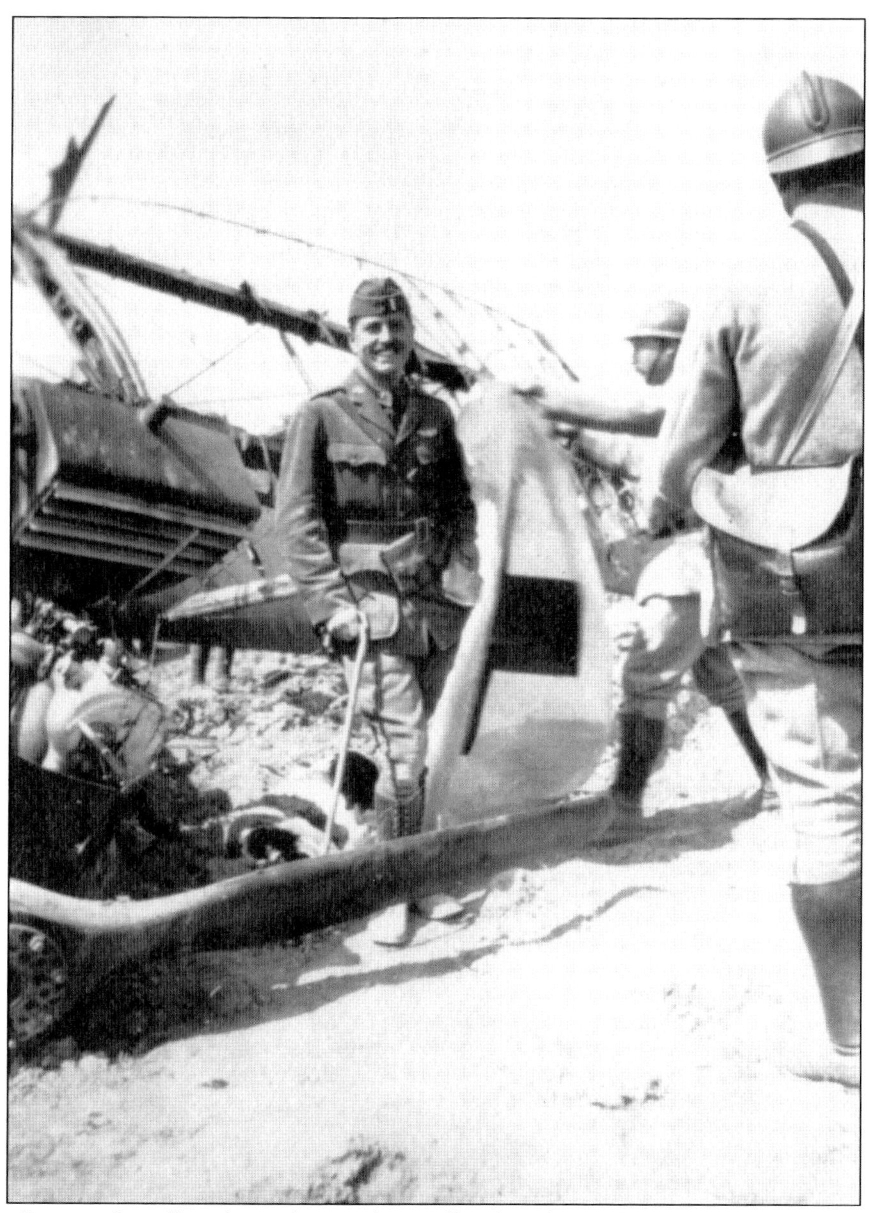

Here, Lt. Sumner Sewall explores the wreckage of his first downed aircraft, a German two-seater, on June 3, 1918, in Dieulouard. A native of Bath, Sewall left Harvard to join the war effort. He first traveled to France in early 1917 to join the Ambulance Field Service and then joined the Signal Corps. A few months later, Sewall joined the Air Corps. A member of the 94th and 95th Aero squadrons, he eventually scored seven victories, making him the only Maine-born ace. He was also credited with two balloons and four other airplane victories, including the downing of German ace Otto Rosenfeld. A fearless fighter, on several occasions he attacked enemy formations, outmanned and outgunned, and in one instance while pursuing a Fokker, he flew within 30 meters of the ground and had bullets pass through his clothing. During his service, he received a Distinguished Service Cross with Oak Leaf cluster and a Croix de Guerre. Following the war, he was elected to the legislature, served two terms as governor, and became an airline executive. (MMM.)

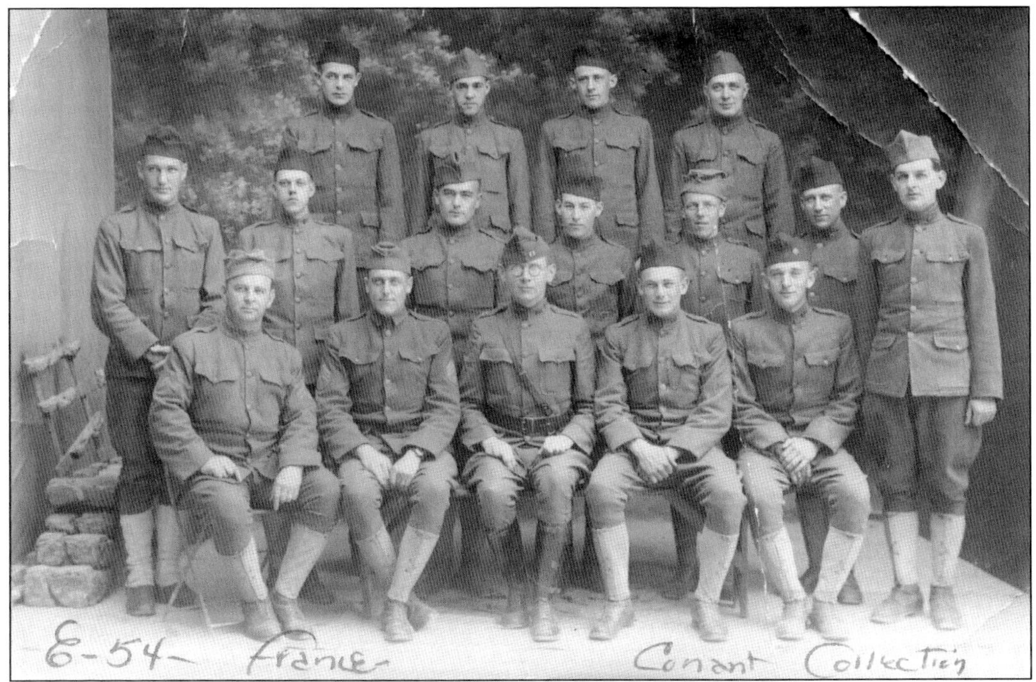

This photograph of Battery E of the 54th CAC was taken in Mailly, France, on July 1, 1918, and features Hiram W. Estey of Westbrook, who is standing at the end. Many members of the battery were originally part of the 28th Company stationed at Fort Williams. After the 54th was called into federal service in January 1918, it was sent to France in March 1918. (Libby.)

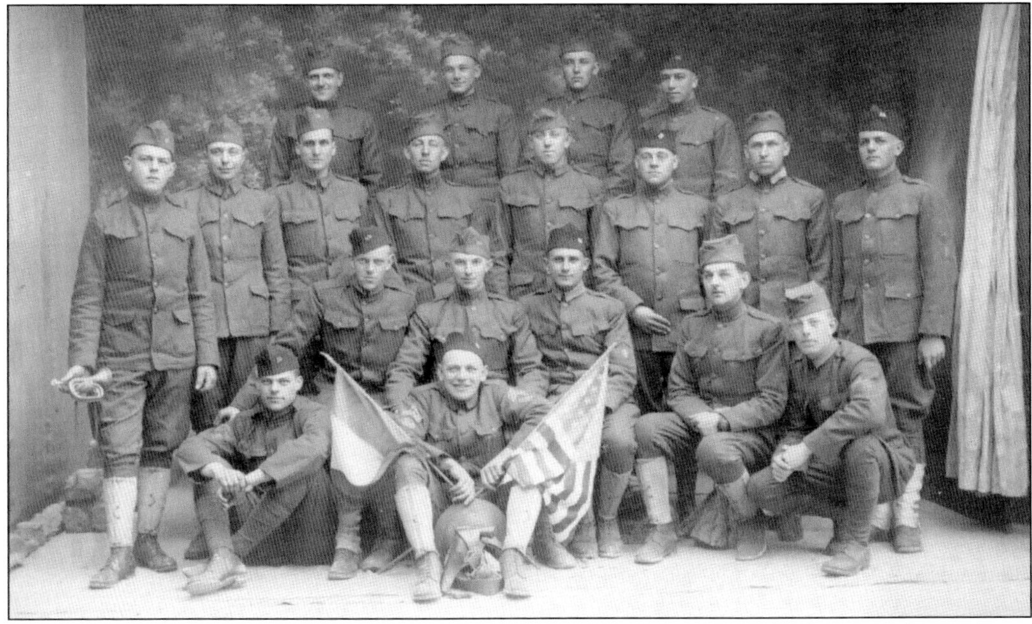

This image of Battery D of the 54th CAC was taken in the same French photography studio in Mailly. Prominent in the image is Sgt. Carl L. Pearson of Falmouth with the flags, helmet, and pistol at his feet. Pearson enlisted in the Maine National Guard in March 1917, was promoted to corporal in July and promoted again while he served overseas. (Gauthier.)

Pfc. Lawrence T, Merriman left his studies at the University of Maine, enlisted in December 1917, and was assigned to Battery E of the 54th Coast Artillery Corps. The 54th was used as replacement artillery, meaning that soldiers were transferred to other artillery regiments as necessary. Merriman went overseas with the 54th in March 1918 and in May was transferred to Battery B of the 60th CAC, also known as "(Col.) Wallace's Red Circus." Merriman is in the image at the right and shown below with two unidentified members of his battery. These two images and those on pages 74–76 are from Merriman's war photo album, a mix of amateur as well as commercial images sold to members of the 60th CAC. (Both, Libby.)

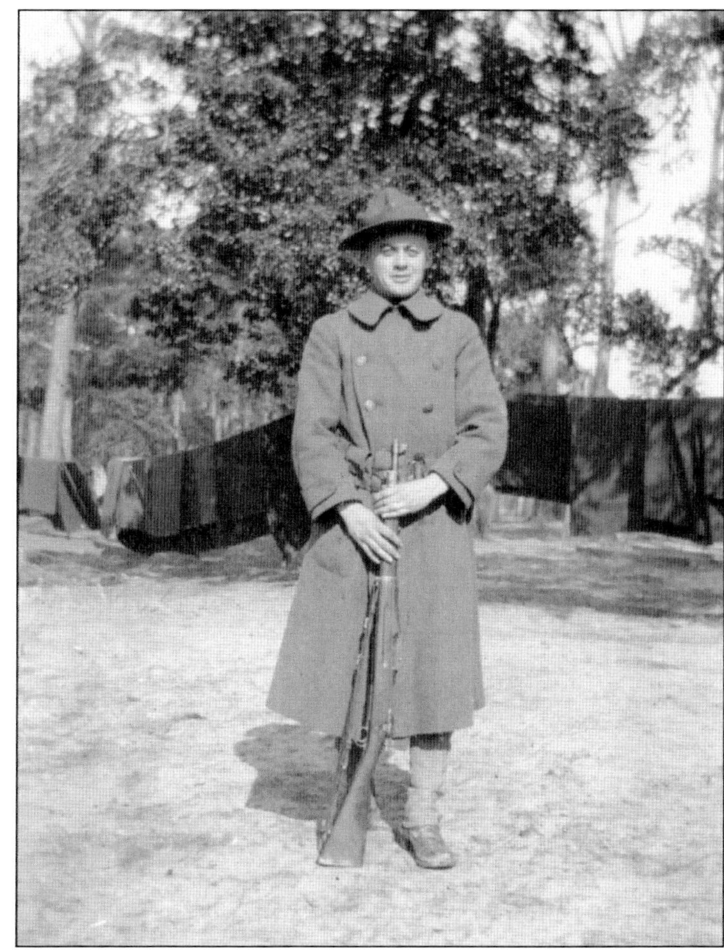

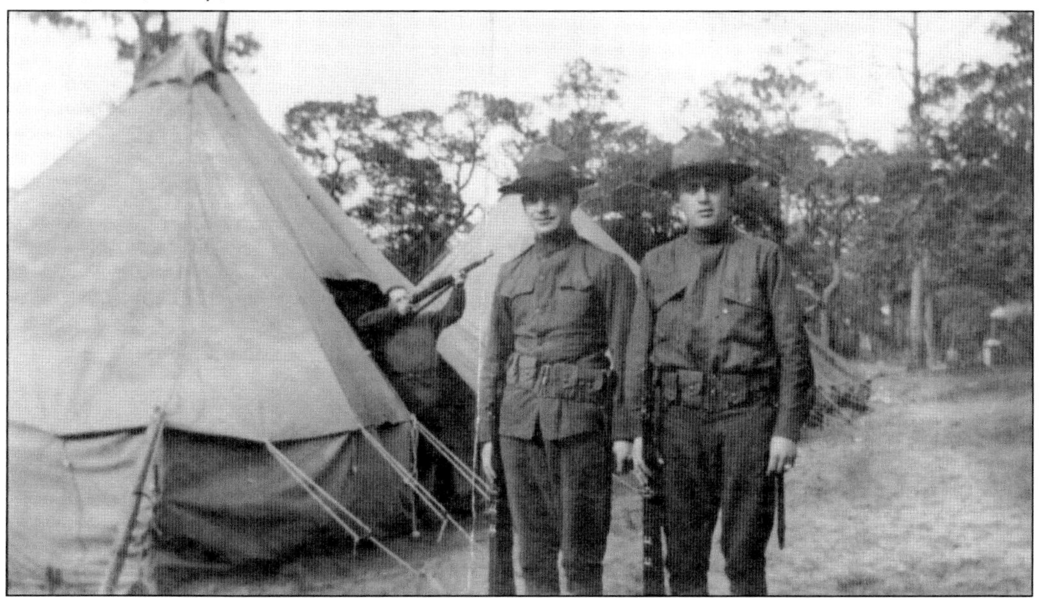

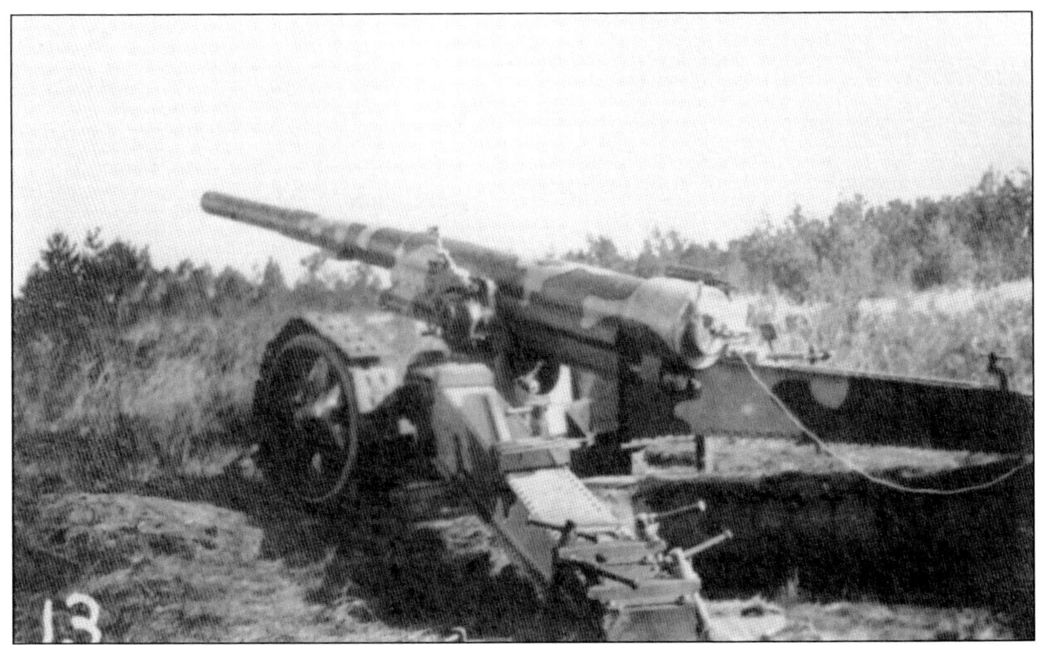

A decision was made early to adopt the artillery that the French army used in order to improve the training of American forces. The French supplied over 200 of 155mm Grande Puissance Filloux (GPF) guns like this one to American forces. This image was taken on August 5, 1918, and is of the first artillery gun of the 60th CAC to fire a service charge. (Libby.)

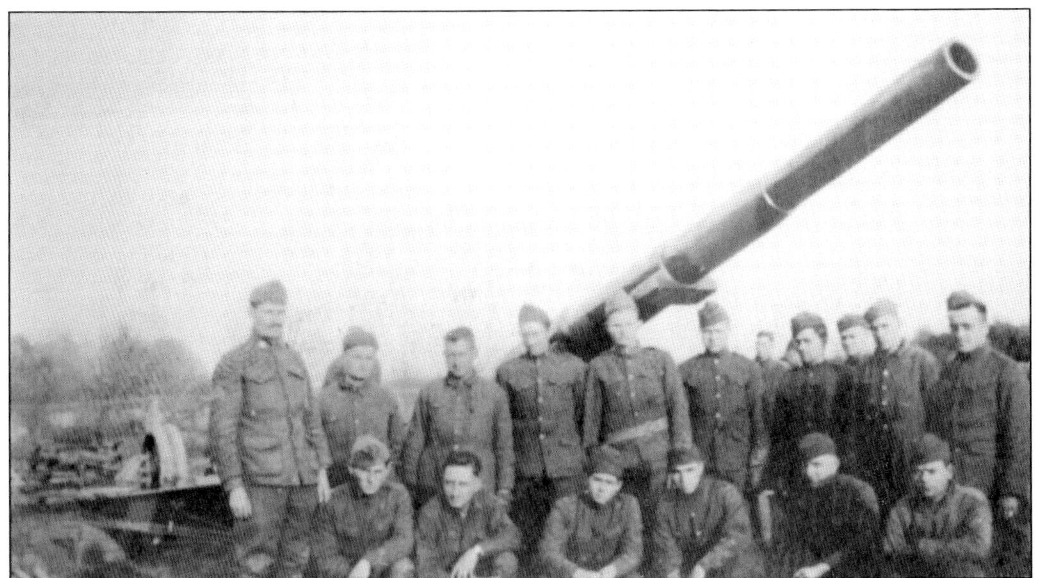

Members of Battery B of the 60th CAC stand in front of a 155mm GPF. The 60th was formed at Fort Monroe, Virginia, and made up primarily of men from that state and the District of Columbia. Others, like Private First Class Merriman, were transferred into the unit. At times, the 60th CAC served as artillery support for the First Corps, which included the 26th Division (Libby.)

Artillery shells came in many sizes, with some large enough for a soldier to sit in. Various types of shells were used, including incendiary, chemical and gas, perforating and exploding. Over a century later, unexploded shells are still unearthed on former battlefields. The 60th CAC alone fired over 34,000 rounds from mid-September 1918 to November 10, 1918, when firing ceased. (Libby.)

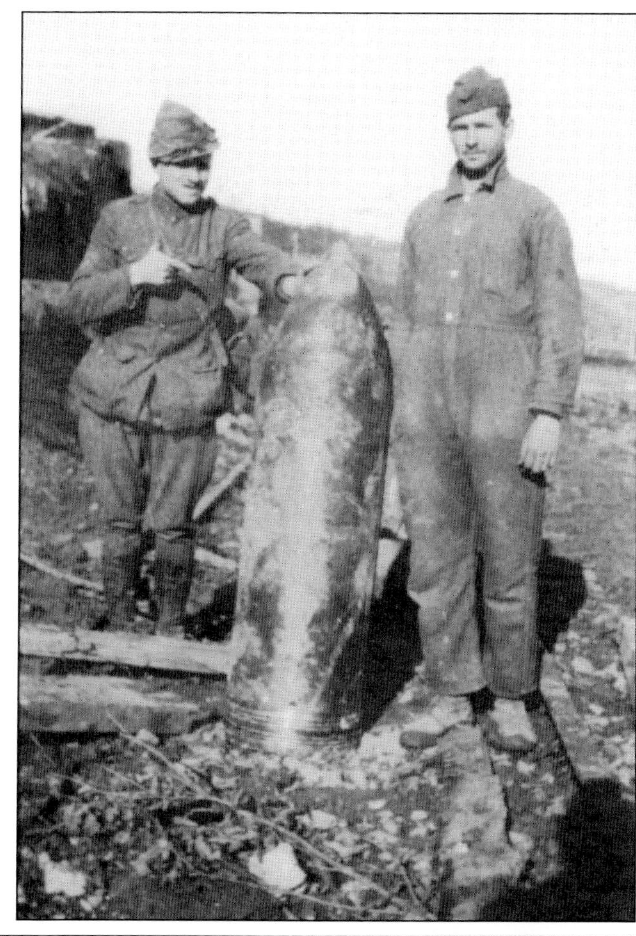

Captioned "the only time the 60th was off the firing line from September 10th to November 11th," this image shows soldiers gathering for a hot meal. Note their vehicles and guns parked on the roadside in the distance. The regiment was ordered to move toward the Verdon sector during the massive Meuse-Argonne Offensive that would last until the close of the war. (Libby.)

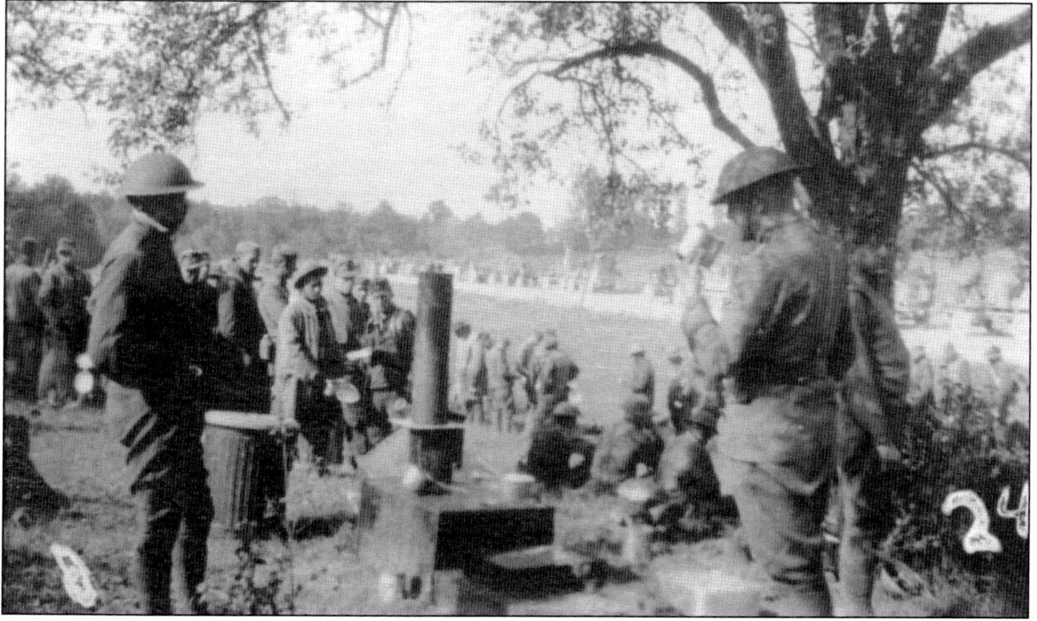

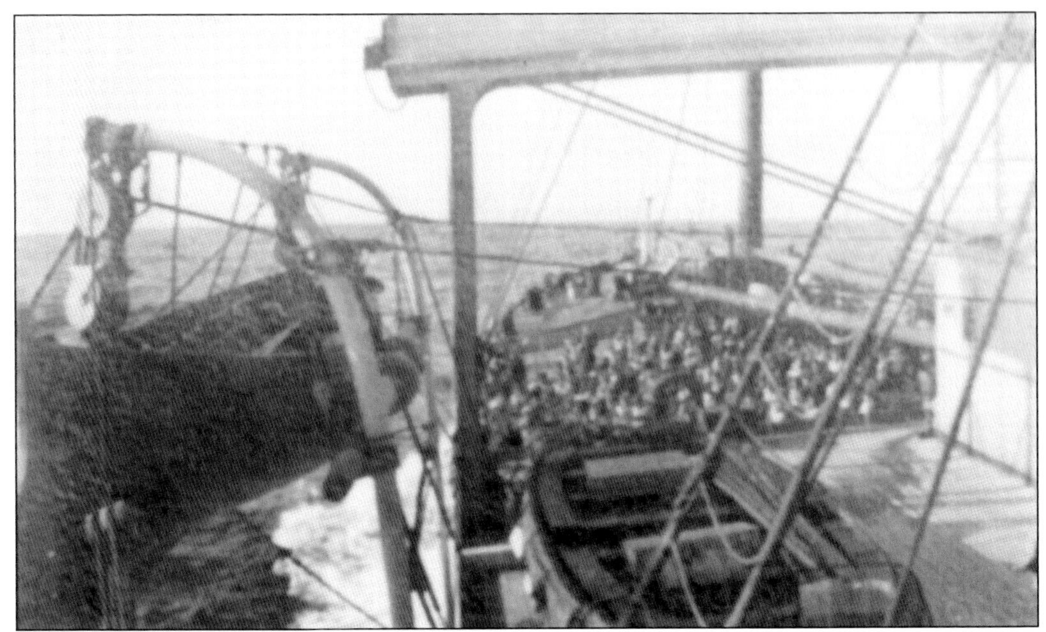

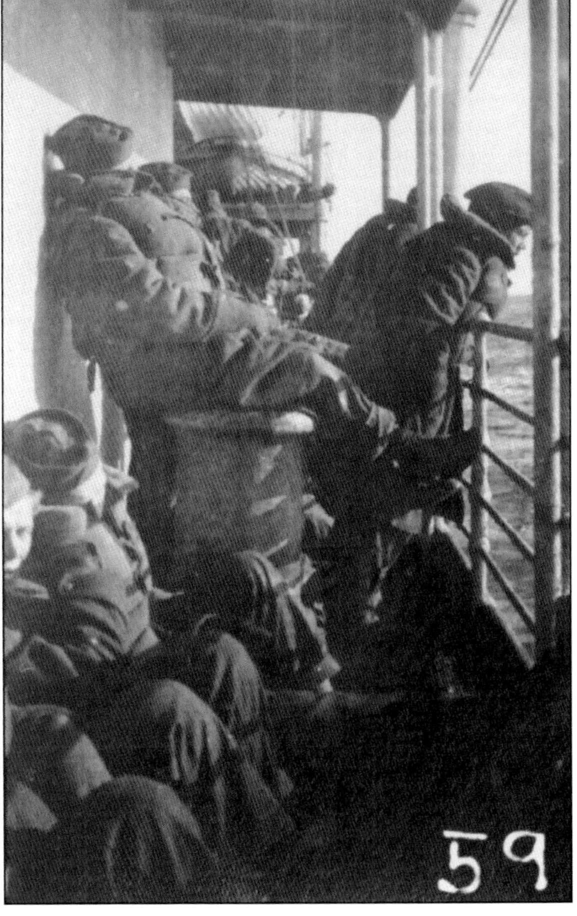

On January 26, 1919, the White Star liner RMS *Cedric*, a passenger ship carrying the 60th and the 44th Coastal Artillery Corps, departed from Brest, France, and set sail for home. Upon demobilization, the 60th CAC was deactivated. As one soldier noted, "It exists only in the memory of those who served in it, though it may be that there are still some Germans who recall it." Like many of his comrades in arms, following his discharge on February 24, 1919, Merriman went home to pick up where he had left off. He returned to the University of Maine to finish his degree, graduating in 1921. He served as superintendent of the Harpswell schools and later worked in insurance and dairy farming. (Both, Libby.)

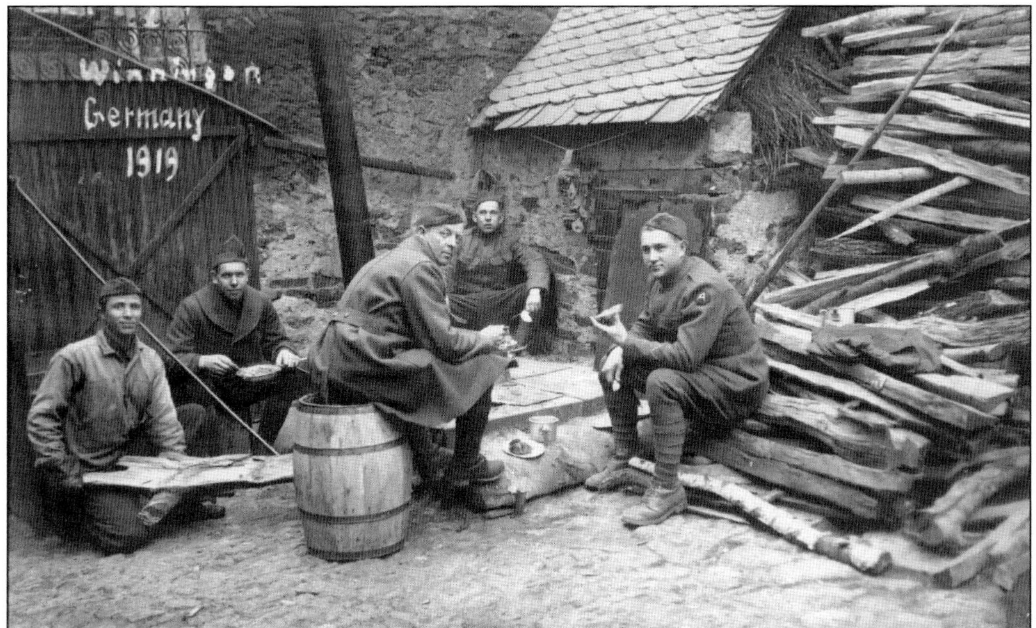

After the 1st Maine Heavy Artillery was designated as the 56th Pioneer Infantry, it was sent to France in early September 1918. The regiment's duties included making trails and roads passable, as well as light construction. After the Armistice, the regiment was stationed in Germany as part of the Army of Occupation. Here, soldiers eat chow while stationed at Winnengen, Germany. (Libby.)

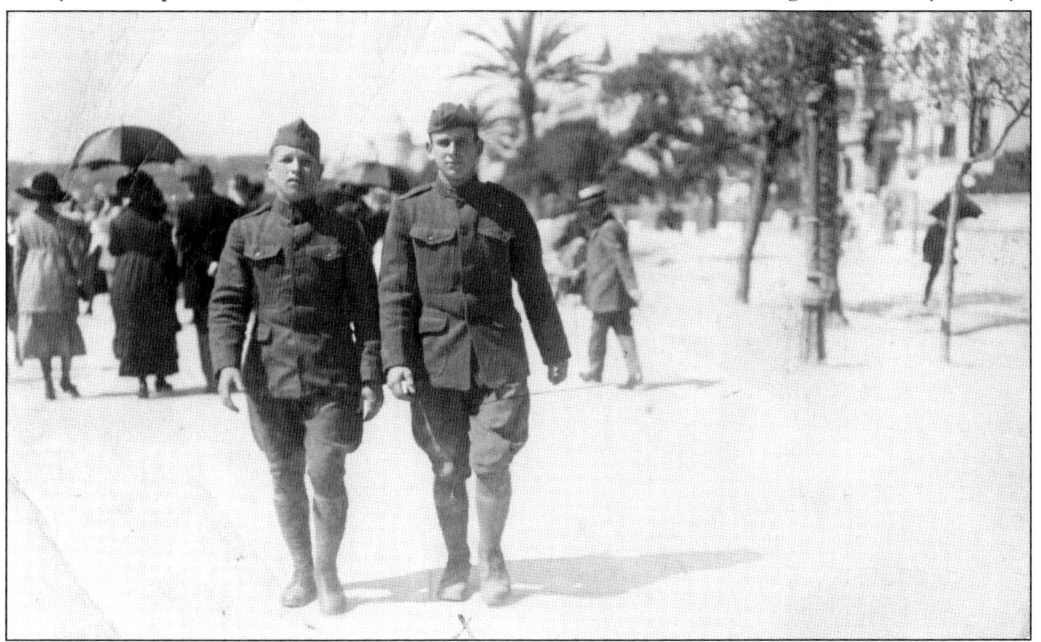

Harold B. Wessenger, on the right, a member of the 79th Division, sent this image to his cousin Hester Wessenger, a student at the University of Maine. Harold and a fellow soldier are seen taking in the sights in southern France in early 1919 while on occupation duty. Soldiers also took the opportunity to take courses in French or other fields, athletic competitions, and other diversions. (Libby.)

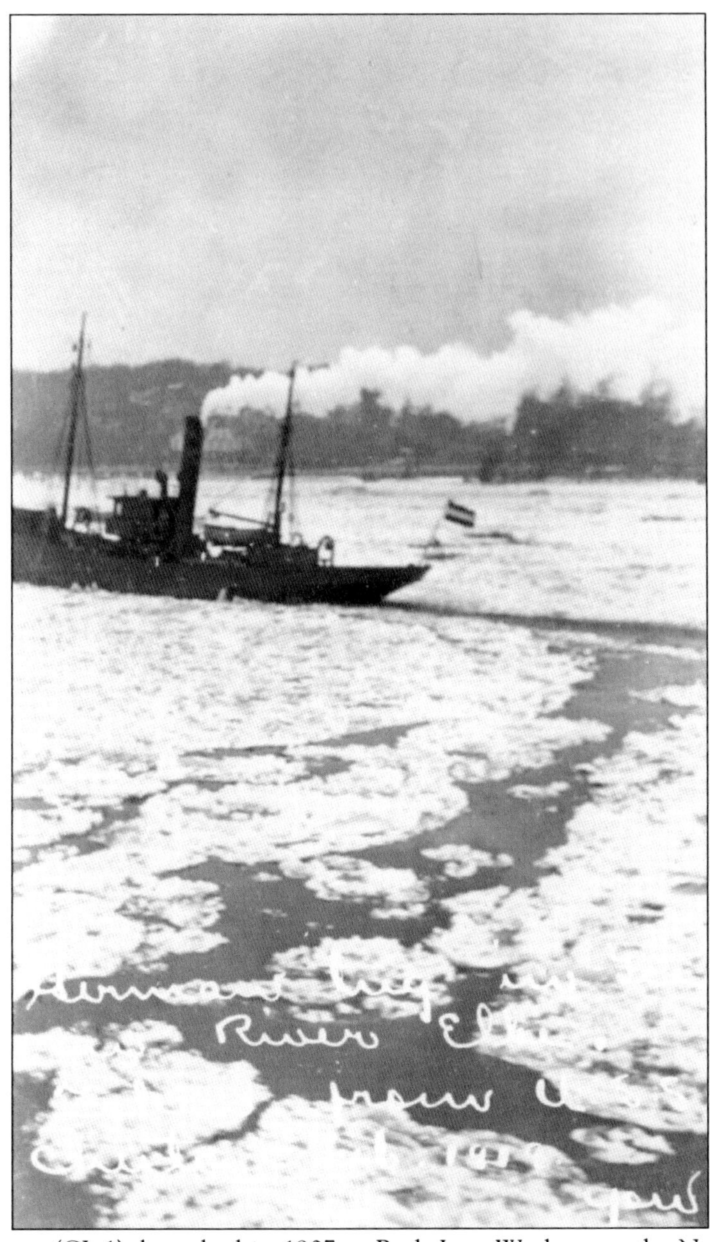

The USS *Chester* (CL-1), launched in 1907 at Bath Iron Works, was the Navy's first scout cruiser, later classified as a light cruiser. During the Mexican Revolution, it patrolled the Gulf of Mexico and anchored at Veracruz, shelling the city to support a landing party which was to protect American interests and citizens. During World War I, the *Chester* was used to patrol the East Coast, and toward the end of the war it escorted ships between England and Gibraltar. On September 5, 1918, the crew sighted a submarine, attempted to ram it, which slightly damaged the ship, and then dropped depth charges but there was no further contact with the vessel. After hostilities had ceased, the *Chester* brought Allied commissions to inspect German ports as a part of the terms of the Armistice and also transported troops to Russia in support of the Siberian Expedition. This image taken from the USS *Chester* and shows an icebreaker during an inspection of German ports on the Elbe River in 1919. (Libby.)

Seven

MAINE PATRIOTS

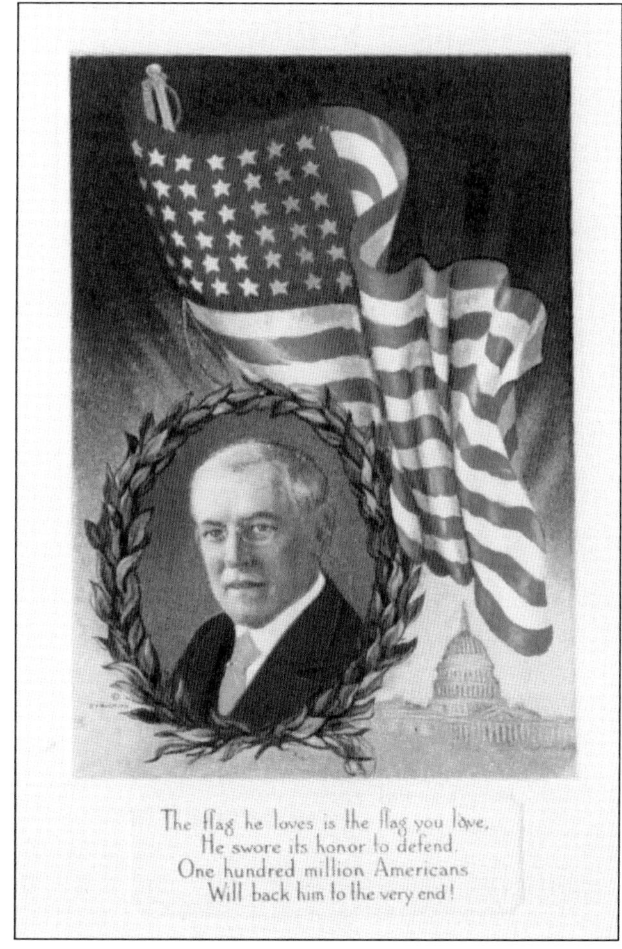

Woodrow Wilson rose to national prominence as president of Princeton University and governor of New Jersey. He won the presidency as a Democrat in 1912 and from 1914 to 1917 strove for American neutrality in World War I. He then led the nation during 19 months of war and sought the elusive goal of a lasting peace through the League of Nations.

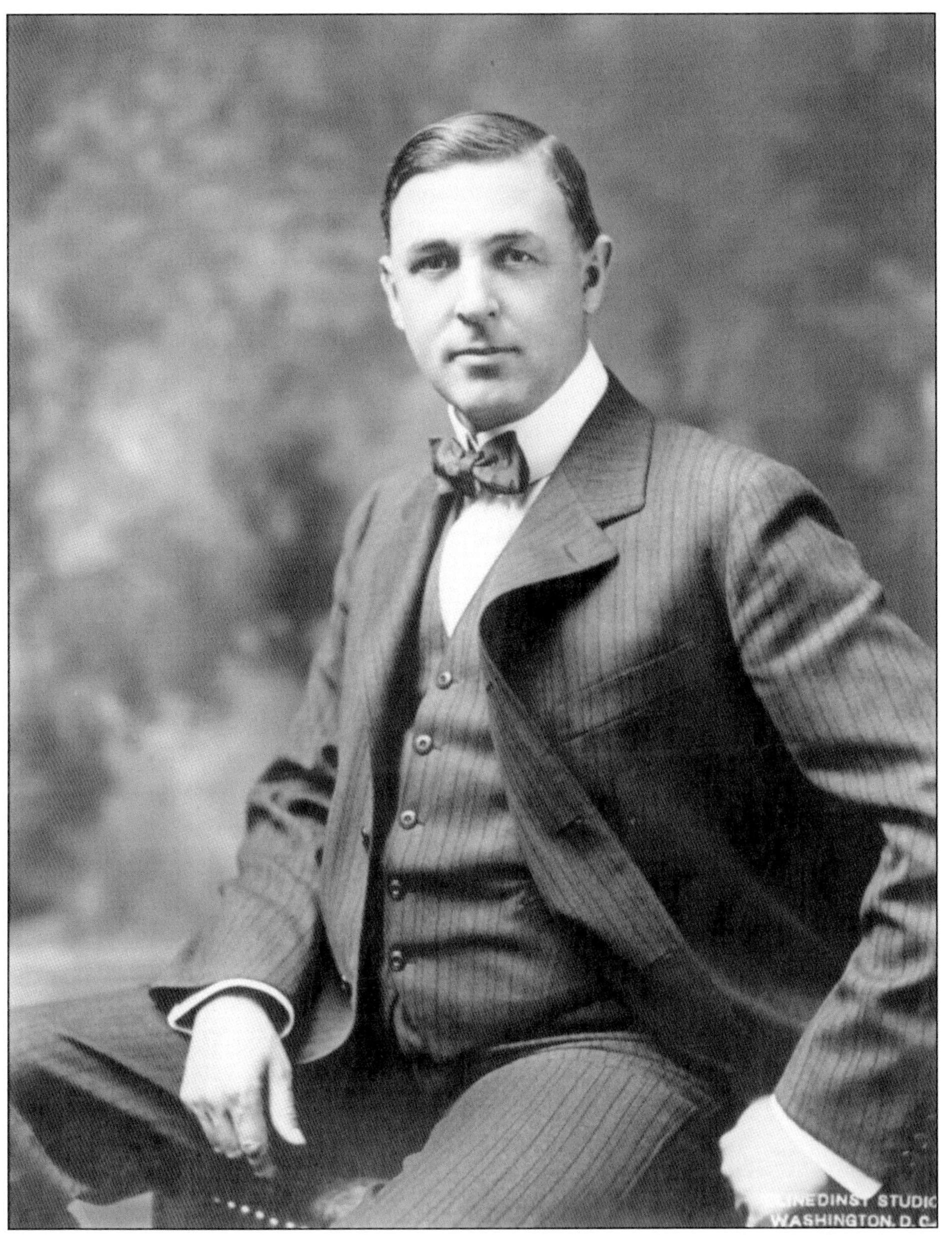

A native of Pittsfield, Carl E. Milliken graduated from Bates College and worked in the lumber business in Aroostook County. He served in the Maine House and Senate before running for governor on the Republican ticket in 1916. That year, he won the first of two terms. Milliken's governorship spanned America's participation in World War I, and he provided Maine with dynamic wartime leadership. In his war message to the legislature on April 3, 1917, he called for the issuance of $1 million in bonds to fund a wide range of war-related programs, including providing for the families of servicemen. His Committee of One Hundred for Public Safety would coordinate these activities in each of the state's 16 counties. A strikingly handsome man who stood six feet tall, Governor Milliken participated in countless public events throughout the state in support of the war. Often dressed in a formal black tailcoat and wearing a tall silk hat, he was every inch a governor for his time.

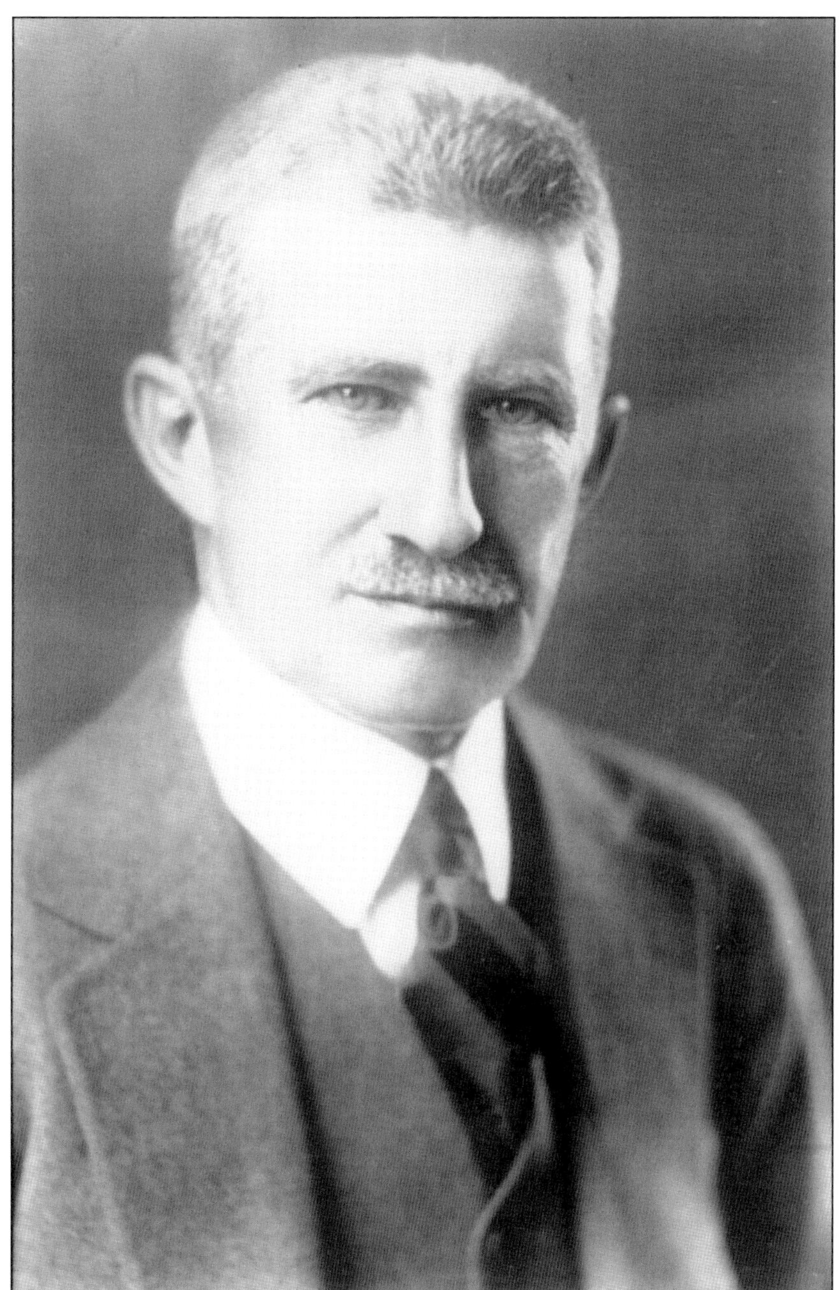

Frederick Hale was a member of a noted American political family. His grandfather Zachariah Chandler and his father Eugene Hale were US senators, while his brother was a diplomat and his cousin was a congressman. Frederick graduated from Harvard, attended Columbia Law School, and began practicing law in Portland in 1899. He was elected to the Senate as a Republican in 1916 and served four terms there between 1917 and 1941 as an influential member of the Naval Affairs and Appropriations committees. He became a forceful advocate for American naval power, which benefited Maine in federal support for the Portsmouth Naval Shipyard in Kittery and the Bath Iron Works. At the time of his death, he was the last living senator who was serving at the time of the United States' declaration of war against Germany in 1917.

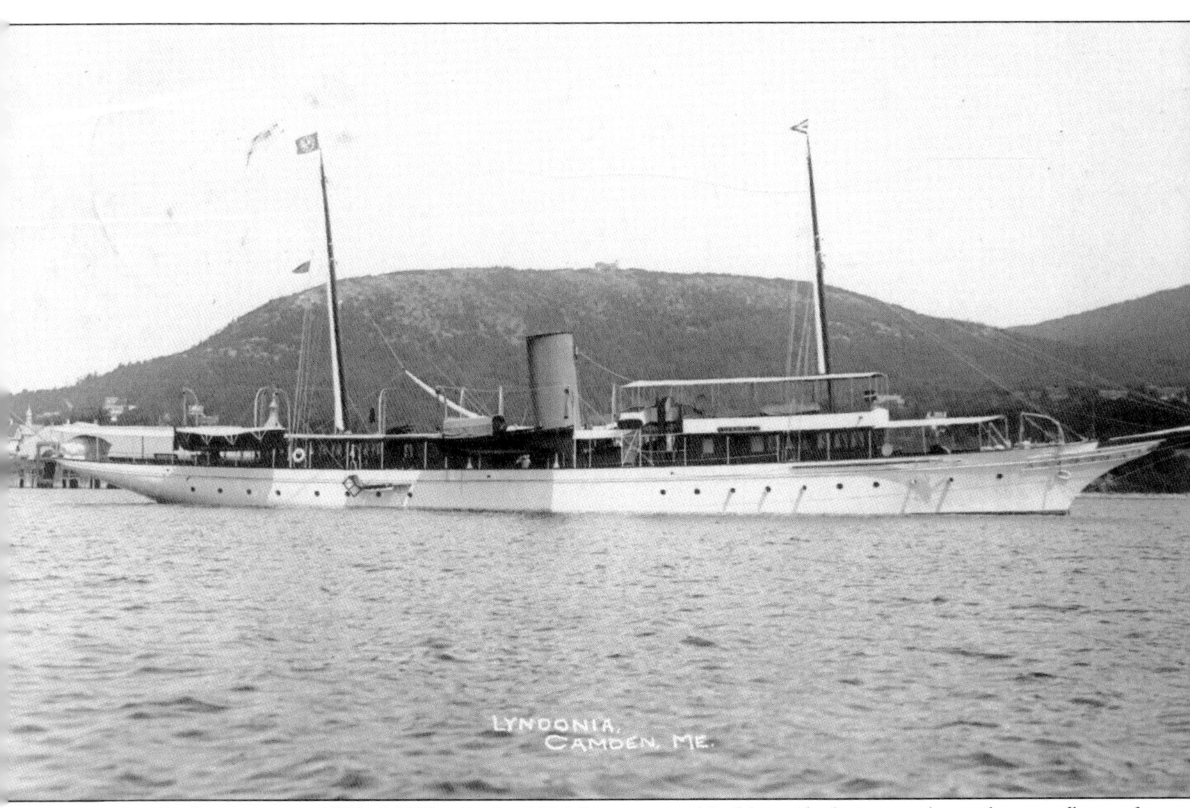

At the beginning of World War I, the US Navy assembled by gift, loan, and purchase a fleet of small craft to use as patrol boats and training ships. One of these was the *Lyndonia*, a luxury yacht acquired from the Philadelphia publisher Cyrus H.K. Curtis in September 1917. The *Lyndonia* was in government service until September 1919, after which she was decommissioned and sold. This elegant vessel was no stranger to Maine waters, having been built for Curtis in New York in 1907 to sail between Philadelphia and his summer home on Beauchamp Point in Rockport. A Portland native, Curtis rose from a modest background to own the *Ladies Home Journal*, the *Saturday Evening Post*, and several Philadelphia and New York newspapers. In 1920, Curtis replaced the first *Lyndonia* with a larger yacht of the same name, which he sailed until his death in 1933.

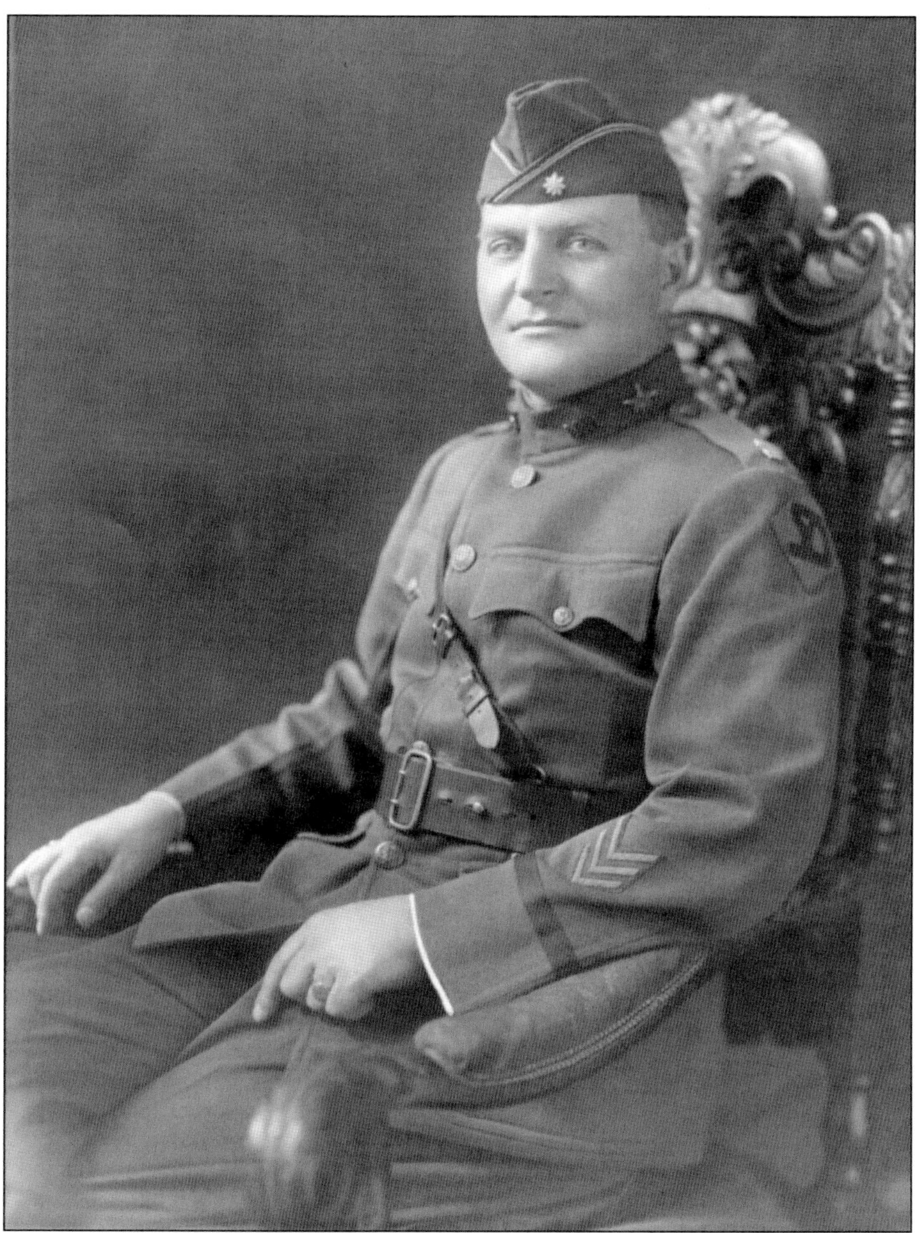

Brig. Gen. Albert Greenlaw of Eastport was a career military man. He began his service in 1894 in Company I of the 2nd Maine and quickly rose through the ranks, being promoted captain in the Quartermasters Corps in 1906. He served in that capacity until he was chosen as adjutant general in 1913 during the administration of Gov. Oakley Curtis. He resigned that post in 1915 and was returned to the grade of captain. Greenlaw was activated with the 103rd, assigned to the 26th Division staff, and was promoted major and lieutenant colonel in October 1918 and March 1919, respectively. Greenlaw was cited with a Meritorious Service Citation. Following the war, Greenlaw and several others from Maine, including James L. Boyle of Waterville, participated in the meeting in Paris in 1919 where the American Legion was established. Greenlaw served as the first chairman of the Department of Maine of the American Legion and remained a strong advocate for veterans. (MSM.)

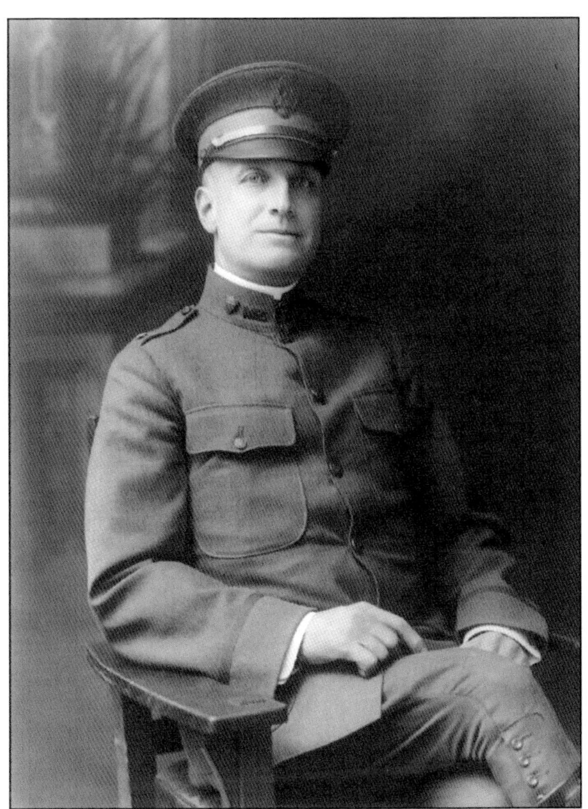

Succeeding Albert Greenlaw as adjutant general was George McLellan Presson of Farmington. During Presson's tenure, he oversaw military matters in the state during the 1916 activation to the Mexican border and throughout the entire war. He frequently spoke at college campuses, town meetings and elsewhere to increase enlistments and encourage civilian support for the troops abroad. Presson served until 1921 and retired with the rank of colonel. (MSM.)

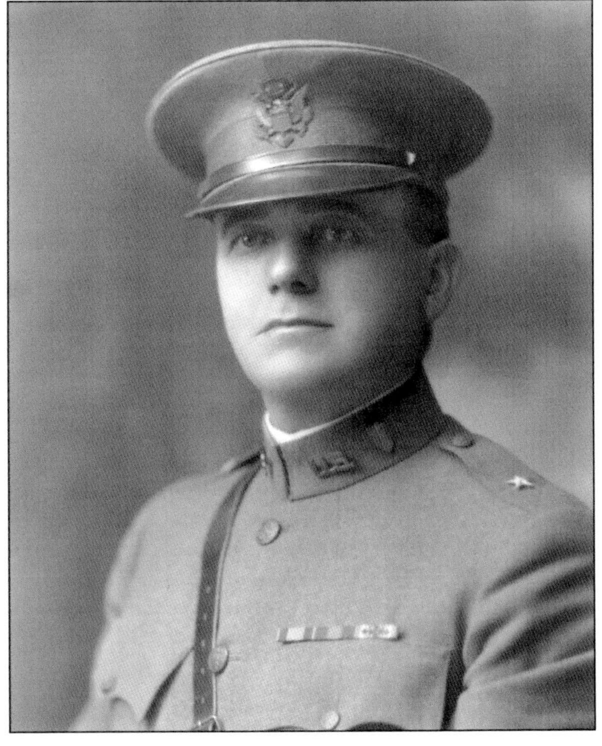

John Austin Hadley, from Rumford, saw service during the Spanish-American War and the Mexican border crisis in 1916. He went to France as a major with the 103rd Regiment and in the 7th and 42nd Divisions. Following the war, he was promoted to colonel and served as adjutant general during Gov. Percival P. Baxter's terms in office, succeeding Presson. Later in life, Hadley served in the Veterans Administration. (MSM.)

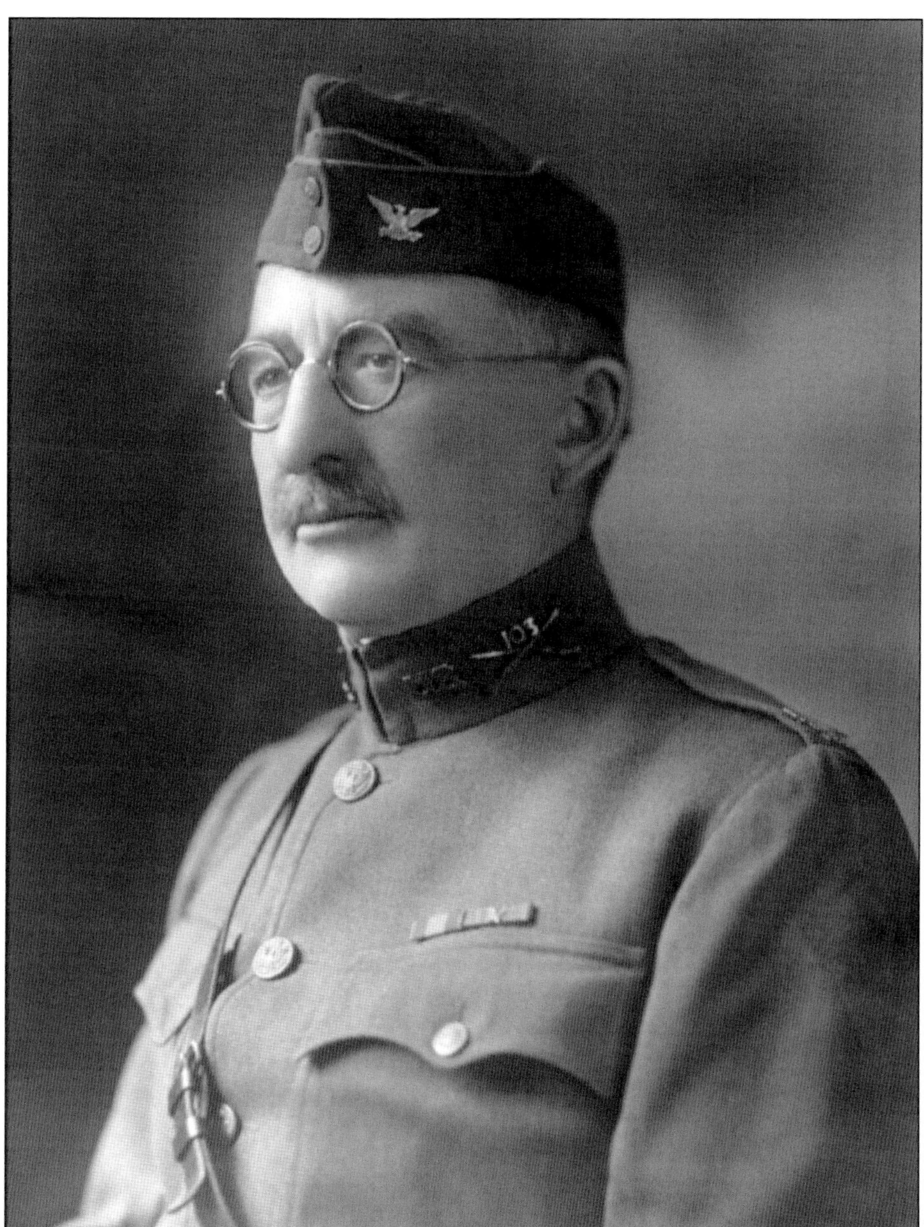

Col. Frank M. Hume of Houlton was beloved by his men. An intelligent man, he was turned down for an appointment to West Point because of health issues and poor eyesight. Instead, Hume went to a military academy and then enrolled in Harvard. He served in Cuba during the Spanish-American War and was colonel of the 2nd Maine Infantry Regiment when it was called into service in June 1916 to go to Texas. When the 2nd Maine was federalized in 1917, Colonel Hume took command of the 103rd Regiment, which consisted of the regiment with additional troops from the former First New Hampshire Regiment. He served the duration of the war and was awarded the Croix de Guerre and the Distinguished Service Cross for his service. Following the war, Hume was a regular visitor to veteran reunions, and a former soldier collected other veterans' accounts of him for a book titled *The Old Man of the 103rd*, published a year after his death in 1939. Hume retired from the Maine National Guard with the rank of brigadier general. (MSM.)

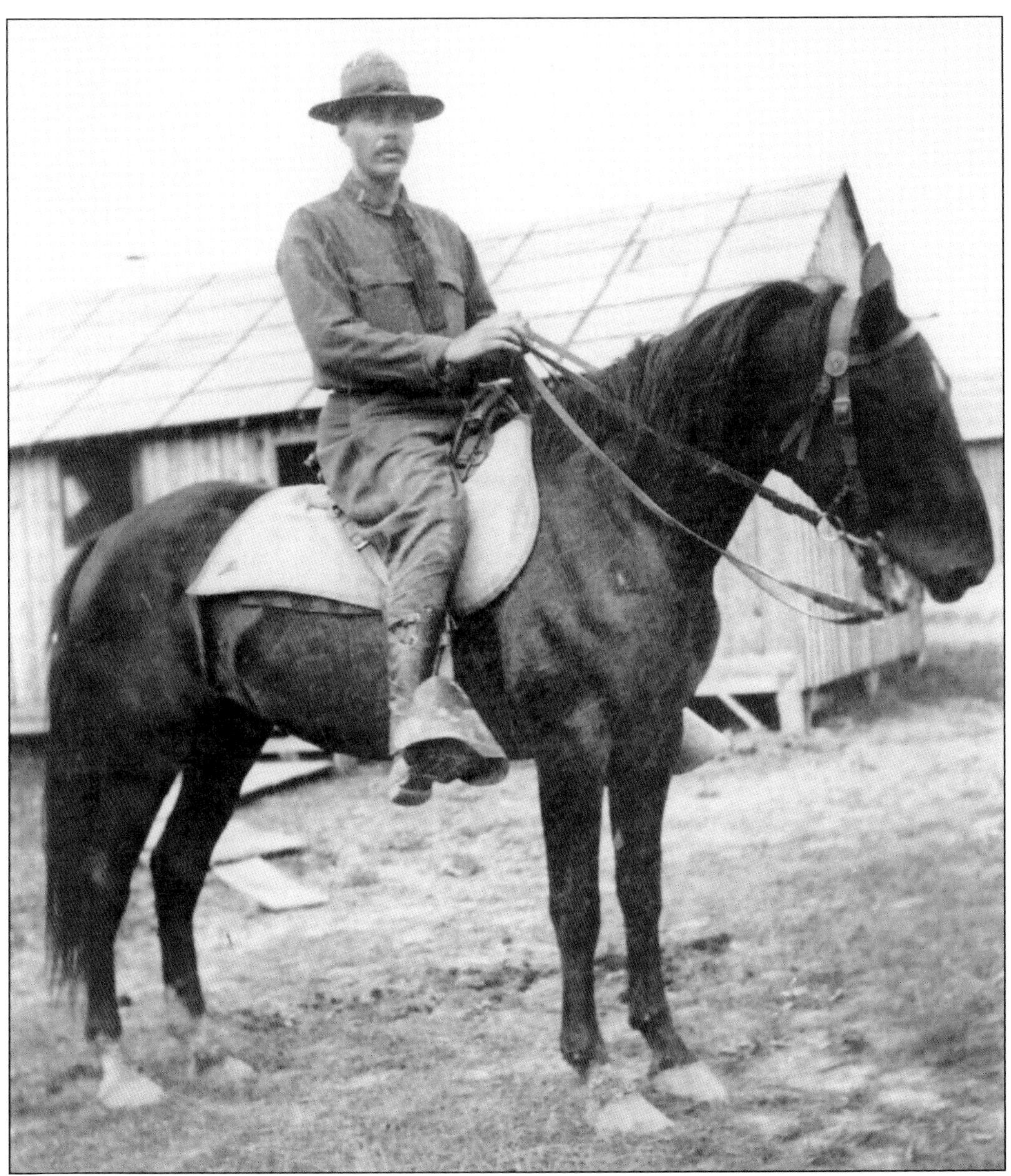

In 1912, Dr. Harrison B. Webster began his practice in Castine. Three years later, he and his wife, Margaret, bought a house and turned part of it into the town's first hospital. In May 1918, Dr. Webster was commissioned a major and sent to France as a regimental surgeon in the 47th Infantry Regiment, Fourth Division. Heroic and hardworking, Dr. Webster was killed in the line of duty as he was attempting to push an ambulance that was stuck in the mud. For his valor, he was posthumously awarded the Distinguished Service Cross. His citation read, "For extraordinary heroism in action near Bois de Brieulles, France from 26 September to 12 October 1918. After seeing that his personnel were functioning properly, he went fearlessly to positions in the front lines. When stretcher bearers were unable to handle the large number of casualties, he personally took a light German wagon to the front lines and gathered the wounded. His personal bravery was an inspiration to his men throughout his service. He was killed by shell fire on October 12, 1918." (CHS.)

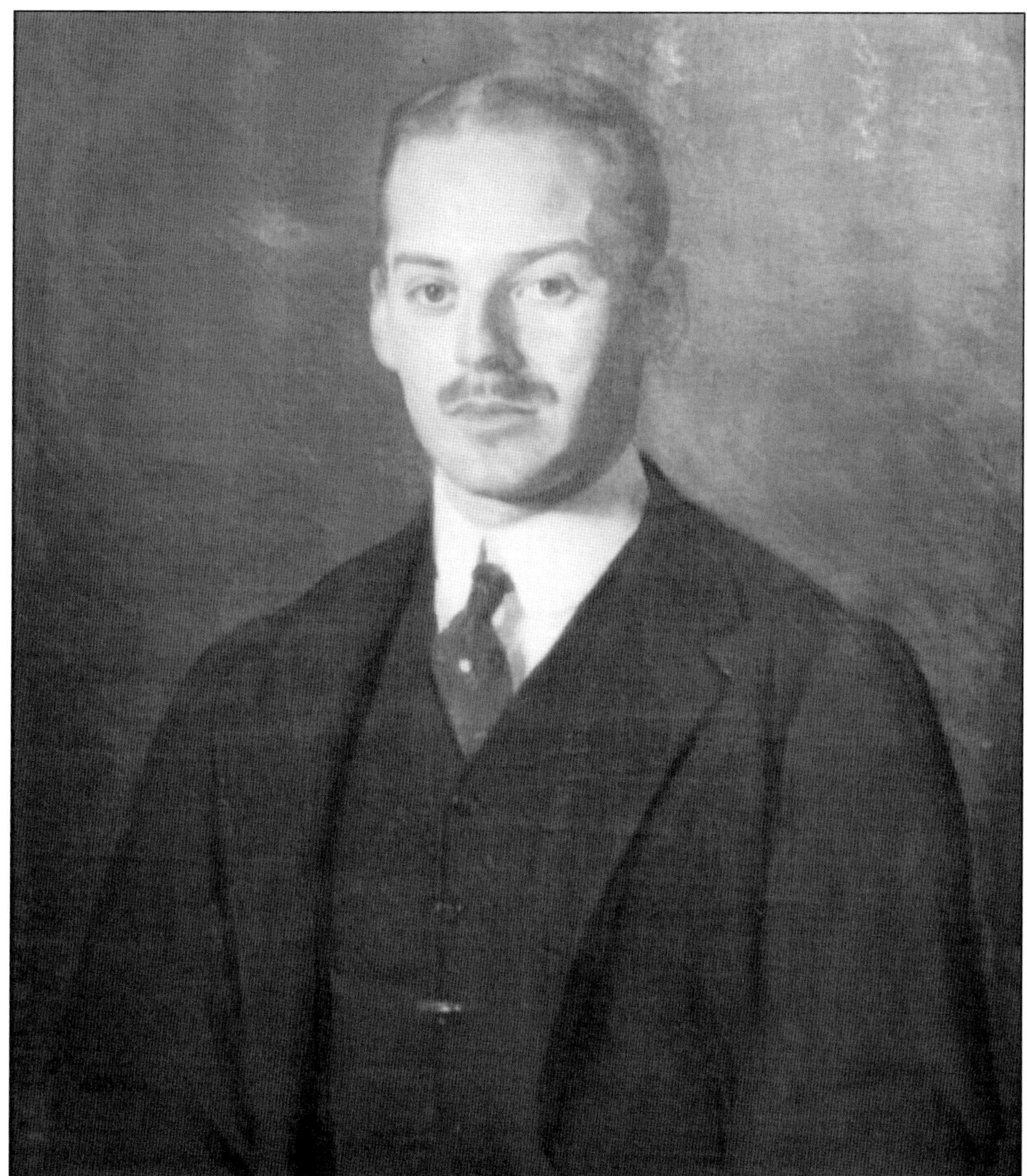

A native of Portland, Walter Goodwin Davis was the son and grandson of successful businessmen. He graduated from Yale in 1908 and from Harvard Law School in 1911 and practiced law in New York City. When the war began in 1917, Davis enlisted as an officer and was commissioned as captain of infantry early in 1918. With his academic and professional background, he was assigned to the Military Intelligence Service and was sent to the American Legation in Berne, Switzerland, where he served as assistant military attaché and liaison officer with the British military office. After the Armistice in November 1918, Davis joined the Commission to Negotiate the Peace in Paris. In this capacity, he was sent to Vienna as part of a group of officers under the direction of Prof. Archibald Cary Coolidge to report to the peace commission on political, military, and economic conditions in the former Austro-Hungarian Empire. After completing that assignment, Davis was discharged in April 1919 and returned to Portland, where he lived for the rest of his life. (MHS.)

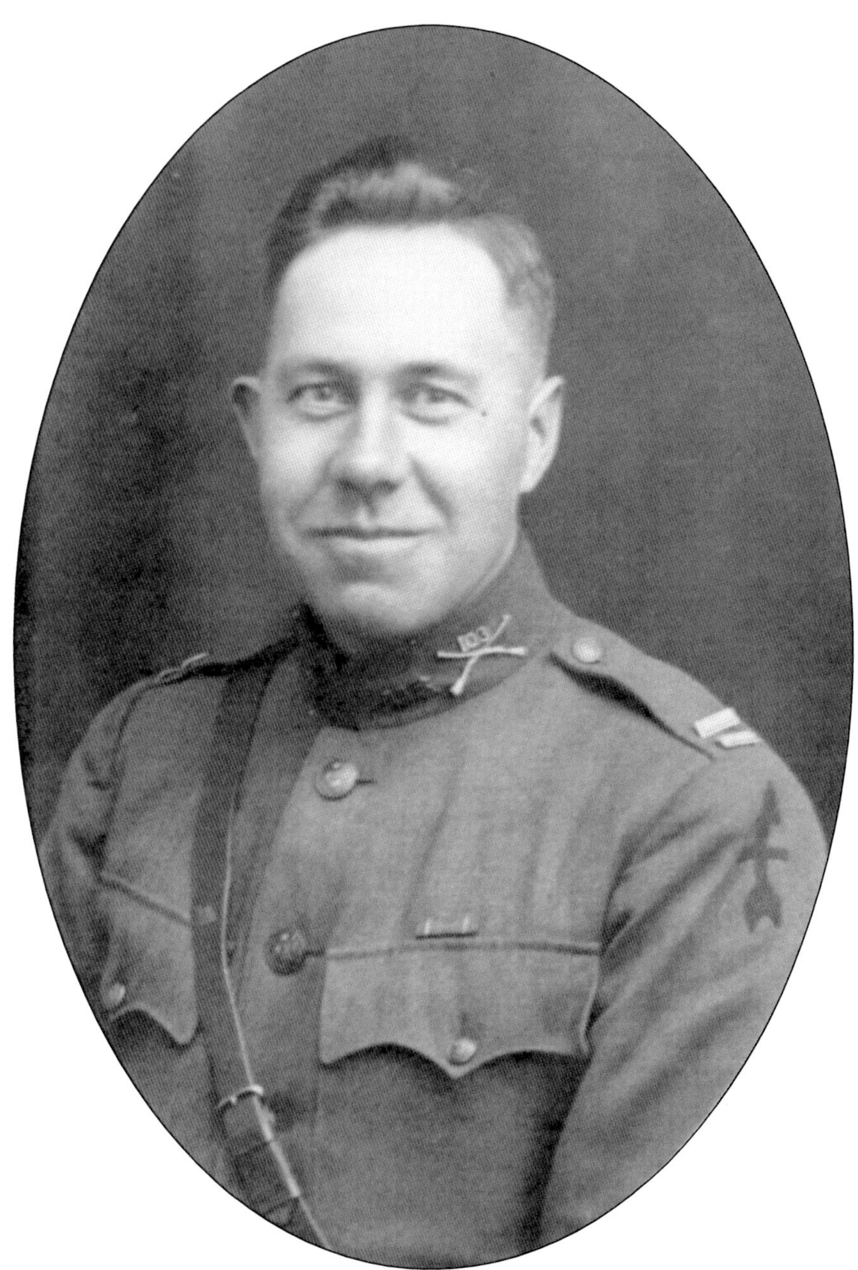

This picture of Capt. Guy I. Swett of South Paris was taken on January 12, 1919, while he was stationed in Selters, Germany, as a part of the Army of Occupation. Originally commissioned as a first lieutenant in the 2nd Maine and then serving with the 103rd Regiment, he was promoted to captain in October 1918. The 103rd Regiment was in the Chemin Des Dames Front when, on February 16, 1918, Swett was slightly wounded in action. At some point during the latter part of the war, Swett was transferred to the 127th Infantry Regiment, which was a part of the 32nd Division, also known as the Red Arrow Division. Most of the soldiers from the 32nd Division were from Michigan and Wisconsin and were assigned duties as a part of the Army of Occupation in Germany. Note the 103rd Regiment collar insignia and the 32nd Division patch on his sleeve. (Gauthier.)

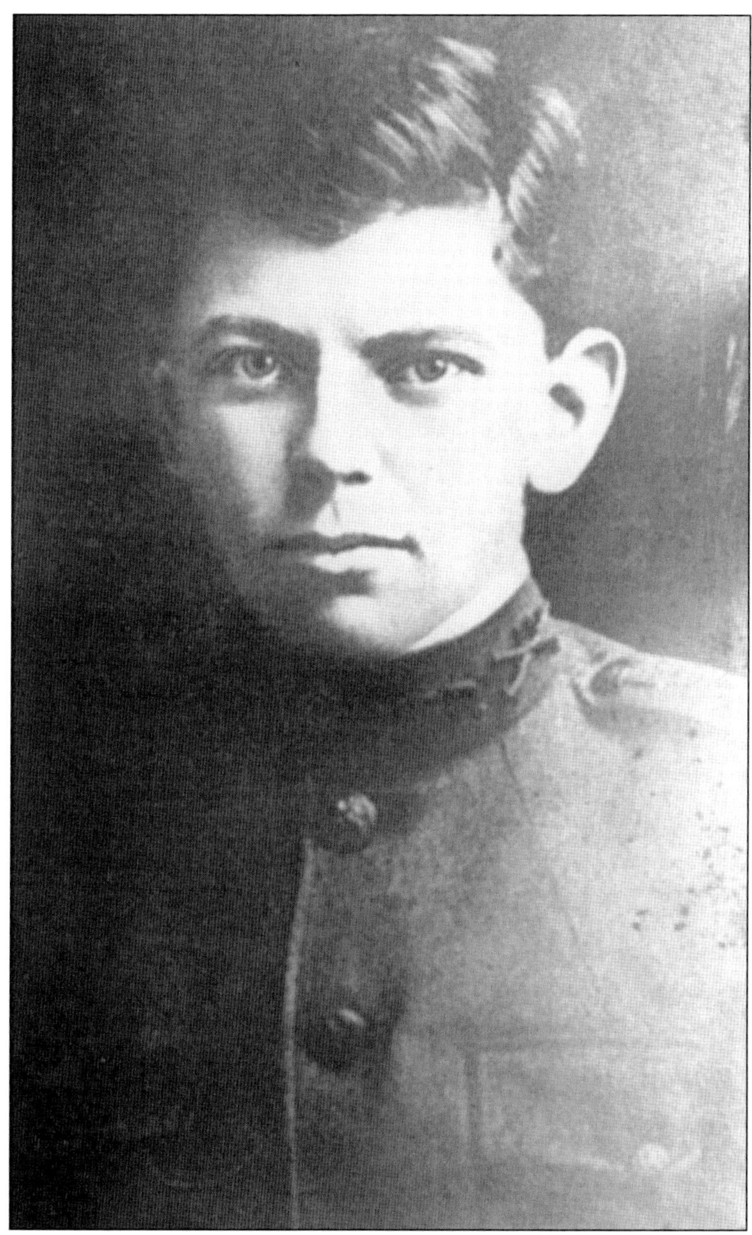

Lt. Walker Blaine Beale was born in Augusta at the home of his maternal grandparents, James G. and Harriet Stanwood Blaine. His father, Truxtun Beale, was a diplomat, and his mother, Harriet Blaine Beale, was the daughter of one of the most famous post–Civil War political figures in America. After attending St. Paul's School, Lt. Beale entered Harvard in 1914 as a member of the class of 1918. Beginning in 1916, he trained as an officer and left Harvard in 1917 to join the 310th Infantry. His unit was sent to the battlefront in France in the summer of 1918, and he was killed at Saint-Mihiel on September 18, 1918, as the result of wounds received in action. As a young man, Lieutenant Beale had inherited his grandparents' home in Augusta, which he offered to the State of Maine in March 1917 for the headquarters of the committee coordinating the state's war activities. After his death, his family gave the Blaine House to the state in his memory to use as the official residence of governors and their families.

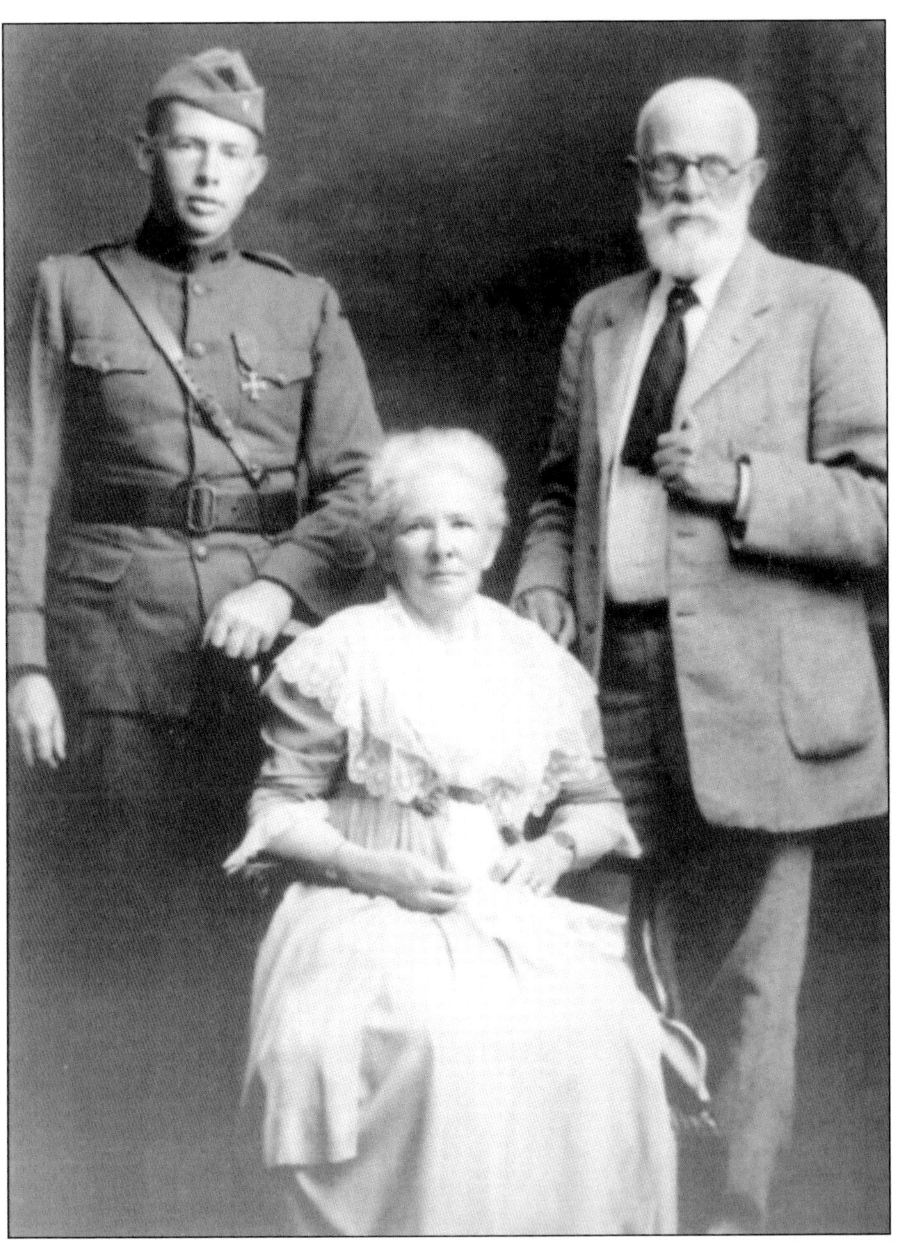

When Lt. John Richards returned to Gardiner from the war, he posed for this photograph with his distinguished parents, architect Henry Richards and authoress Laura E. Richards. Born in Gardiner, Richards graduated from Harvard in 1907 and began teaching English at St. Paul's School in 1912. His parents founded Camp Merryweather for boys in 1900 in North Belgrade, and Richards spent his summers there as an instructor. He served as a first lieutenant in the Army from July 1917 to March 1919. He was severely wounded in the Fourth Battle of the Champagne in France in 1918 and was awarded the Croix de Guerre and the Purple Heart. From November 1918 to his discharge, he was an officer in the 369th Infantry Division, the famous New York African American regiment popularly known as "the Harlem Hellfighters." In later life, Richards credited his survival on the battlefield with the training that he had received at his parents' summer camp.

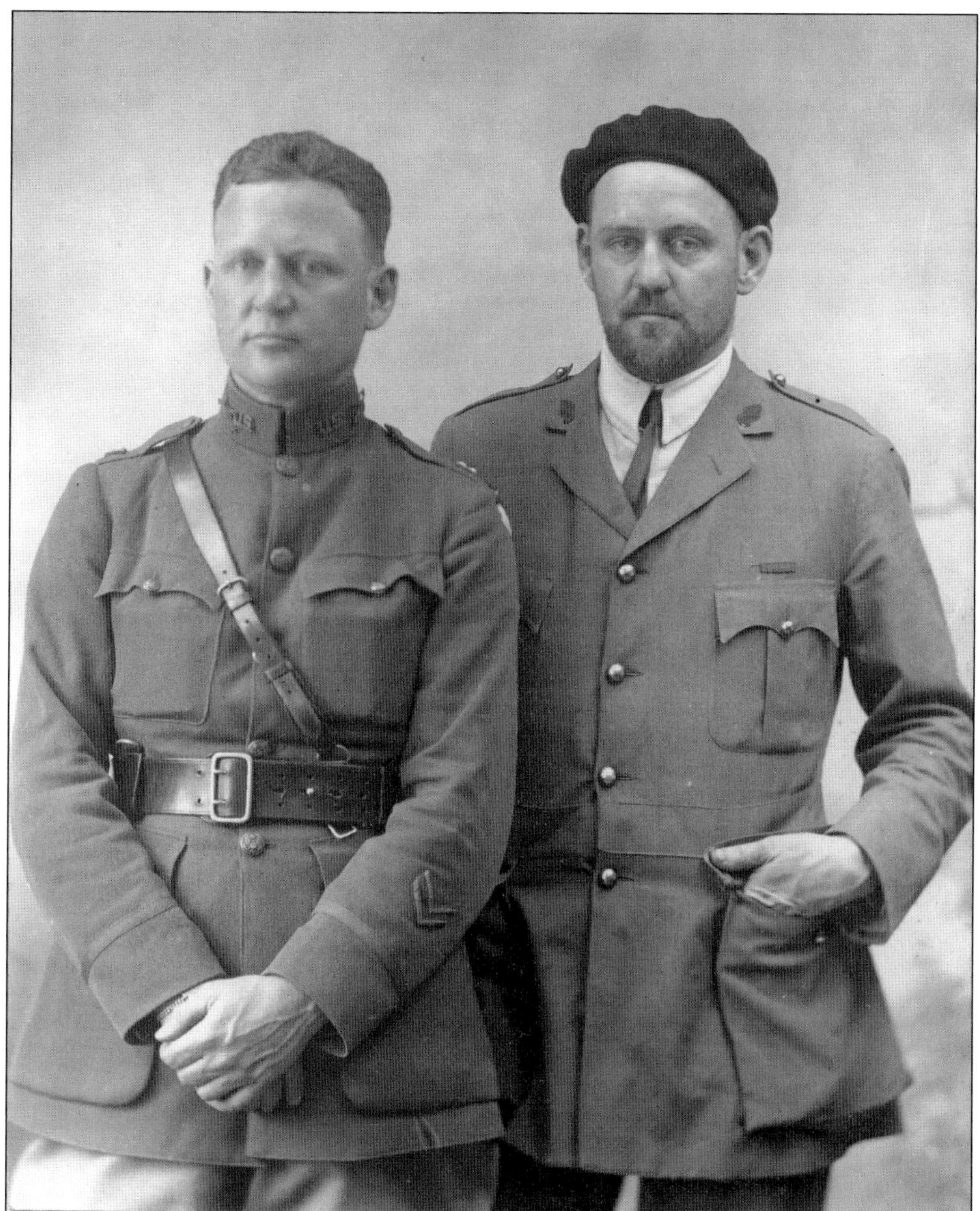

Hayford Peirce (left) and his younger brother Waldo Peirce (right) were born in Bangor, attended Milton Academy, and graduated from Harvard. A noted authority on Byzantine art, Hayford was an Army intelligence officer in France from March 1918 to December 1919. His duties included analyzing aerial reconnaissance photographs and serving with the American delegation at the Versailles Peace Conference. Waldo Peirce was not a commissioned officer, but rather a volunteer ambulance driver for the American Field Service in France in 1915. In this capacity, he was awarded the Croix de Guerre for his bravery at the Battle of Verdun. Two years later, he was attached to the French army as a war artist. Peirce was a larger than life figure who devoted his life to painting and counted journalist John Reed and writer Ernest Hemingway among his friends. (BPL.)

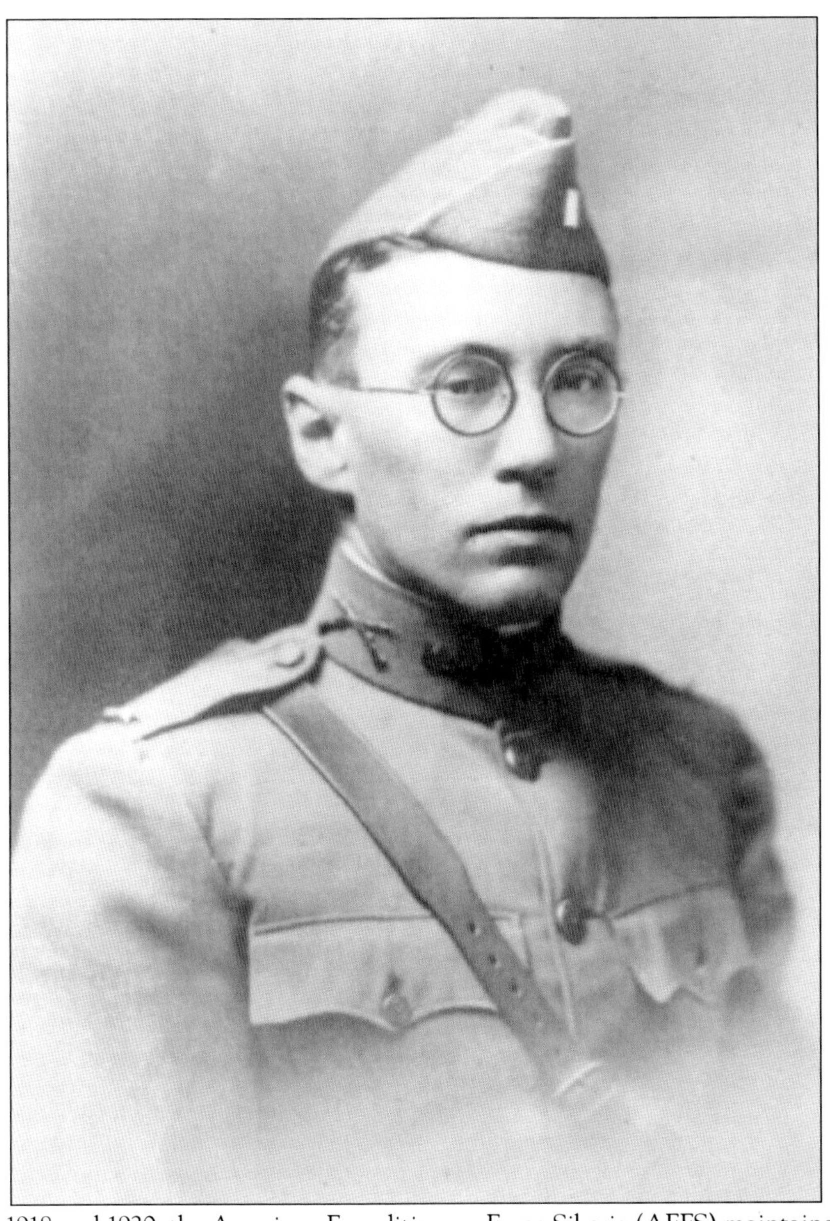

Between 1918 and 1920, the American Expeditionary Force Siberia (AEFS) maintained several thousand troops in Vladivostak, Russia. President Wilson dispatched this force to Russia to help free 40,000 Czech soldiers who were being detained by the Bolsheviks and to protect military supplies and trains that the United States had sent to the Eastern Front. A native of Farmington Falls, Lt. Ben Stinchfield joined the military intelligence branch of the Army in July 1918 and was ordered to report to General Pershing's headquarters in France. However, the Army decided that his language skills were needed in Russia, and he was reassigned to Vladivostak, where he handled secret codes, ciphers, and postal censorship. While there, he worked with a fellow Mainer, Capt. Kenneth L. Roberts, who later became a popular historical novelist. After serving eight months with the AEFS, Stinchfield returned to the United States to begin a 36-year career as a French teacher in New York City. He spent each summer in Farmington Falls and was instrumental in preserving the home of the famed opera singer Lillian Nordica in Farmington. (MSL.)

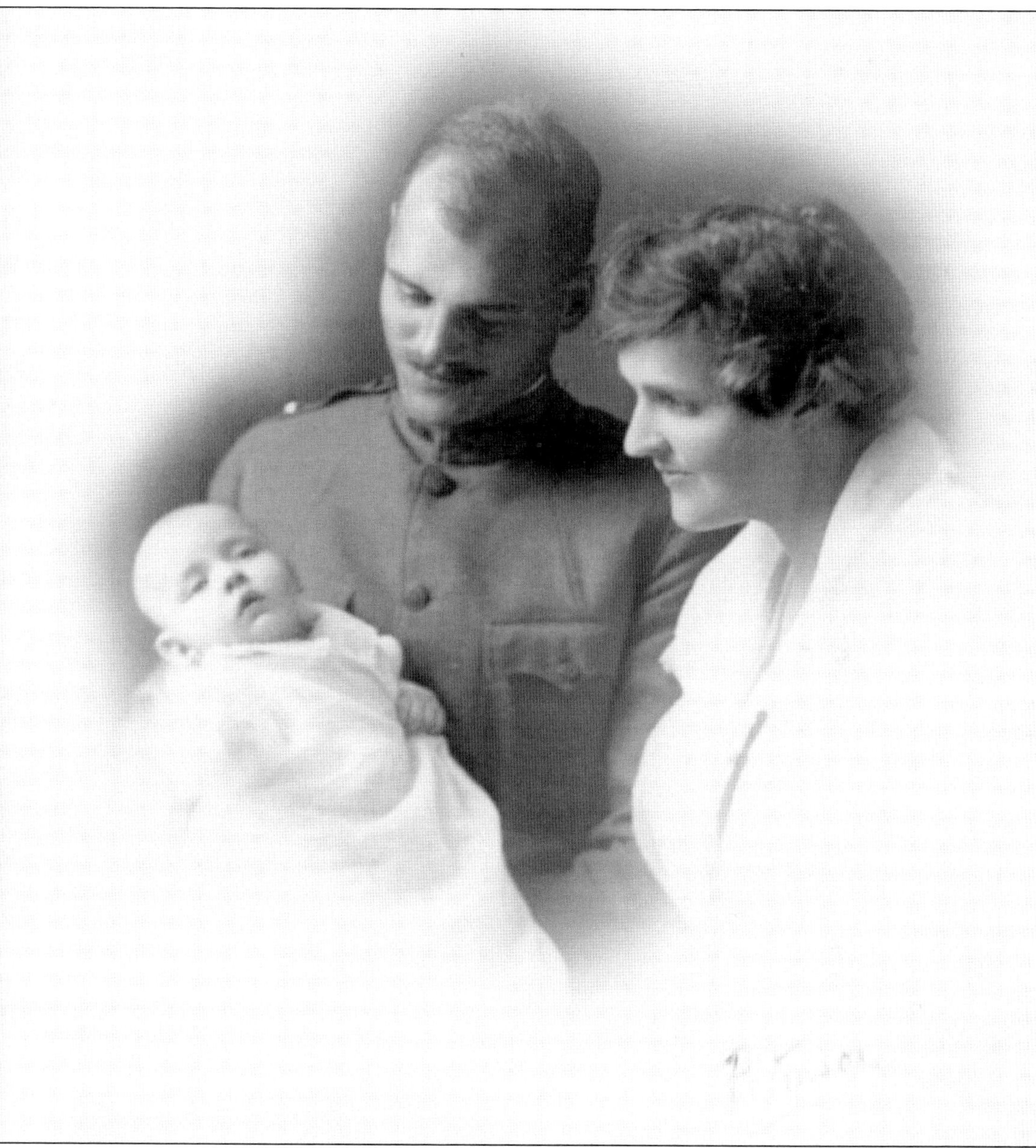

Wearing his Army uniform, William Tudor Gardiner and his wife, Margaret Thomas Gardiner, are shown in this 1918 photograph with their young son Tudor. Born into one of Maine's most distinguished families, Gardiner attended Groton and Harvard. Between college and Harvard Law School, he served with an American ambulance at the Battle of the Marne in France. When America entered the war in 1917, Gardiner enlisted in the First Maine Heavy Field Artillery, rising in the ranks from private to first lieutenant. Reorganized as the 56th Pioneer Infantry, the regiment saw nine months of service in France, including the Meuse-Argonne Offensive and the occupation of Germany. Once back in Maine, Gardiner practiced law and entered Republican politics, serving as governor of Maine from 1929 to 1933. During World War II, he had a highly decorated career as a staff officer in the US Army Air Force. Gardiner died in a plane crash in 1953 while returning home from a 56th Pioneer Infantry reunion. (Gardiner.)

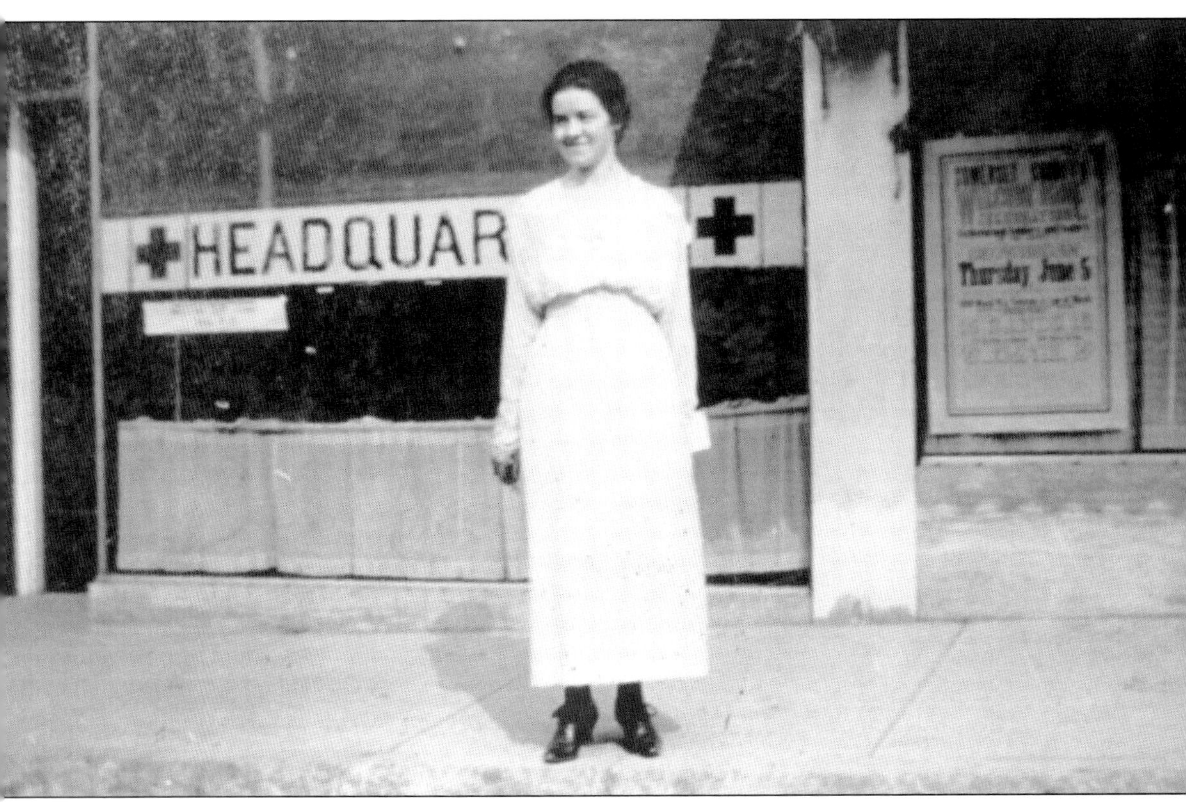

One of Maine's most admired 20th-century political figures was Margaret Chase Smith. Born in Skowhegan, she graduated from high school in 1916 and taught school for a year before becoming a telephone operator. Like many young women across the state, she volunteered for the American Red Cross in World War I. She is shown here in her white uniform standing in front of the Skowhegan Red Cross headquarters. This photograph records Margaret Chase Smith's first experience in public service, to which she devoted much of her life. Upon the death of her husband, Clyde Smith, in 1940, she was elected to fill his seat in the US House of Representatives, where she served until her election to the US Senate in 1948. Senator Smith was the first woman to be elected to both houses of Congress. She is remembered for her legislation to give women full status in the military and for her courageous stand against Sen. Joseph McCarthy in her 1950 "Declaration of Conscience" speech. (MCSL.)

Sgt. James F. Lacey of Portland stands in front of a photographer's backdrop reminiscent of a Civil War–era tintype. Lacey was initially assigned to the 156th Depot Brigade, and one day after being promoted to corporal, he was assigned to Battery C of the 41st Field Artillery stationed at Fort Monroe in Virginia, where he was later elevated to sergeant. Lacey did not see service overseas.

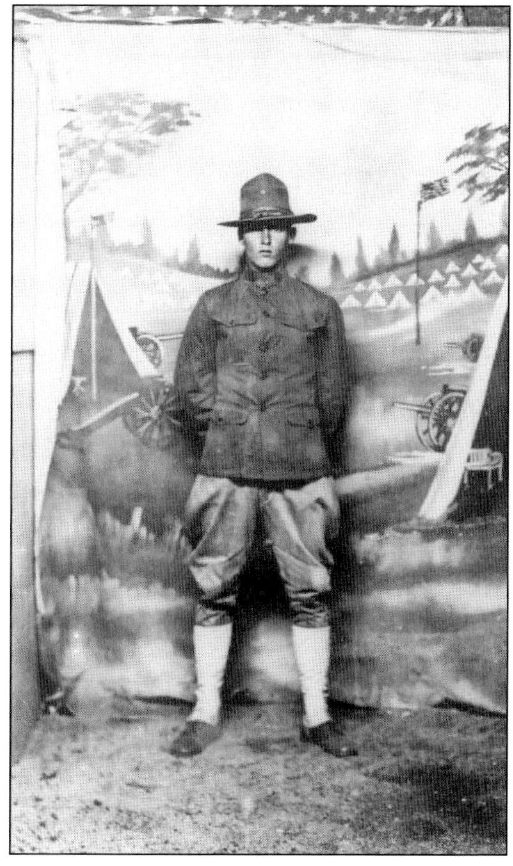

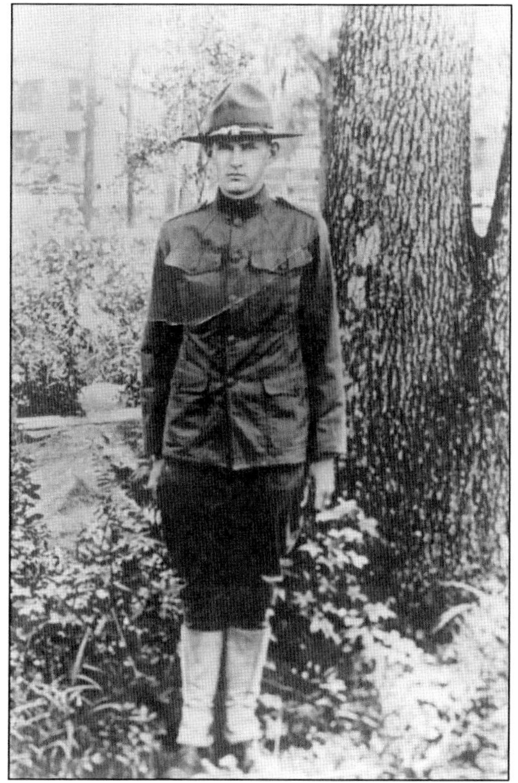

Cpl. Edward R. Blaisdell of Oakland was inducted at Fort Slocum in New York in June 1918 and, six weeks later, was promoted to corporal. His initial assignment was with the 1st Road Regiment and later assigned to the 448th Motor Truck Company before his departure for France. While overseas Blaisdell fell ill and died from disease. He was one of four Oakland soldiers not to return home. (Libby.)

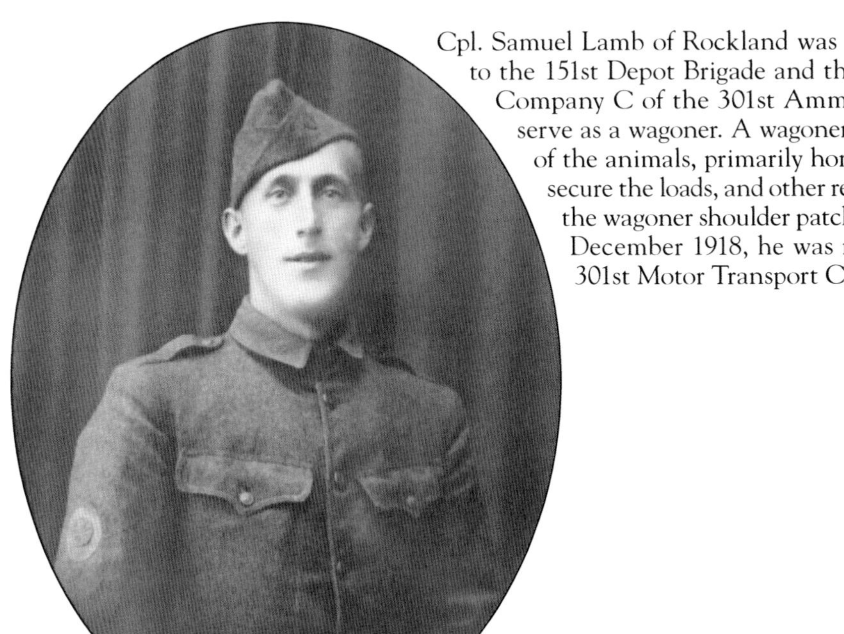

Cpl. Samuel Lamb of Rockland was initially assigned to the 151st Depot Brigade and then transferred to Company C of the 301st Ammunition Train to serve as a wagoner. A wagoner had to take care of the animals, primarily horses, know how to secure the loads, and other related duties. Note the wagoner shoulder patch on his sleeve. In December 1918, he was reassigned to the 301st Motor Transport Company. (MSM.)

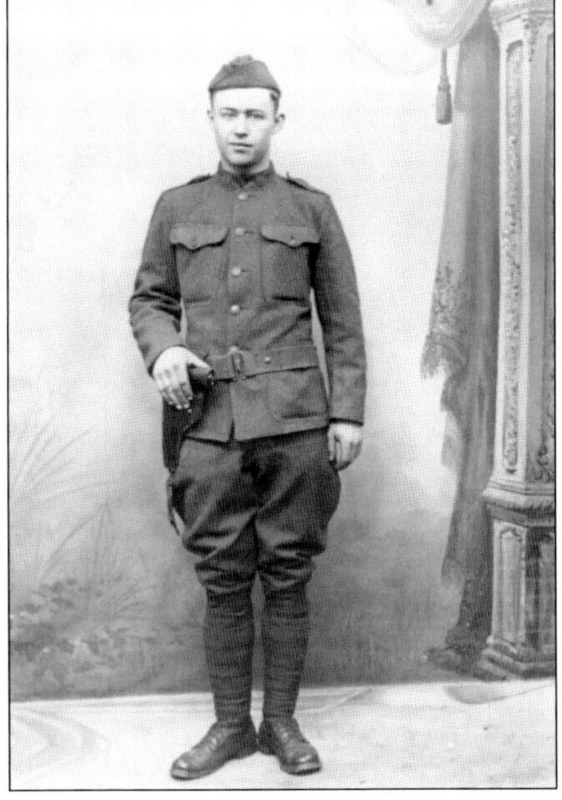

Cpl. William H. Betts of Gardiner, Quartermasters Corps (QMC), enlisted in July 1918, trained at Camp Joseph E. Johnston in Florida, and went overseas that September. Betts was assigned to the Conservation and Reclamation Company of the QMC, which oversaw the repair of clothing, shoes, and other equipment. Following the war, Betts returned to Maine and later served in World War II in the Navy Reserves. (MSA.)

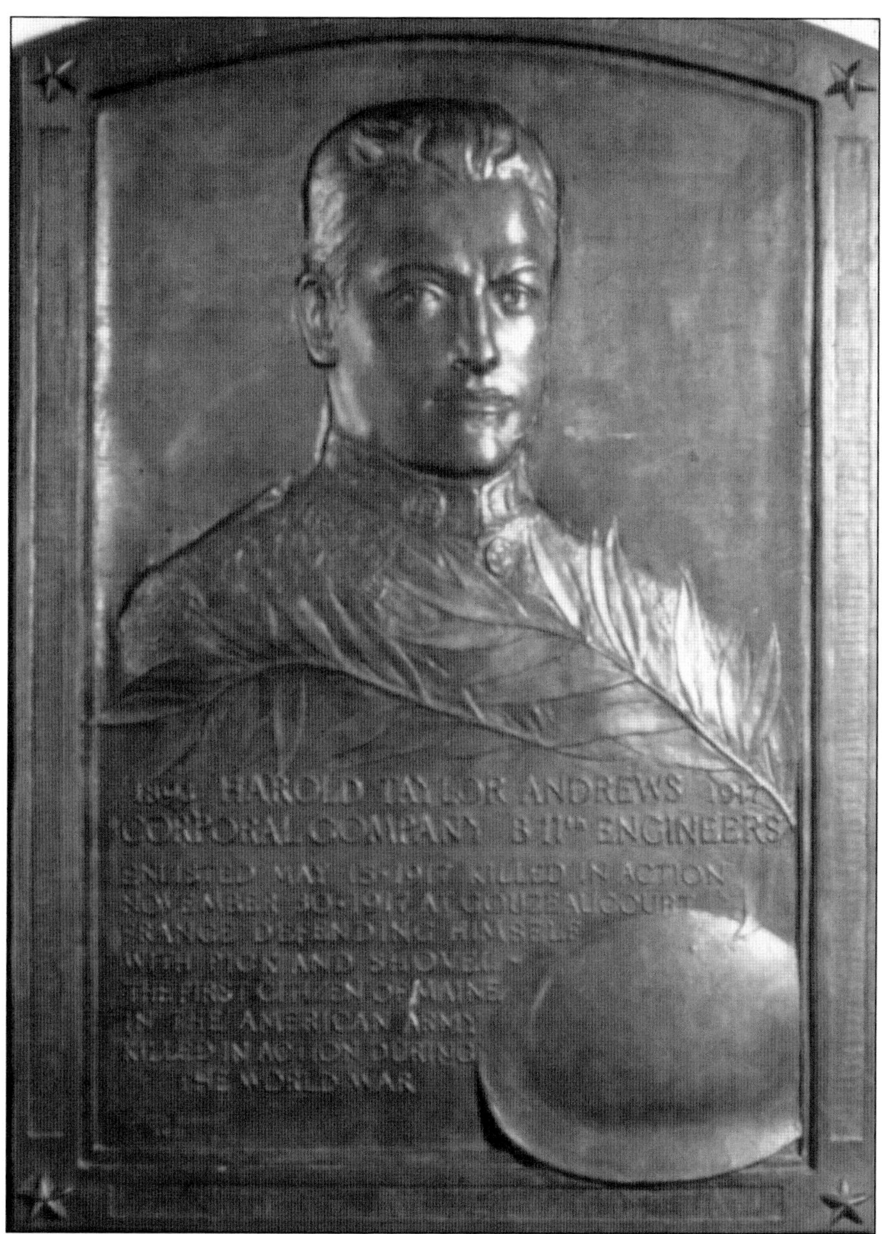

Cpl. Harold Taylor Andrews was the first Maine citizen to die in battle in World War I. A native of Portland, Andrews attended Portland High School and the University of Maine. He enlisted in the 11th Regiment of New York Engineers in May 1917. Arriving in France the next month, his unit was assigned to repair rail lines that had been seized from the Germans. Near Cambrai, France, on November 30, 1917, Andrews was killed in a German attack, having only a pick and shovel with which to defend himself. Corporal Andrews is remembered in two memorials: Andrews Square in Portland and a memorial plaque in the Hall of Flags at the Maine State House in Augusta. Dedicated in 1921, the Portland memorial consists of a bronze plaque on the granite base of a flagpole. The bronze plaque in the State House was unveiled in 1931 by its sculptor, Victor Kahill of Portland. It bears a bronze relief portrait of Corporal Andrews holding his helmet. (MSM.)

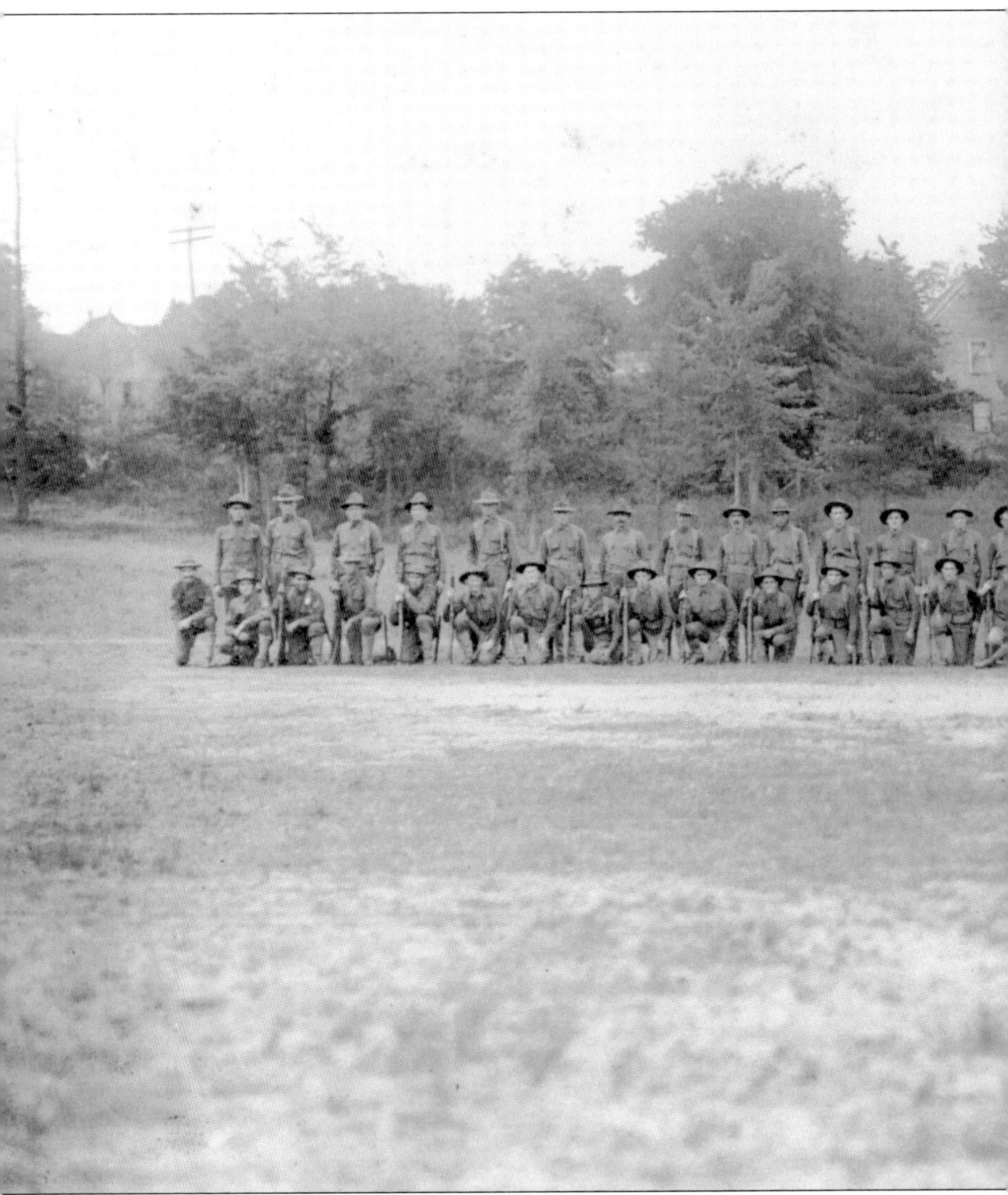

Here is a picture of Company C of the 2nd Maine Regiment, based in Livermore Falls before they were activated for federal service. Men primarily from Livermore Falls, Livermore, and Jay made up the original unit. After being redesignated as Company C of the 103rd Infantry Regiment, men from other areas of the state and elsewhere were added to its numbers. The company suffered the loss of 42 soldiers during the war, more than any other company in the regiment except for

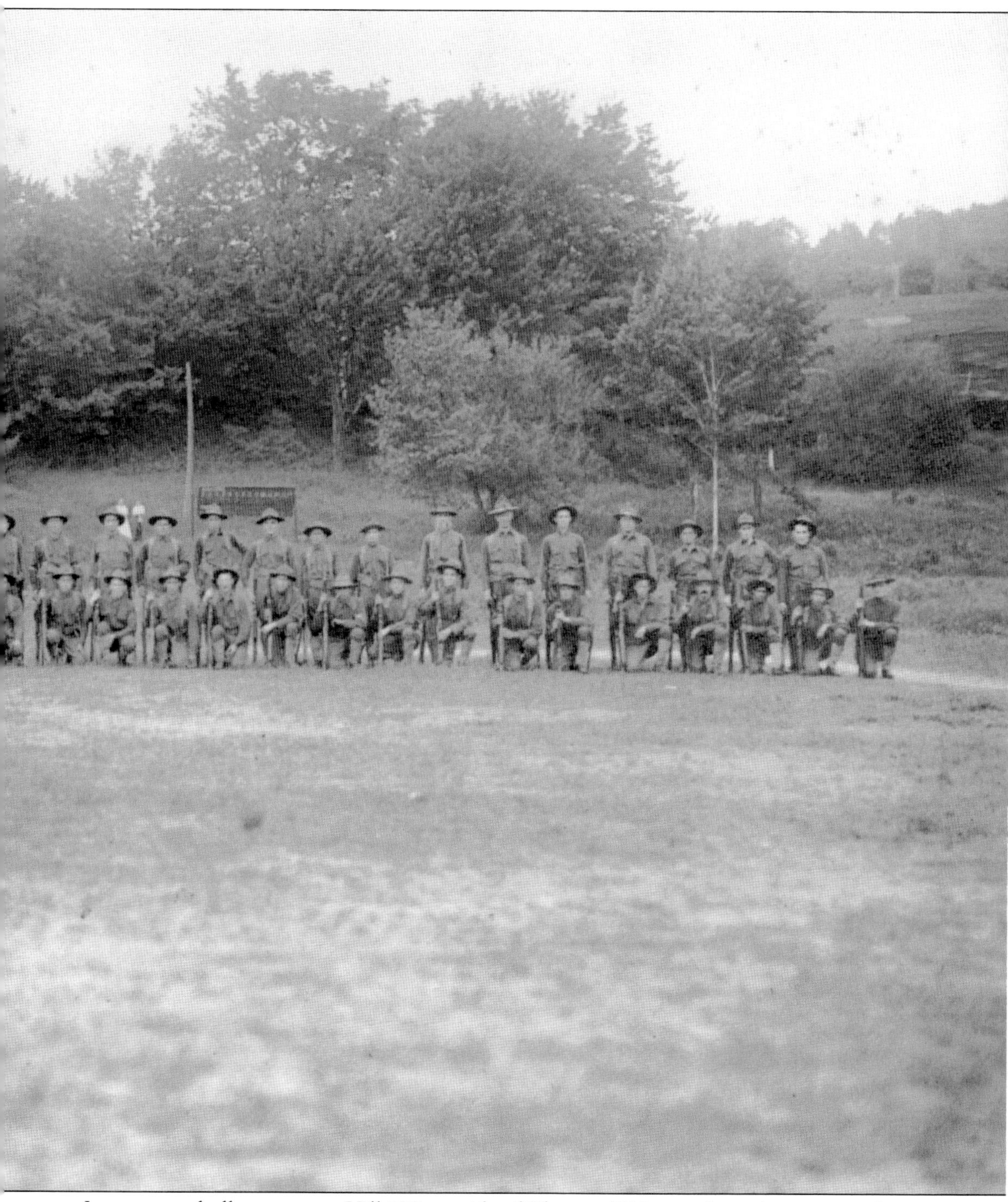

one. Its greatest challenge was at Hill 190, outside of Chateau Thierry, where the company lost Livermore Falls natives Sgt. George T. Bunten, Pfc. Forrest E. Merrill, Pvt. Arthur F. Alden, and Pvt. George E. Ryder. Following the engagement, Lt. Frank J. Burbank and Pvt. Eugene Dube, both of Livermore Falls, were awarded the Distinguished Service Cross. (Libby.)

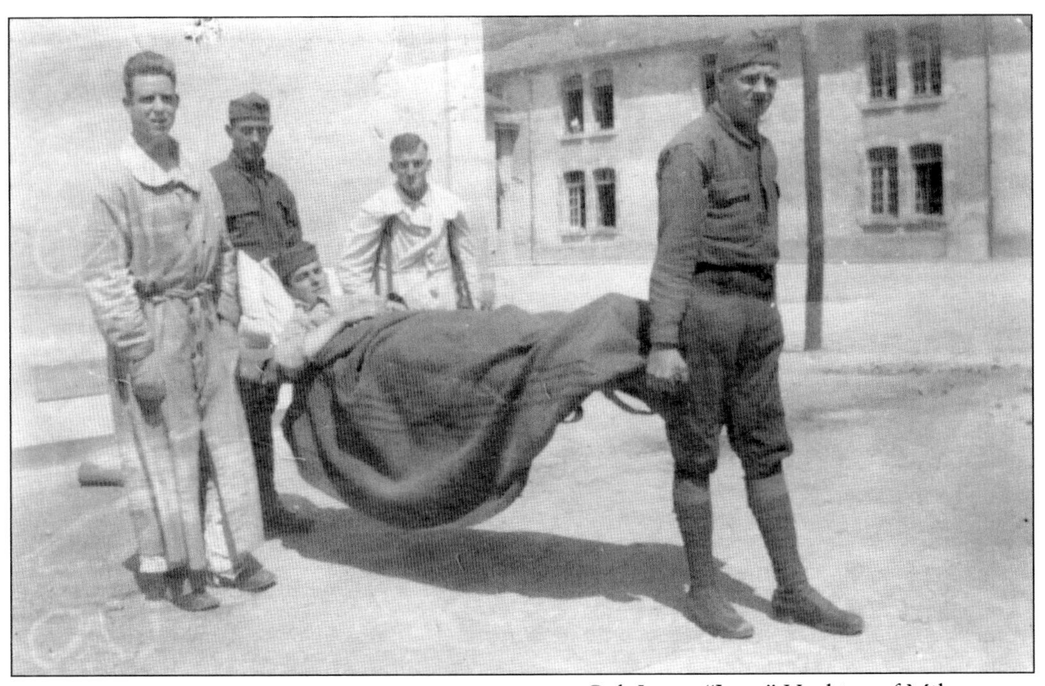

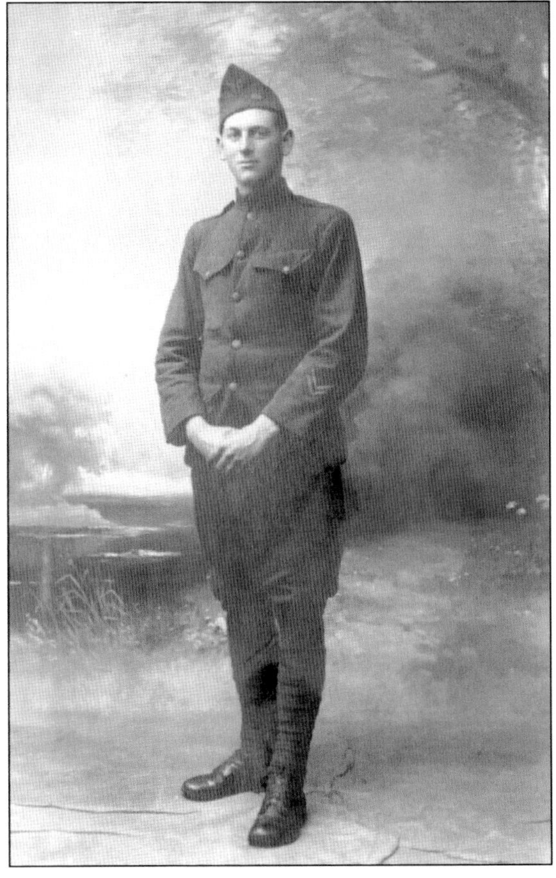

Cpl. Leroy "Jerry" Hoskins of Milo, enlisted in Company F of the 2nd Maine, later the 103rd Regiment, a week after war was declared. Promoted to corporal before the regiment's departure for France, Hoskins was severely wounded in action on July 10, 1918, at Chateau Thierry. Hoskins is the soldier in the stretcher. He served the rest of the war and was honorably discharged in May 1919. (MSM.)

Pvt. Christopher Grover of South Portland enlisted in May 1917 and was assigned to Company C of the 14th Engineers. He was sent overseas in July 1917, one of the earliest American troops to arrive in France. Like most of the members of his unit, Grover was involved in the railroad industry. The overseas chevrons on his left sleeve indicate that at this time he had completed a year overseas.

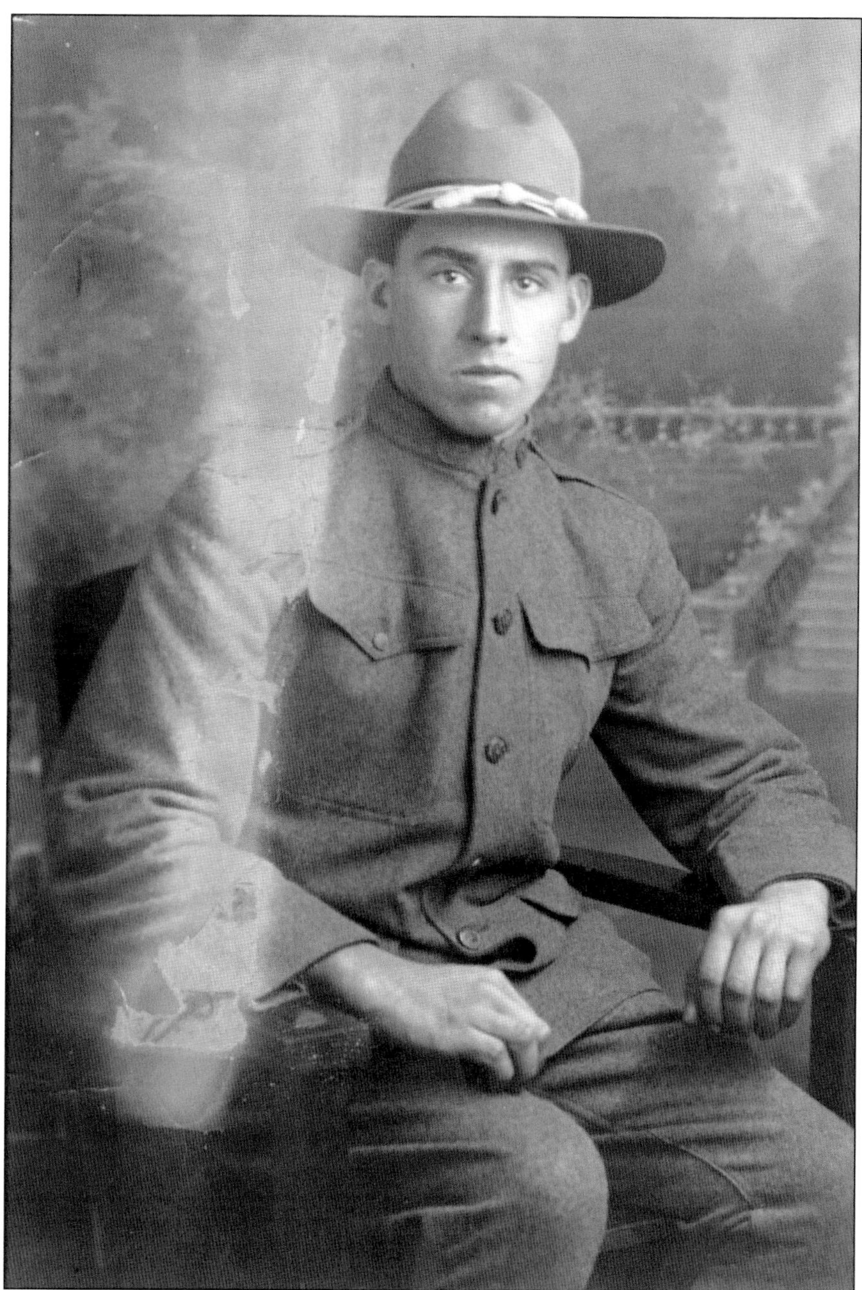

Pvt. Ralph Spaulding was born in Pleasant Pond but is claimed by Embden, where he lived throughout his school days. Spaulding was working in Fairfield when the war broke out and he joined Company H of the 2nd Maine Infantry. Sent overseas as a member of the 103rd Regiment, on February 13, 1918, Spaulding was digging trenches with other members of his company in the Chemin de Dames Sector when they were fired upon by the enemy. Not used to being under fire, as he ran for cover, Spaulding noticed he had dropped his hat, and when he went to retrieve it, he was instantly killed. This was the first of the soldiers in the division to die at the hands of the enemy and one of the first, if not the first, National Guardsman to be killed in action in the war. Spaulding left behind his parents, four brothers, and five sisters. (MSM.)

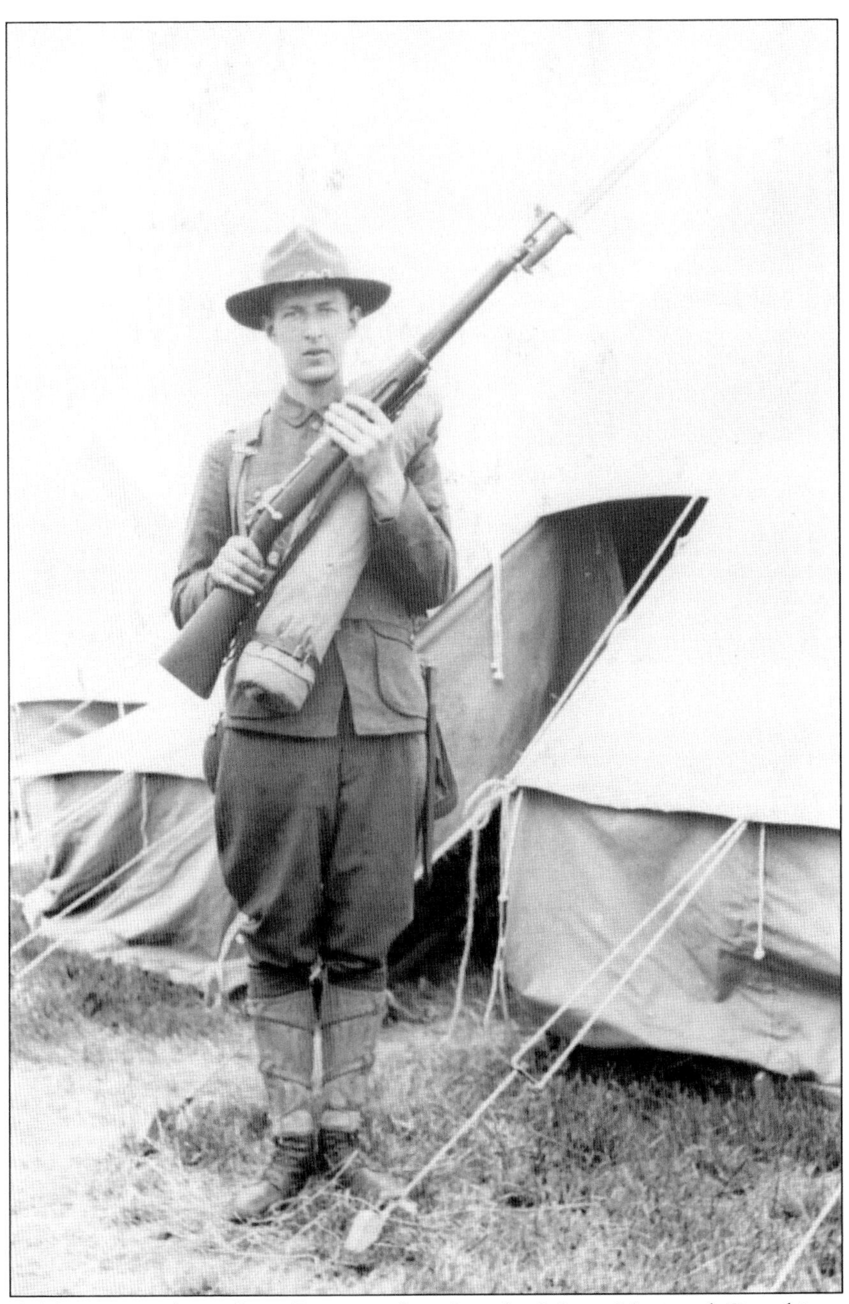

Pvt. Winfield Scott Hodgins from Brewer enlisted in the Maine National Guard in early June 1916 and served with the 2nd Maine on the border in 1916. When the war broke out, Hodgins was assigned to Company G of the 103rd Regiment. Hodgins kept a journal during his time overseas and noted some mundane things, like the weather, writing letters, marching, taking a bath, and drill. Other things were more sobering, like in August 4, 1918, when he wrote about attending a memorial service "for our boys that have gone West." His reaction to the Armistice was slightly understandable, as he had been on guard duty all night the previous night. He wrote, "The war stopped at 11 a.m. Was some glad to see the finish but the bells woke me and I didn't like that." He followed the next day: "On duty again tonight. Not a shot fired!" (Thompson.)

Pfc. Charles A. Corey of Auburn sits "somewhere in France" in a photograph he sent home to his family. He enlisted shortly after war was declared and was assigned to Battery F of the 54th CAC. He went overseas with the 54th and then served at the Training Center for Tractor Artillery No. 3, which operated tractors to transport heavy artillery guns. (Libby.)

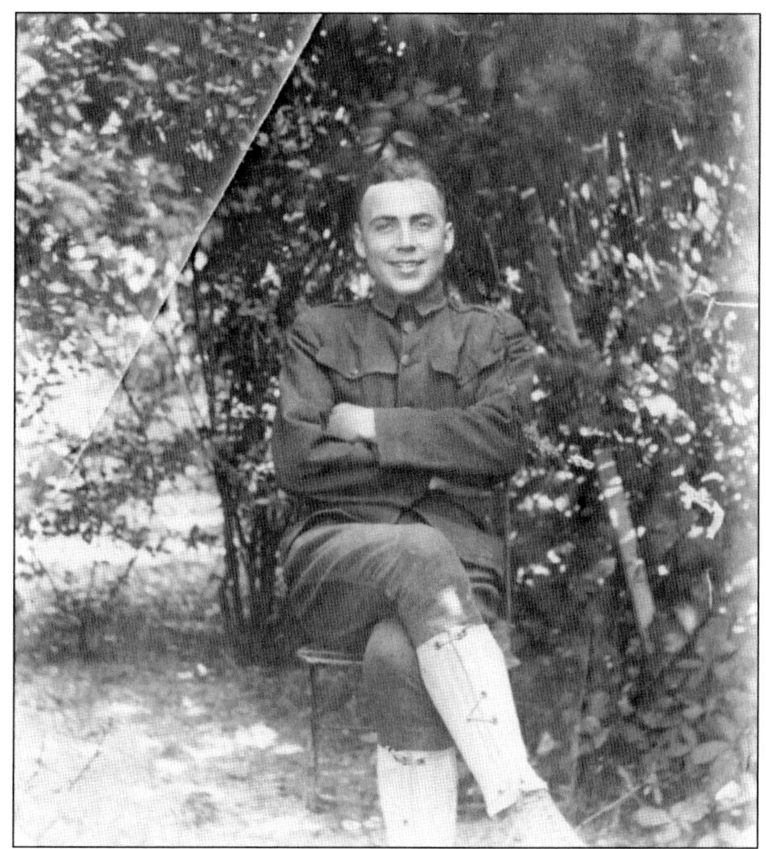

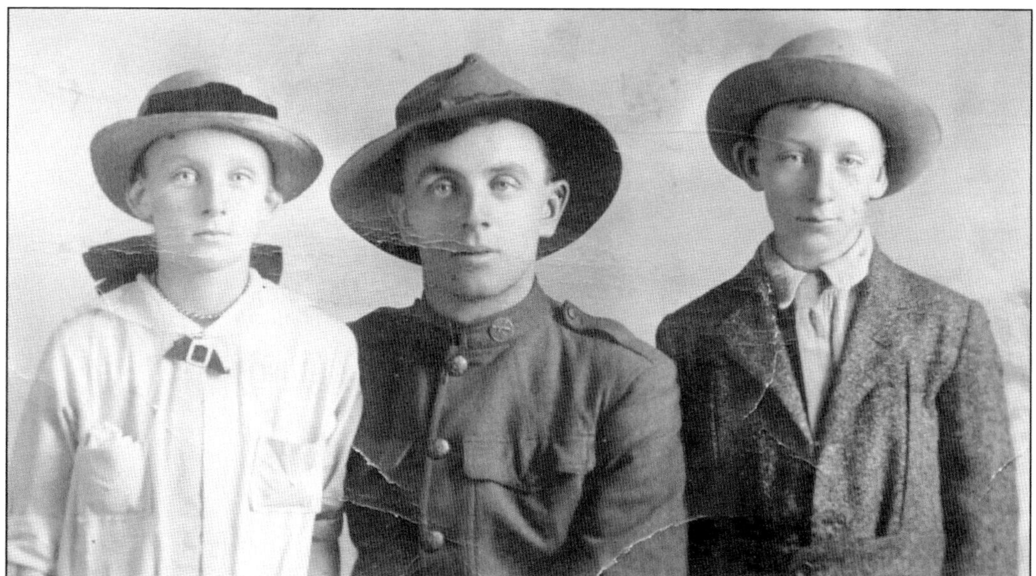

Pfc. Wilbur Emmons of Springvale enlisted in the National Guard in June 1917 and was assigned to Coastal Artillery Corps stationed at Fort Levett in Portland. In March 1918, he went overseas as a member of Battery D of the 54th CAC and served until his death of pneumonia in February 1919. He is pictured here with two of his siblings before he left for France.

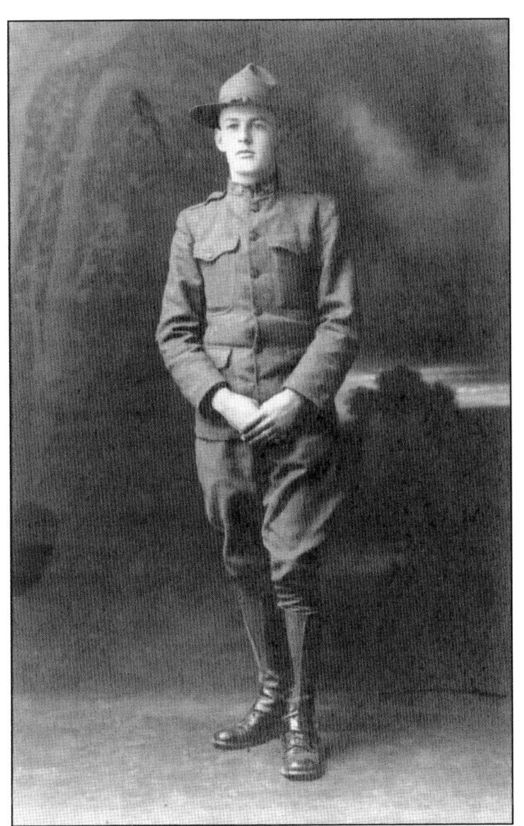

Pfc. Ralph Norton of Falmouth originally enlisted in the Maine National Guard in July 1917 and served in the 56th Pioneer Infantry Regiment until September 1918 when he was transferred to the newly formed Company C 5th Anti-Aircraft Machine Gun Battalion. These battalions were organized late in the war to combat the threat of airplanes and balloons.

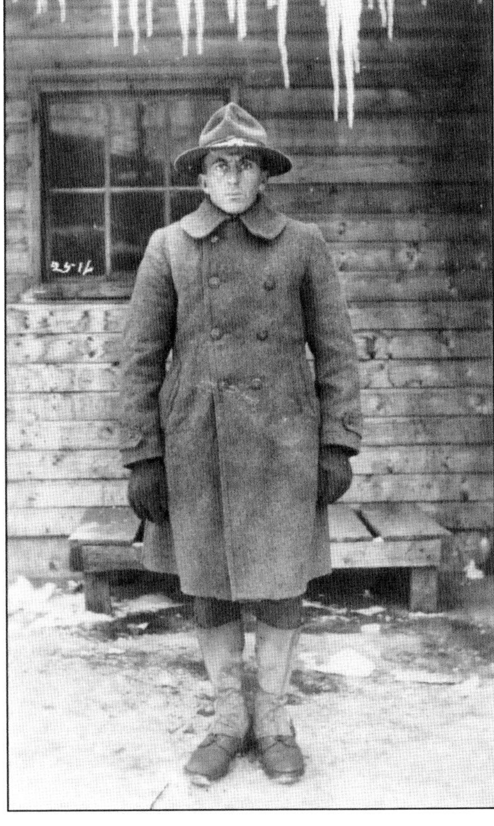

Pvt. Edmund Cyr of Van Buren was inducted in May 1918 and originally assigned to the 151st Depot Brigade at Camp Devens, now Fort Devens, in Massachusetts. Cyr was later transferred to the 303rd Infantry Regiment but was not sent overseas. The depot brigades were based at a number of stateside training camps and organized unassigned troops, equipped them, and sent them to France. (MSA.)

Pvt. Bruce McLain of Waite mailed this real-photo postcard of himself taken in France to his sister Dora in 1918. McLain, a laborer for the Bangor & Aroostook Railroad, enlisted in the Coastal Artillery Corps in October 1917 and was assigned to Battery F of the 54th CAC. He was later transferred to the 43rd CAC and served until demobilization in 1919.

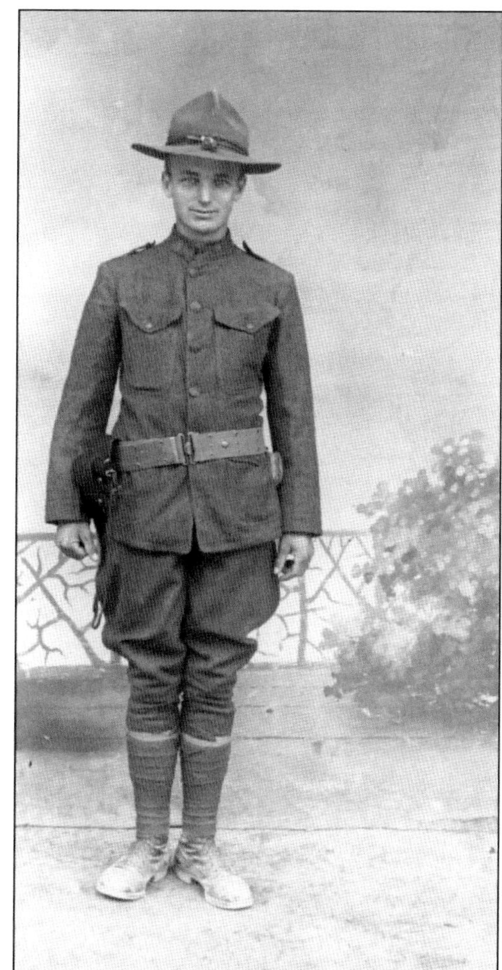

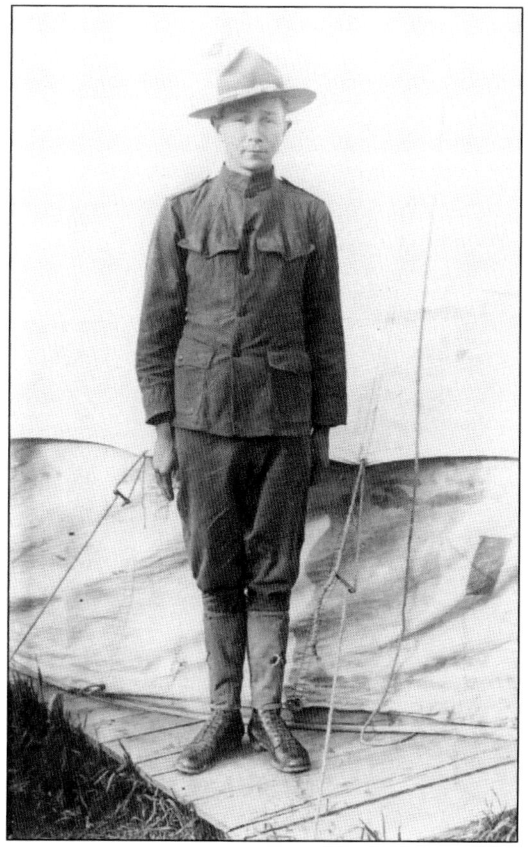

Pvt. Charles H. Storer of Union, a member of Company C of the 103rd Regiment, is seen here in a real-photo postcard taken while he was at Camp Keyes in June 1917. On July 20, 1918, the 26th Division was engaged in heavy fighting at Hill 190 outside Chateau Thierry when Storer was struck by an enemy bullet and killed. (Thompson.)

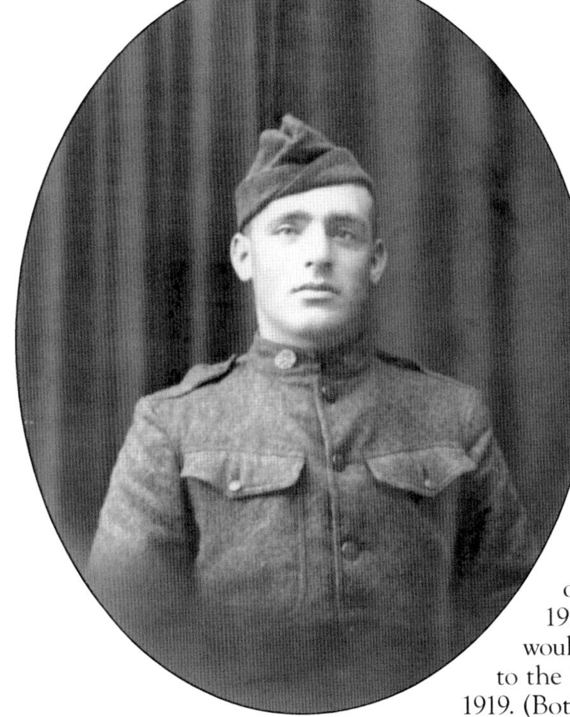

Pfc. Herbert T. Curtis (pictured at left) of South Thomaston and Pfc. Maynard H. Shaw (below) were both inducted into the Army on May 28, 1918, at Rockland. The two soldiers, from neighboring communities, were assigned to Company M of 302nd Infantry Regiment and later to the 163rd Infantry in the 41st Division, which was made of National Guard troops from northwestern states of Idaho, Oregon, Washington, Montana, and North Dakota. Curtis would later serve in the PWE (Prisoner of War Escort) Company 235 from December 1918 until his discharge in October 1919. Shaw would remain in the 41st Division but was assigned to the 161st Infantry until his discharge in March 1919. (Both, MSA.)

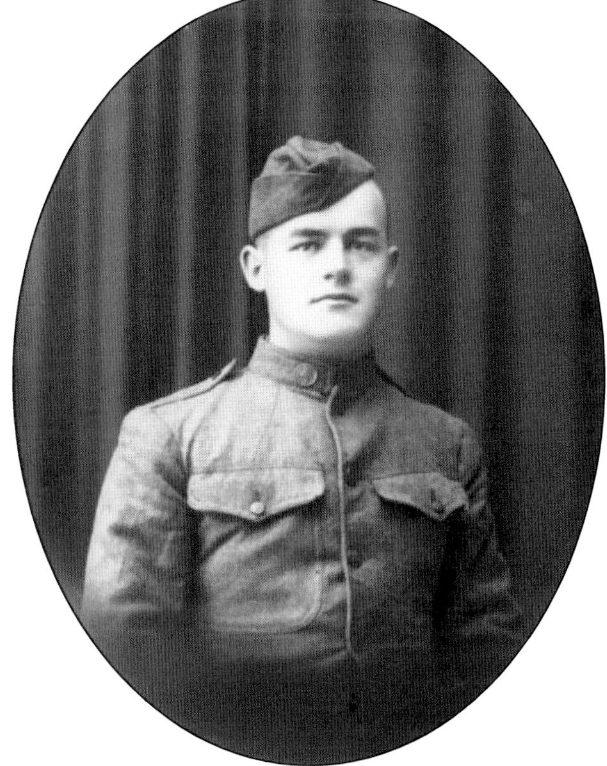

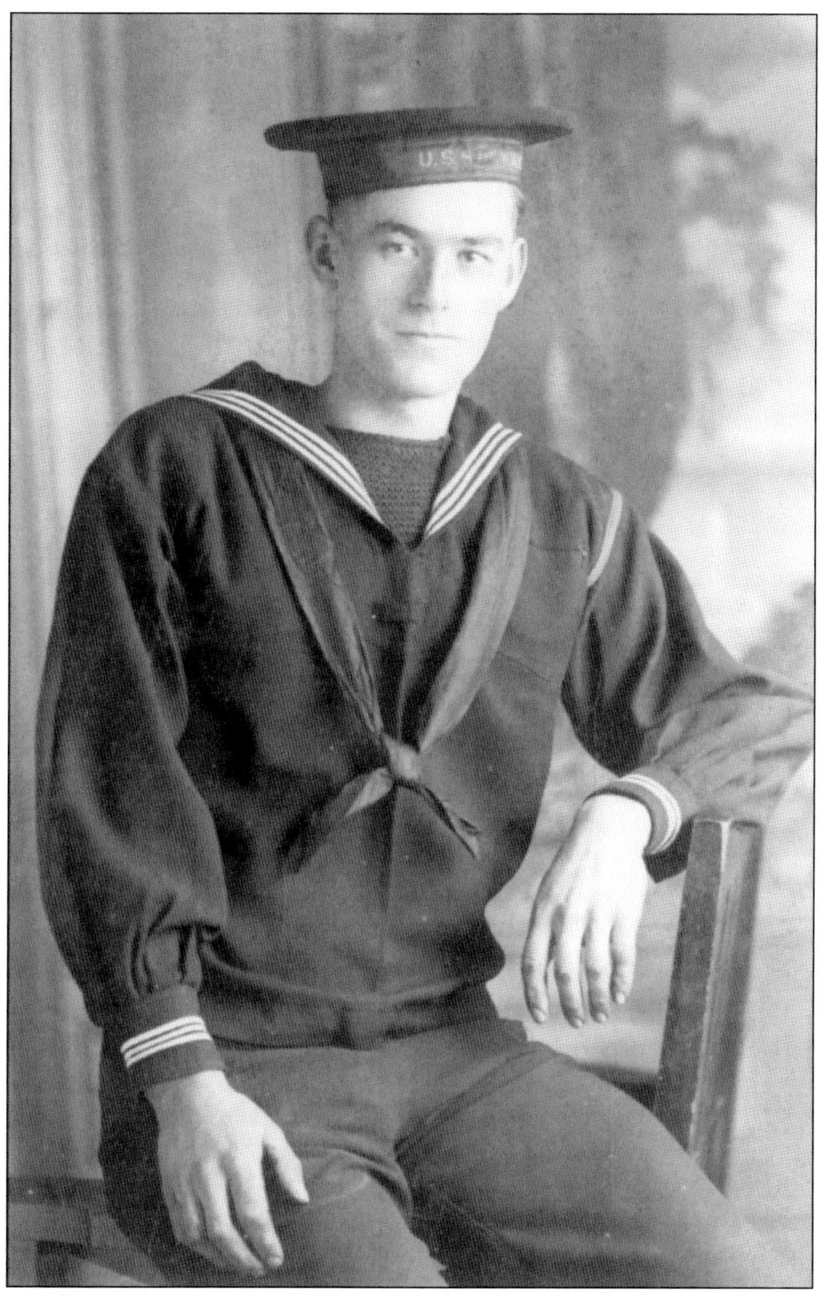

Fireman 2nd Class Arthur A. Carr, from Westbrook, enlisted in the Navy in June 1918 and was sent to the Naval Training Station in Newport Rhode Island. Carr was later assigned to the USS *DeKalb* (ID-3010), a troop ship. Note Carr's tally on his cap, which bears the name of the ship. The vessel, originally a German mail ship, was later converted into a warship, the SS *Prinz Eitel Friederich*. In 1915, during its service in the Imperial German Navy, it sank the schooner *William P. Frye*, the first US vessel to be sunk in the war. The *Frye* was built by Bath Iron Works and named in honor of Maine's longtime senator. In 1917, the German raider was interned and seized by the United States and commissioned as the USS *DeKalb*. After the war, the ship would be transferred to the US Shipping Board. It would later be turned into a passenger ship for transatlantic use.

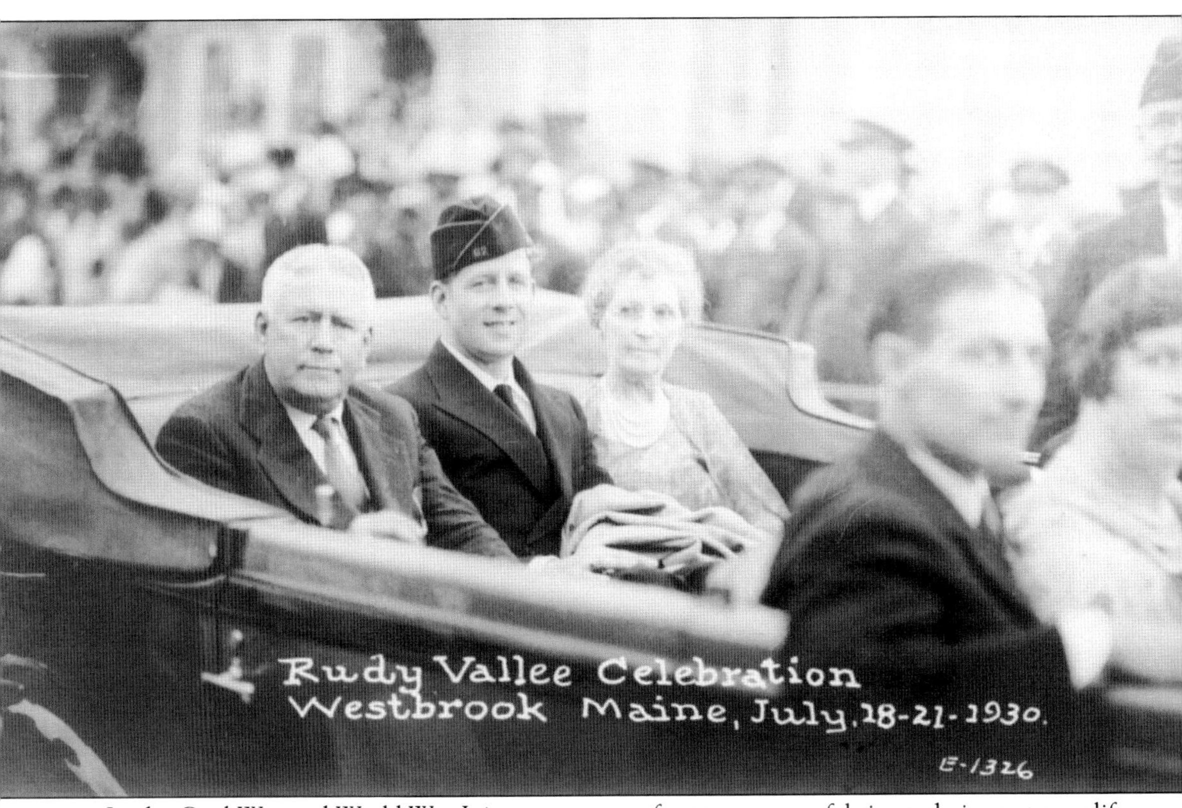

In the Civil War and World War I, it was common for teenagers to fabricate their age to qualify for enlistment in the military. One of the most famous Americans to do so was young Hubert P. Vallee of Westbrook, who claimed that he was about to turn 18 years old when he was actually 15. He enlisted in the Navy in Portland in March 1917 and trained at the Naval Training Station in Newport, Rhode Island, for 41 days before being discovered and discharged as underage. In the celebrity-crazed decade of the Roaring Twenties that followed the war, Rudy Vallee became a wildly popular singer, actor, bandleader, and entertainer. To celebrate his fame, Vallee was invited in 1930 to return to Maine, where he was the center of attention in parades on Congress Street in Portland and Main Street in Westbrook. Here, he posed for the camera with his parents, Charles and Catherine Vallee, wearing an American Legion cap as a proud reminder of his brief service in World War I.

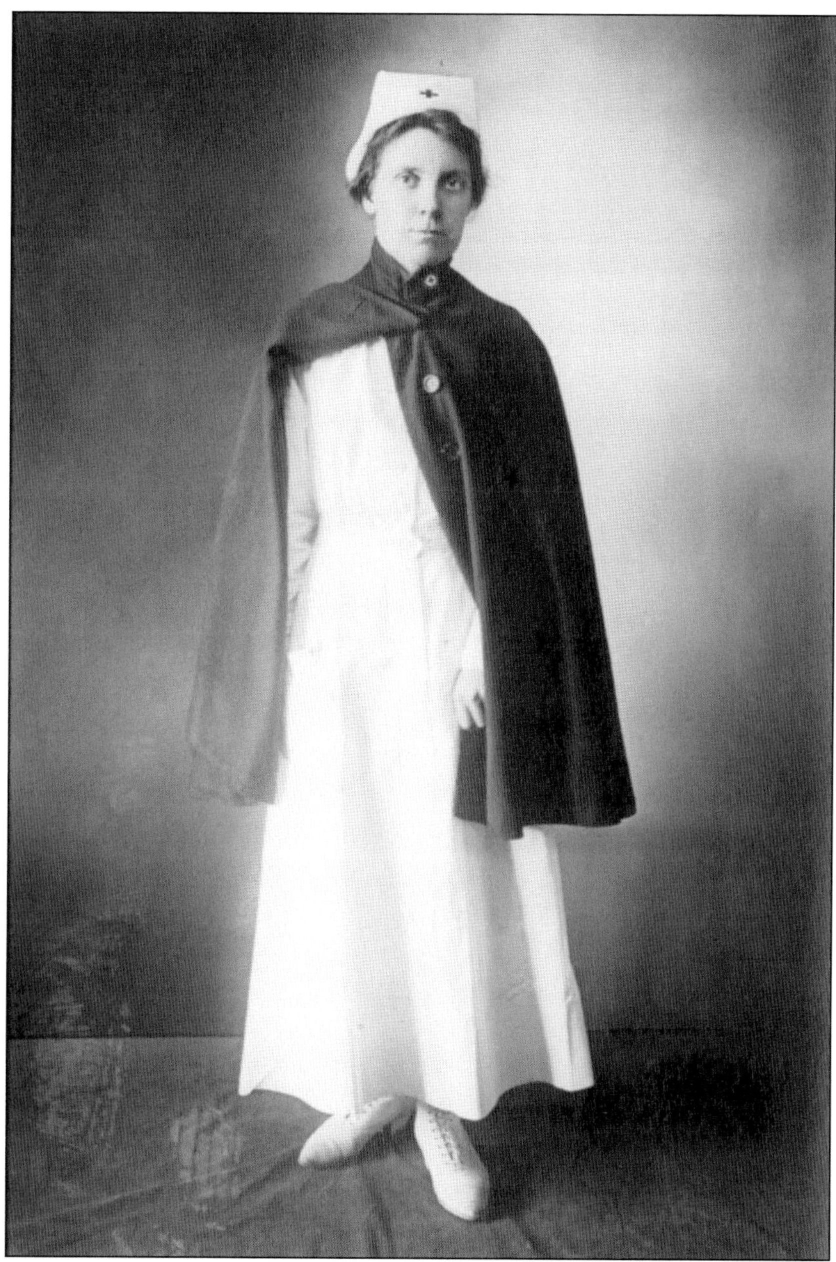

The Army Nurse Corps had only been established in 1901, but it quickly proved how important it would be to the well-being of the troops abroad as well as those training stateside. To qualify, nurses had to have graduated from a nursing school, be single, and be between the ages of 25 and 35. Thousands of nurses were sent overseas but thousands of others like Army Nurse Bernice Ames of Jefferson remained stateside at training camps. Ames was stationed at Camp Merritt in New Jersey, a military installation rapidly constructed after the declaration of war. Its site was chosen due to the close proximity to Hoboken, where several thousand soldiers embarked for overseas daily. She remained on duty through September 1919 as troops returned to the states. After the war, Ames continued in her profession serving in hospitals in Connecticut, California, and Arizona before returning to Maine. (Stegna.)

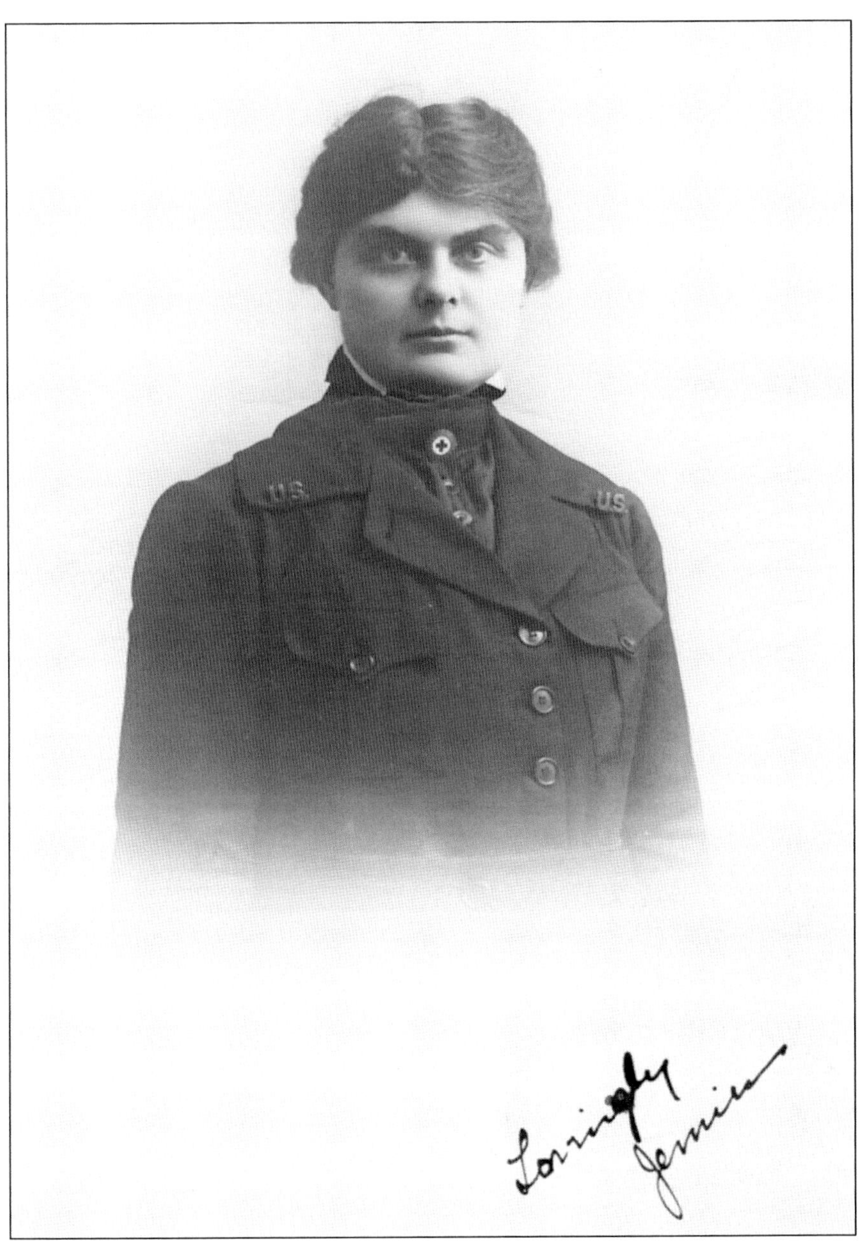

Jane Jeffery, born in England, went to the United States to assist her aunt and uncle with their health needs. When the United States declared war, she joined the Red Cross and, in 1917, went to France to serve in a refugee hospital. She was later transferred to an Army hospital at Jouy-sur-Morin. On July 15, 1918, German airplanes bombed the hospital, severely injuring Jeffery. For her actions during the attack, she received the Distinguished Service Cross. Her citation read, "Miss Jeffery was severely wounded by an exploding bomb during an air raid. She showed utter disregard for her own safety by refusing to leave her post, though suffering great pain from her wounds. Her courageous attitude and devotion to the task of helping others was inspiring to all of her associates." After the war, she worked in several hospitals and then moved to Maine to work in the bath department of the Poland Spring Resort. She married Alvan Bolster Ricker, one of the owners of the resort, and remained in Poland until her death in 1960. (PSPS.)

Eight

Peace and Remembrance

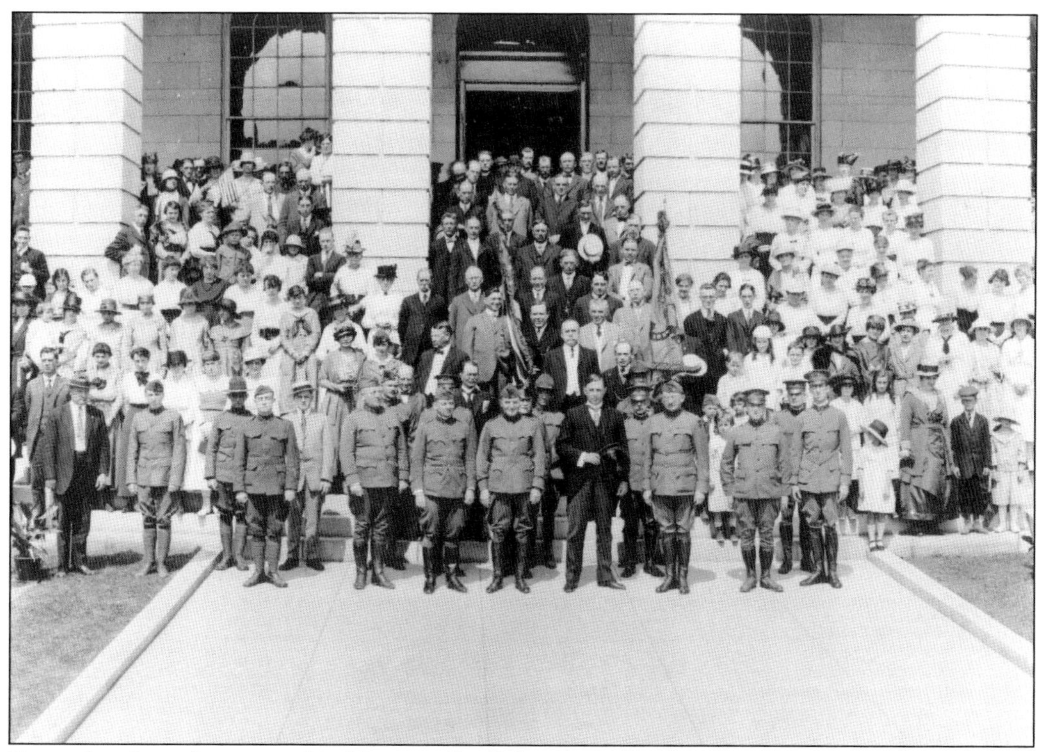

Dressed in formal attire and holding a tall silk hat, Gov. Carl E. Milliken stands in front of the Maine State House in Augusta, having accepted the flags of the 103rd Infantry Regiment from Col. Frank Hume, the officer to the right of the governor. These colors were placed in the State House Hall of Flags, where they may be seen today with Maine's Civil War battle flags.

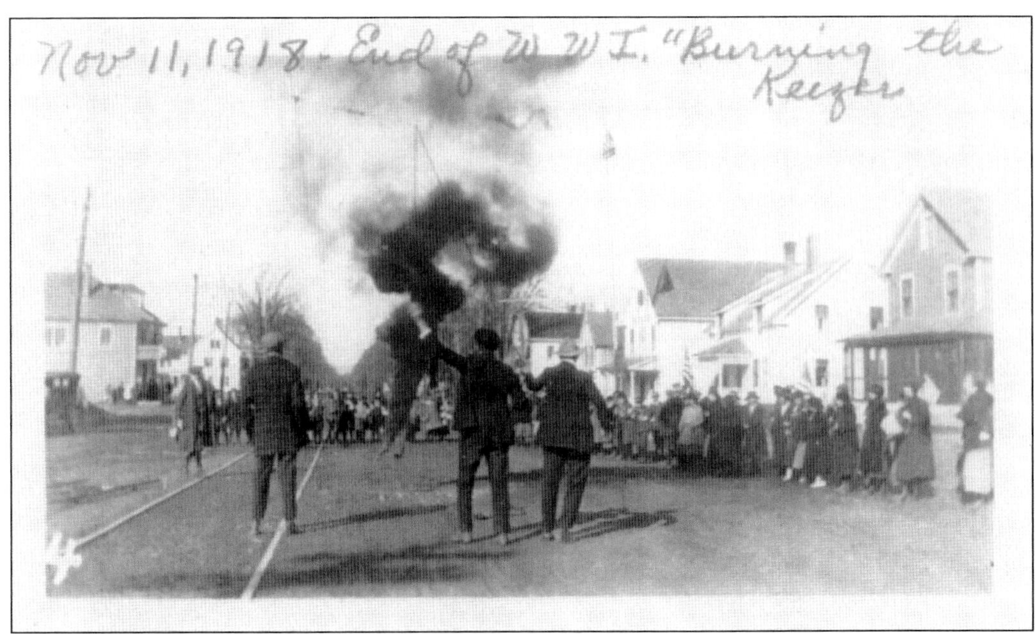

Here, citizens of the small rural community of Corinth burn the kaiser in effigy on November 11, 1918. As the news of the war's end reached Mainers, church bells tolled, mill and fire station whistles blew, and people gathered in the streets to celebrate the Armistice. Many communities closed their schools as impromptu parades were launched and patriotic celebrations commenced. (Shaw.)

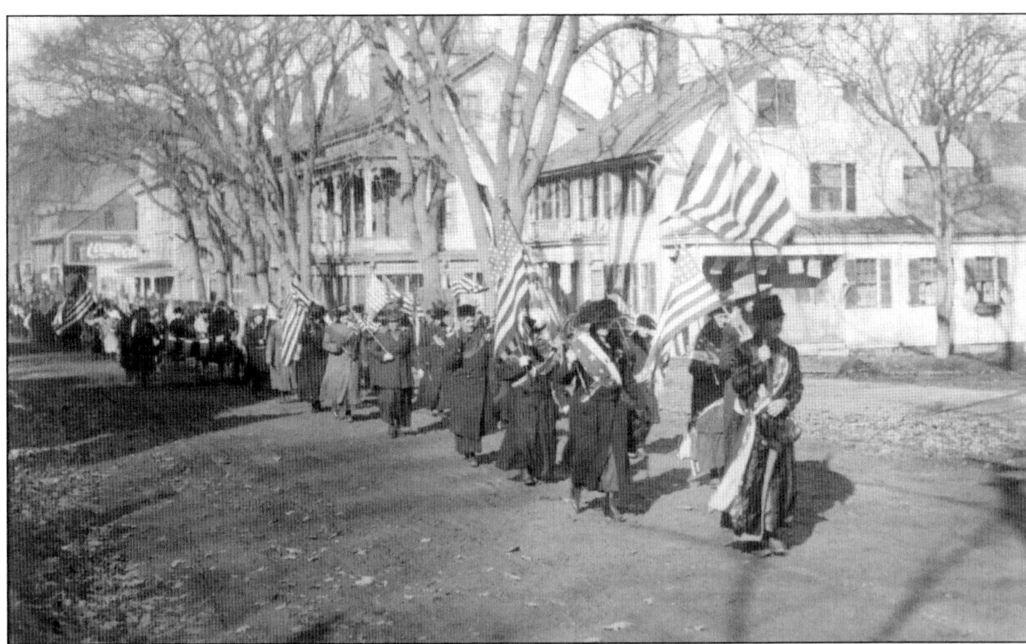

As word of the war's end reached Maine on November 11, 1918, people gathered in town squares to celebrate the news. Here, a line of flag carrying women lead a procession down High Street in Belfast in what they called a peace parade. A year later, these ladies won the right to vote, a victory achieved in part through women's important contributions to the war effort. (MSM.)

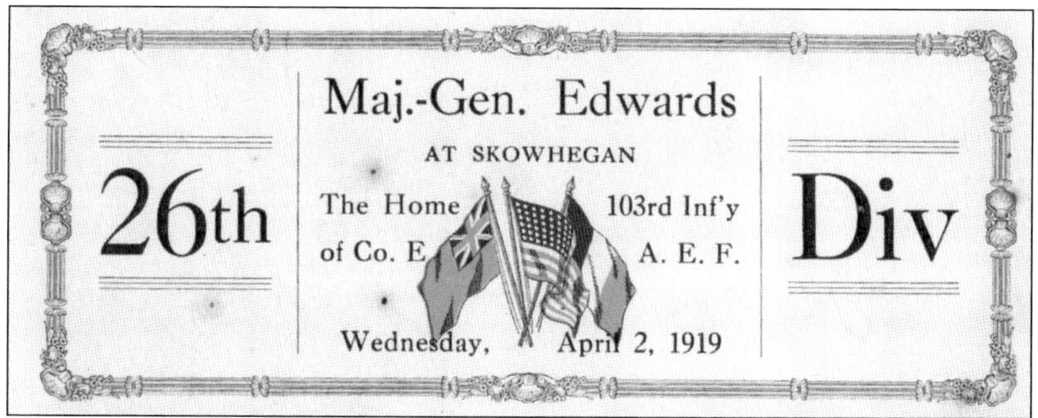
Maj.-Gen. Edwards
AT SKOWHEGAN
26th
The Home of Co. E
103rd Inf'y A. E. F.
Div
Wednesday, April 2, 1919

In April 1919, Maj. Gen. Clarence R. Edwards, commander of the 26th Division, popularly known as the Yankee Division, made several appearances in Central Maine to celebrate America's victory in the war. This souvenir ticket commemorated Gen. Edwards visiting Skowhegan on April 2, 1919, greeted by Col. Roy L. Marston, who had supervised the landing of the division in France in September 1917.

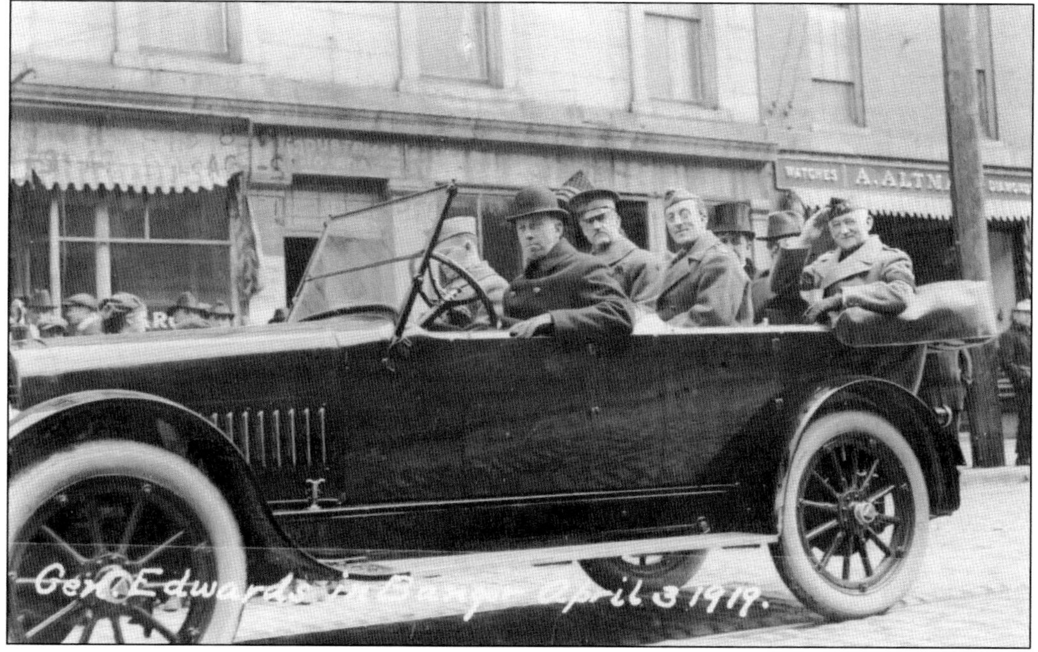

On April 3, 1919, Bangor gave Major General Edwards a hero's welcome that included greetings at the railroad station, a luncheon, a dinner, and two speeches at city hall—one for schoolchildren and the other for servicemen and their families. Here, Edwards (right) salutes well-wishers from the back of an open car that also carries Gov. Carl E. Milliken, third from the right, in the tall silk hat. (Shaw.)

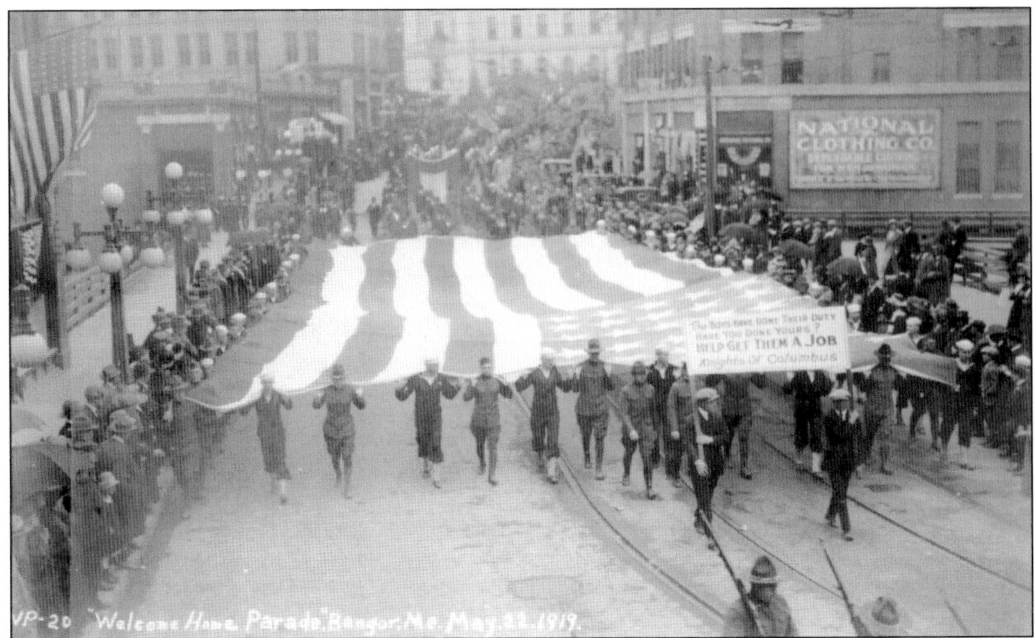

Bangor followed Maj. Gen. Edwards's visit with a huge Welcome Home parade on May 22, 1919. Crowds lined Central Street as soldiers and sailors led the parade with a large American flag. To the right, two young men in civilian dress carried a sign with a plea for helping veterans to find jobs. This message echoed Edwards's call the month before to "give each man his place when he returns."

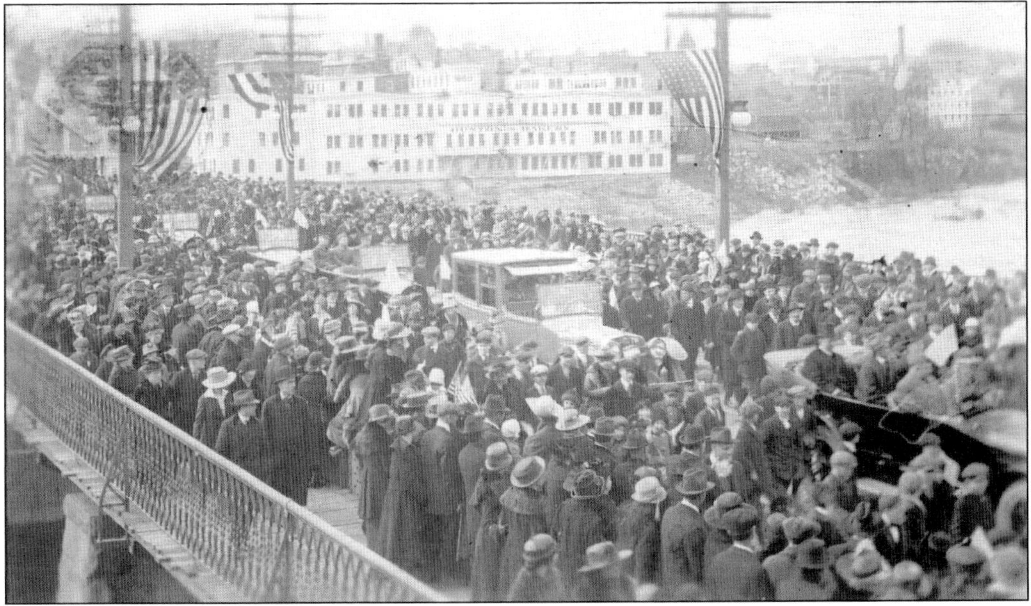

The next stops in Maj. Gen. Edwards's tour were Auburn and Lewiston on April 4, 1919. Accompanied by Governor Milliken, the general arrived in Auburn at 2:30 p.m., and the two dignitaries drove through the crowded streets of the twin cities, followed by a parade of 1,500 service members. The lead car carrying the general and the governor is shown at right as it crosses the bridge into Lewiston. (LePage.)

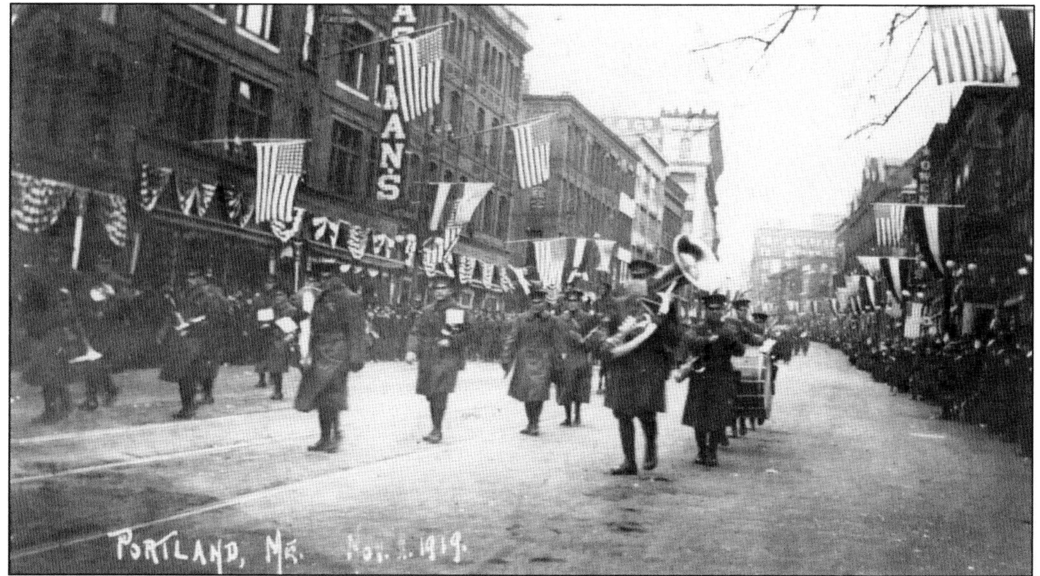

Portland observed the first anniversary of the Armistice on November 11, 1919, with a parade, a band concert, a football game, a dinner, a dance, a boxing match, and fireworks. Here, an Army band marches down Congress Street toward Monument Square as part of an hour-long parade comprised of 10,000 men and women. Many thousands more cheered from the sidewalks.

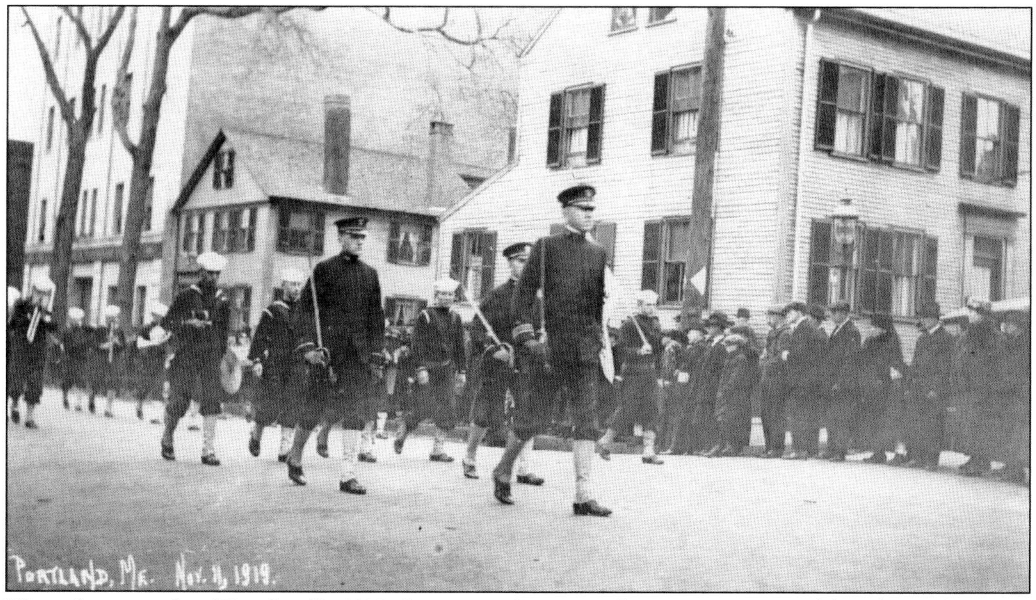

This photograph of Portland's 1919 Armistice Day parade captures a naval band marching on Cumberland Avenue between Preble Street and Brown Street. The star attraction of the parade was Maj. Gen. Clarence R. Edwards. In remarks made in Portland, General Edwards stated, "Let the American public rejoice on this day for a worthy cause well won."

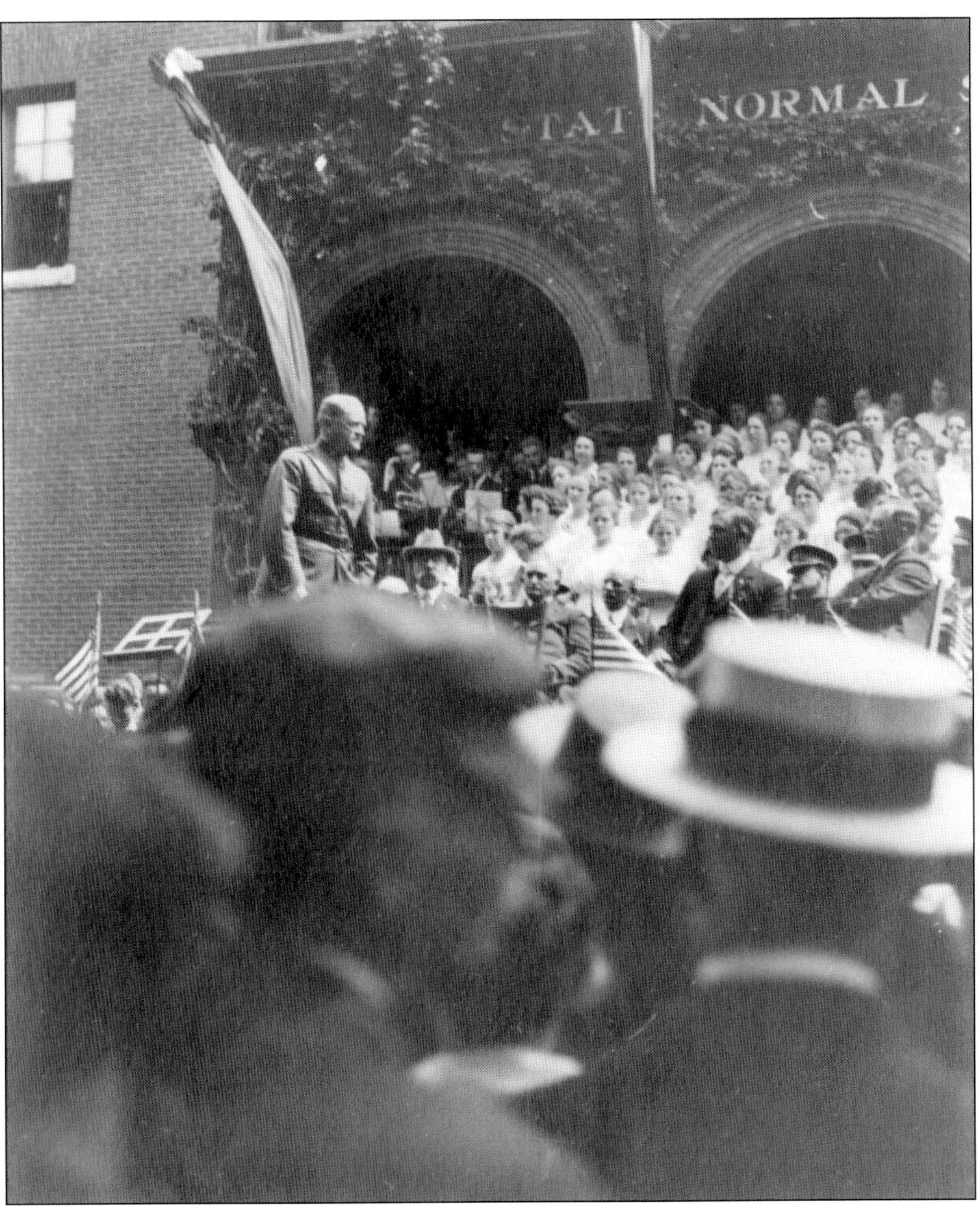

In 1920, Gen. John J. "Black Jack" Pershing, commander of the American Expeditionary Force, set out on a three-day tour of Maine. Here he is on June 4, 1920, at Farmington Normal School, now known as the University of Maine at Farmington. After his speech at the college, the female students, all clad in white, sang a song that wove General Pershing's name into a verse. Pershing also spoke in Biddeford, Brunswick, Portland, Lewiston, Waterville, Bangor, Rockland, Skowhegan, and Augusta. While in Augusta, he was the first official guest at the new executive mansion, the Blaine House. Regarding his speech in Lewiston, the *Lewiston Daily Sun* reported that General Pershing "paid tribute to the sons of Maine who fell in battle, to those who fought and came through unscathed, and to the people who remained at home and their prayers which instilled the expeditionary forces with the spirit that it returned victorious."

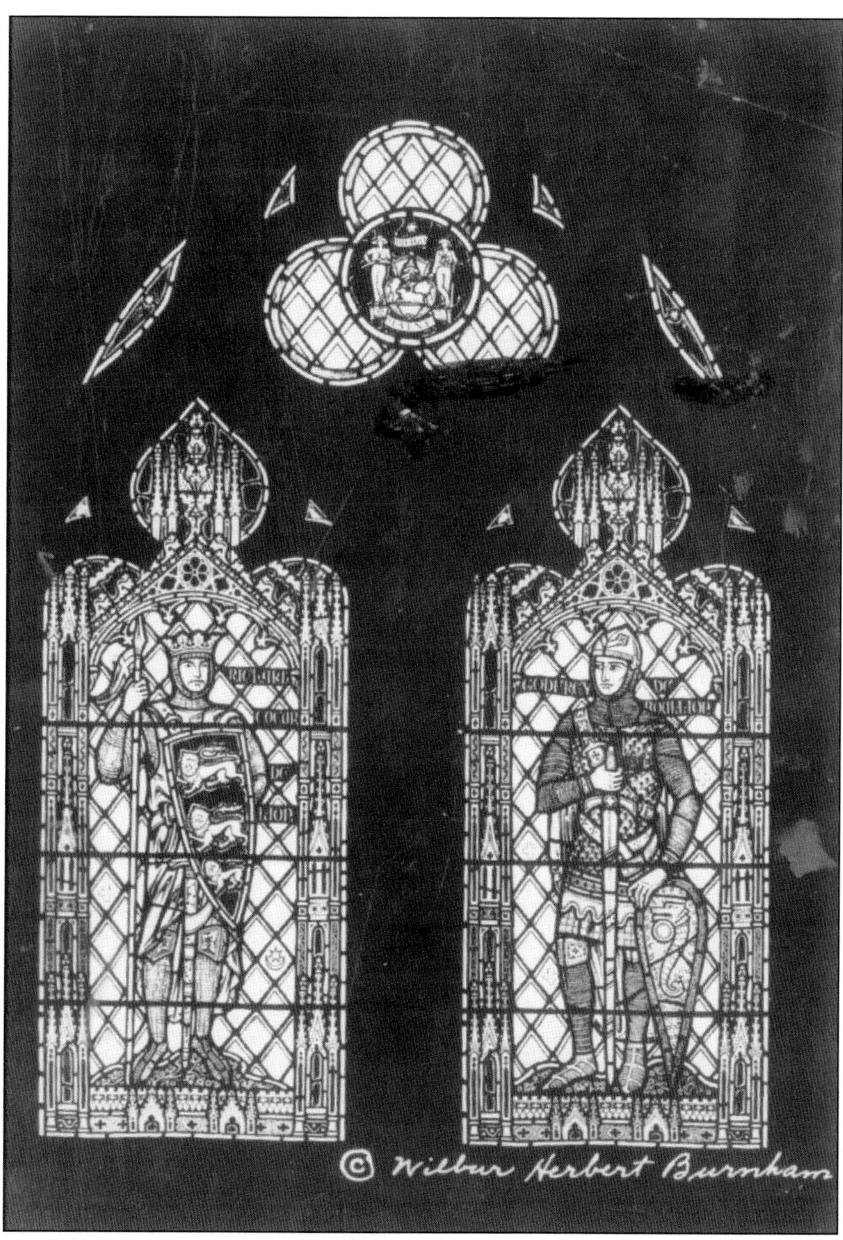

In June 1918, troops from the Second Division, including a brigade of Marines, fought against the Germans at Belleau Wood near Chateau Thierry. In July, the 26th Division was ordered into Belleau to take the village, but they met with heavy resistance. During the battle, the village church was destroyed, but Gen. Clarence Edwards, commander of the division, promised the church would be rebuilt. Following the war, veterans raised money, and on October 10, 1929, the 26th Division Church was dedicated. Memorial stained-glass windows depicted individuals such as George Washington and Lafayette and the seals of the New England states. This window shows crusaders Richard Coueur de Lion and Godfrey de Bouillon as well as the seal of the State of Maine. A plaque at the church reads, "This church, destroyed during the world war, has been reconstructed by the veterans of the 26th Division of the American Expeditionary Force in memory of their comrades who fell on the soil of France fighting for a communal cause." (Libby.)

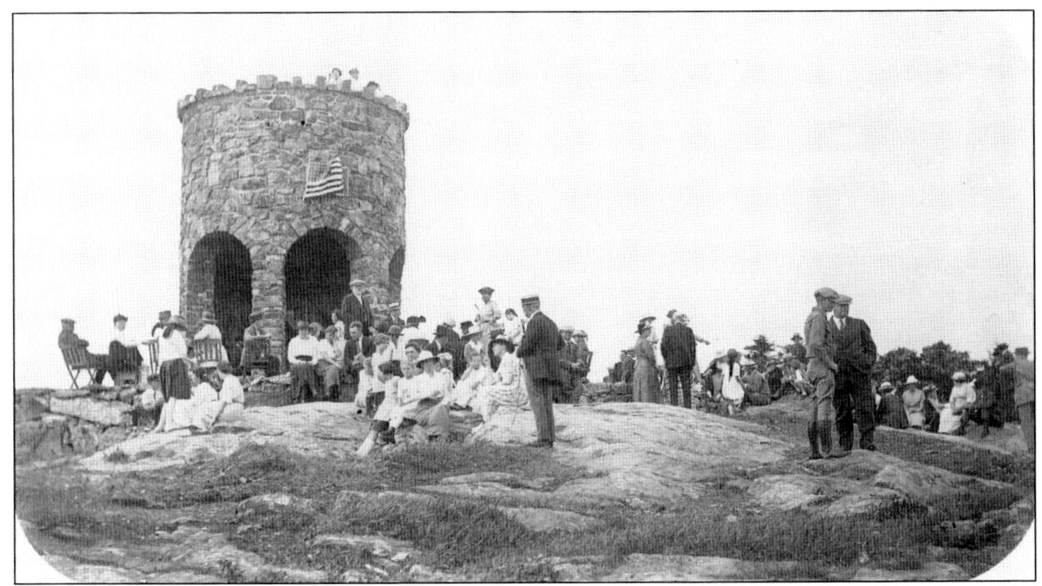

One of Maine's most well-known World War I memorials is the Mount Battie Memorial Tower in Camden. Based on the Old Stone Mill in Newport, Rhode Island, this 26-foot stone monument was designed by Parker Morse Hooper, a New York architect who summered in Camden. The tower was dedicated in 1921 to "the men and women of Camden in the World War."

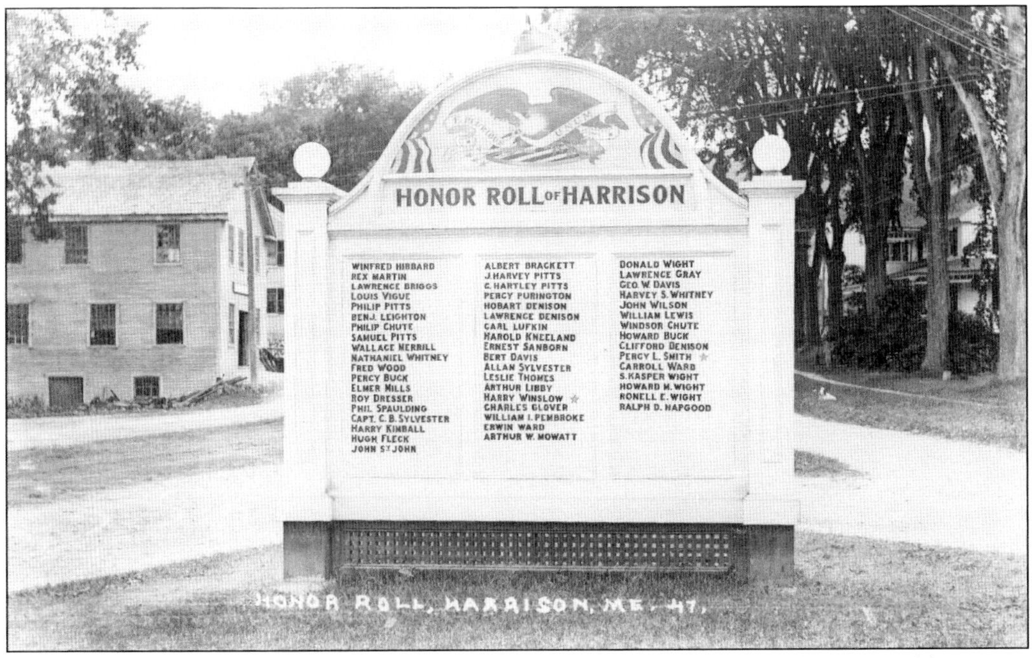

Many Maine communities recognized their servicemen by erecting honor rolls in central locations. Constructed of wood, these honor rolls listed the names of local soldiers and sailors. A gold star next to a name indicated that the individual had died in service. With a population of 900, Harrison sent 42 men to the war, of whom two did not return.

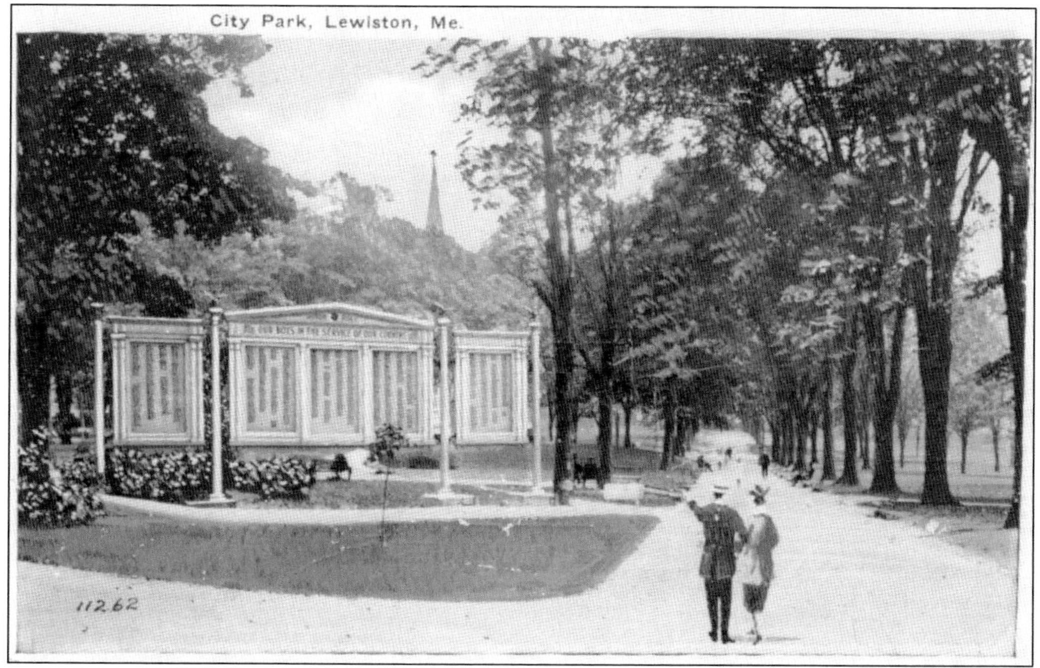

Lewiston was Maine's second largest city in 1917, and its honor roll in City Park, now Kennedy Park, featured 16 columns of the names of "our boys in the service of our country." In 1919, the honor roll was replaced by a marble tablet of names that was displayed at Lewiston High School until 2005, when it was mounted on granite and moved to Veterans Park.

A World War I memorial, such as this one at Camp Androscoggin in Wayne, was personal in nature. In 1907, Edward M. Healy founded one of the first boys' camps in Maine, and his three sons spent summers there. When Healy's oldest son, Lt. Jefferson A. Healy, was killed at Chateau Thierry in France in 1918, Androscoggin campers erected this monument to his memory in 1921.

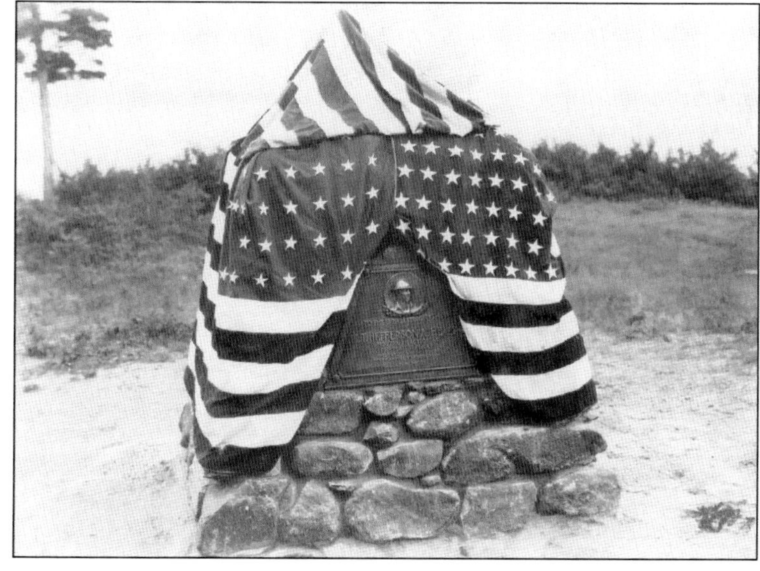

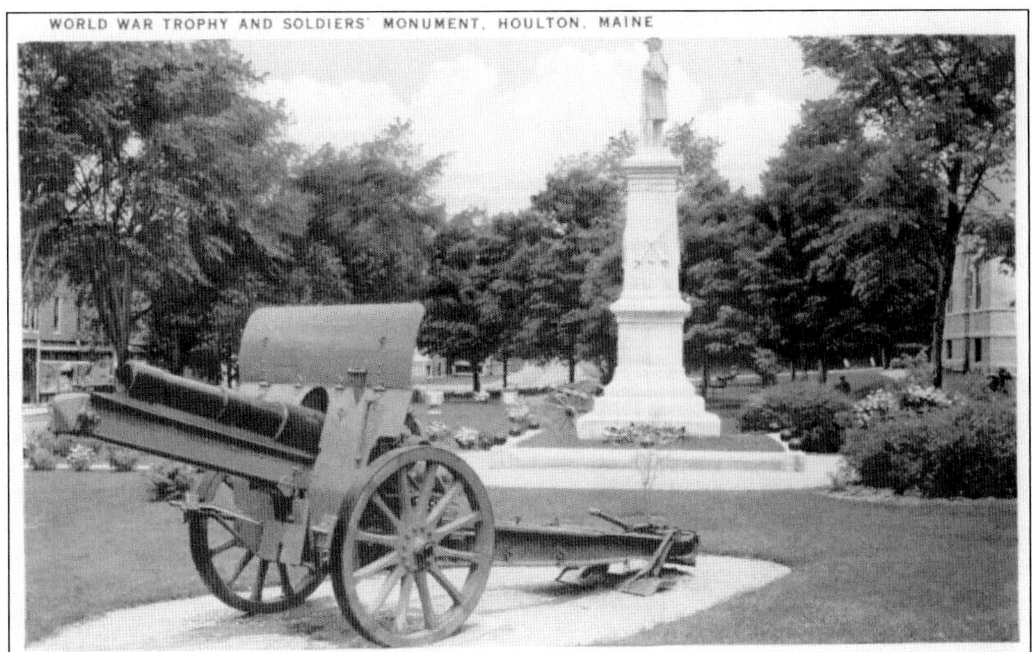

Following the tradition of Maine's more than 170 Civil War monuments, the state's World War I monuments ranged from sculptures to cannons. Houlton's Civil War monument was erected in 1909 in the park adjacent to the Cary Library. After World War I, it was joined by this captured German artillery piece, which served as the town's world war memorial.

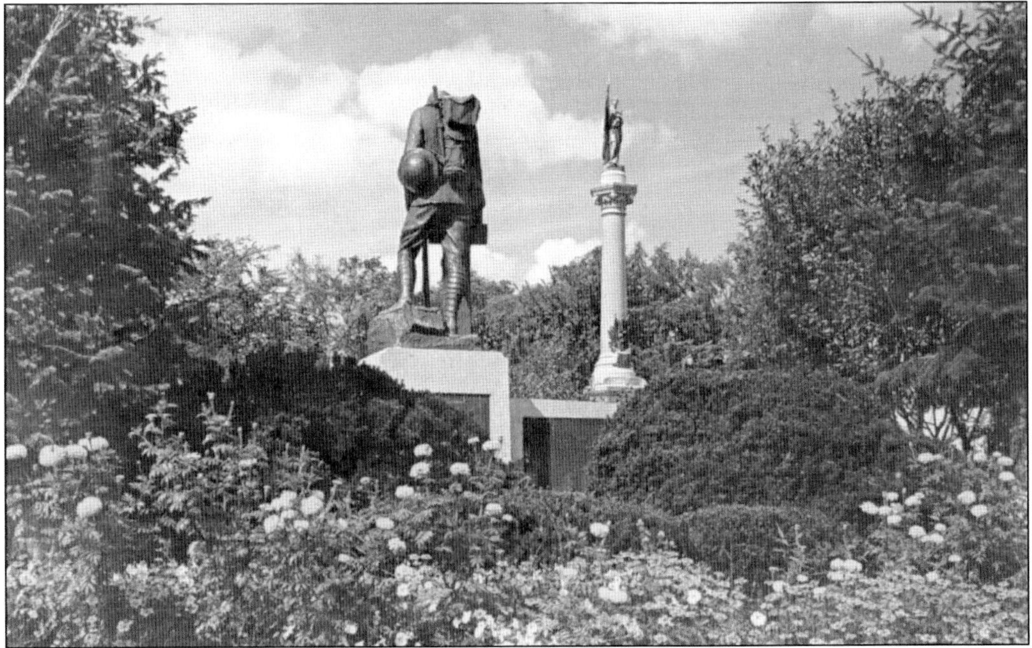

On November 11, 1929, Augusta's World War I monument (left) took its place next to the Civil War memorial in Memorial Park. The 12 local servicemen who died in the war and 680 who served were honored by Canadian sculptress Frances N. Loring's bronze statue of a soldier looking down at a comrade's grave while holding a rifle in one hand and a laurel branch in the other.

One of Maine's most dramatic World War I monuments is the bronze statue of the *American Doughboy* in Lincoln. Created by sculptor E.M. Viquesney, this figure of an infantryman in battle was reproduced throughout the country. Dedicated on May 29, 1927, Lincoln's copy of the statue is the only one in Maine.

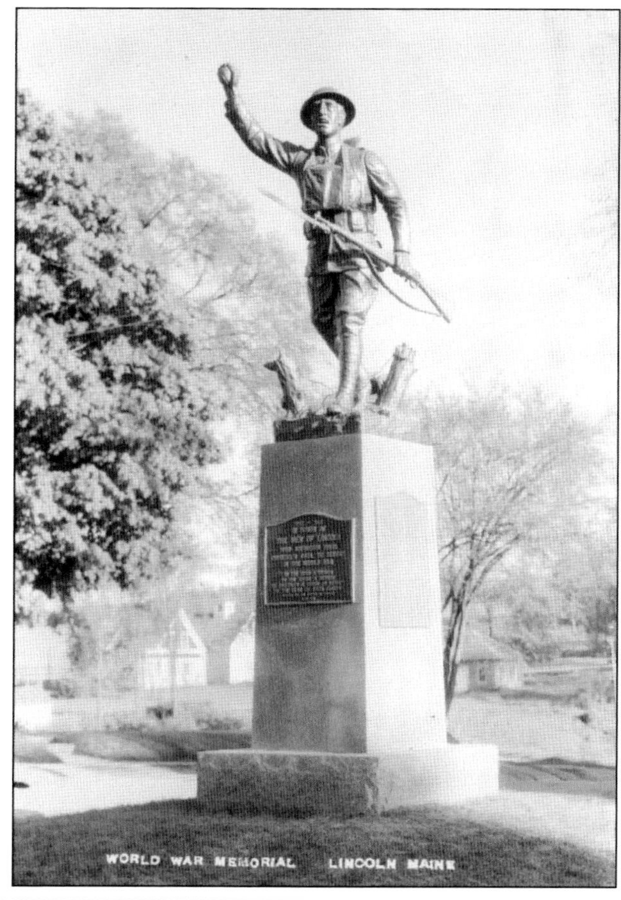

Bangor commemorated its World War I soldiers and sailors with a bronze statue of a heroic female figure holding a torch in one hand and a palm leaf in the other. Prominently sited at the center of the city in Norumbega Park, the statue was erected by the Veterans of Foreign Wars and dedicated on May 31, 1939. The sculptor was Charles E. Tefft, a Brewer native.

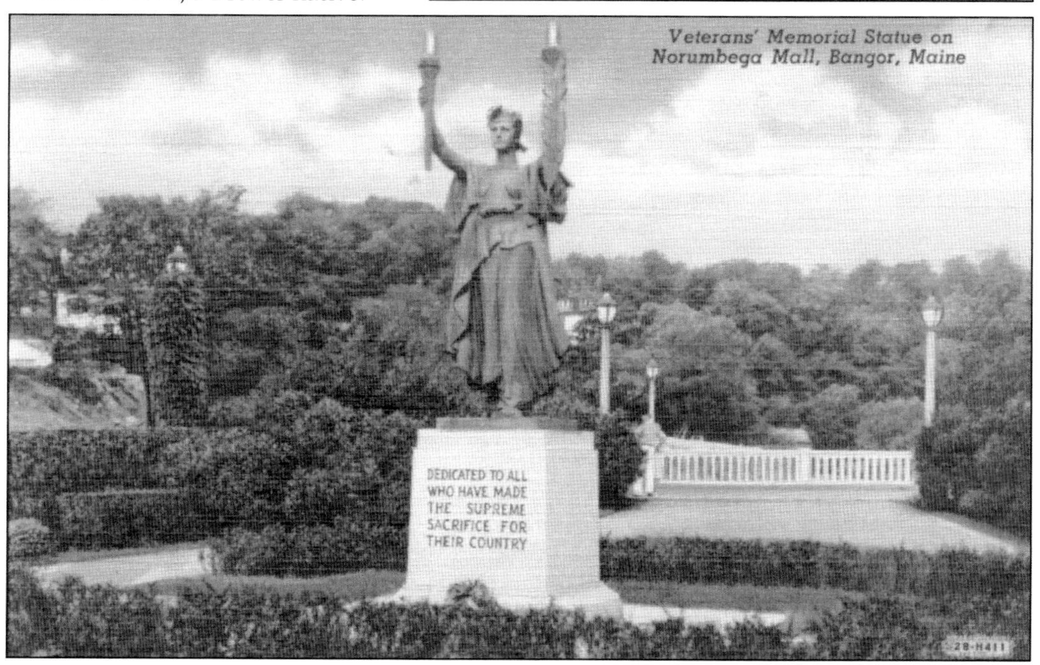

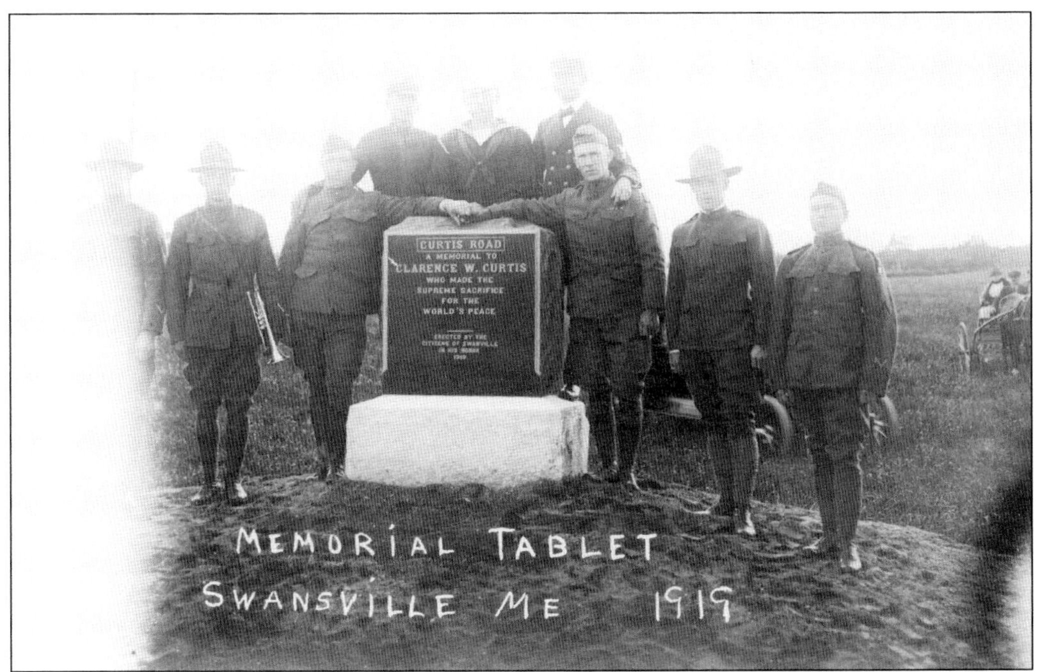

The Waldo county town of Swanville, population 396, lost resident Clarence W. Curtis to the war. In his memory, his fellow townspeople named Curtis Road for him and erected a tablet in his honor. The 1919 dedication of this monument was attended by nine Swanville soldiers and sailors who had survived the war.

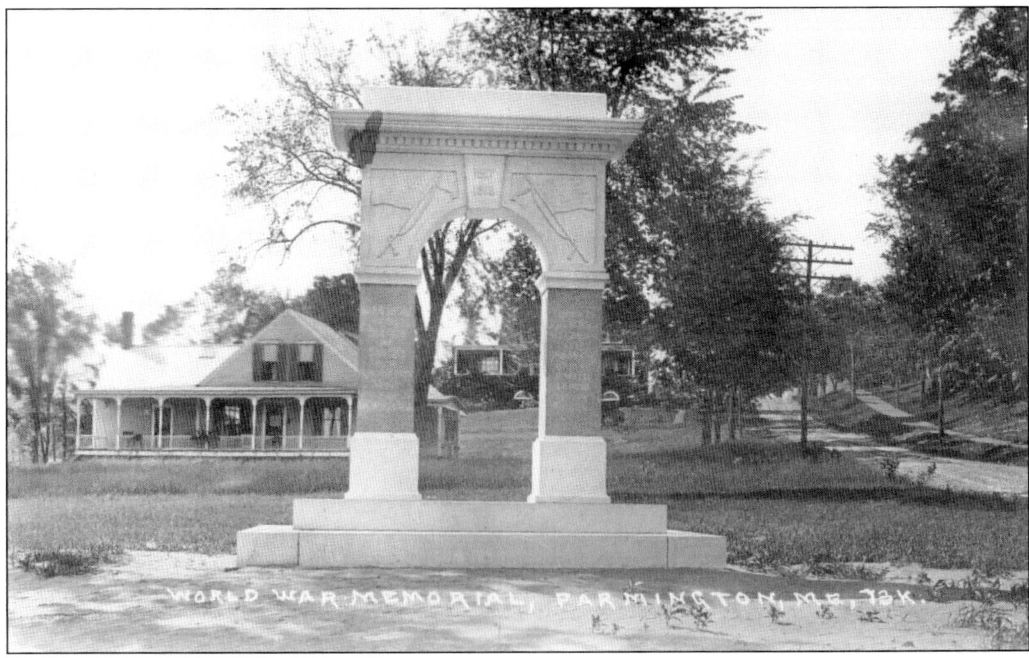

The Teague Memorial Arch was dedicated on May 30, 1924, to those who served in World War I from Franklin County. Prominently located in a park at the north end of downtown Farmington, the arch was the gift of Civil War veteran John M. Teague and his wife, Henrietta Teague.

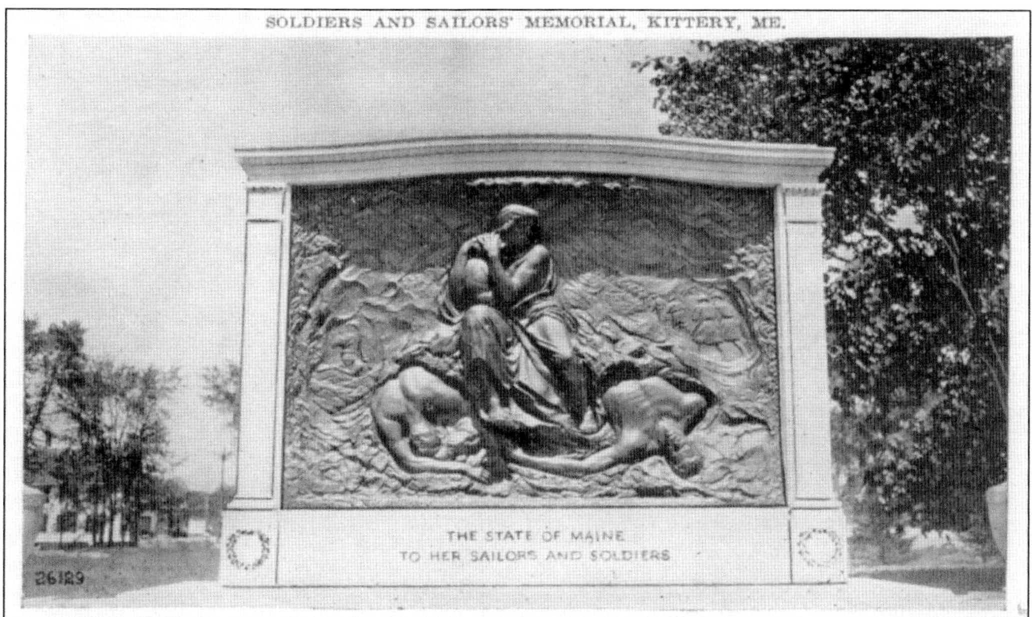

The State of Maine's Sailors and Soldiers Monument was built in John Paul Jones Memorial Park in Kittery between 1924 and 1926. The memorial was located at the beginning of Route 1 in Maine. Planning for the monument began in 1923 under the direction of Gov. Percival P. Baxter, and Russian sculptress Bashka Paeff's design was chosen in May 1924.

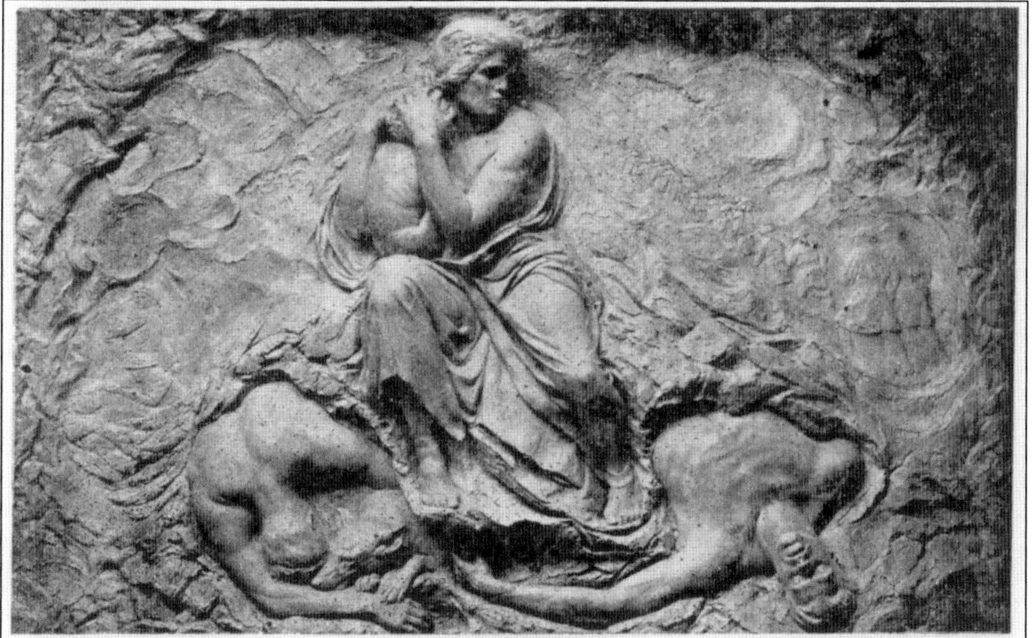

Unlike most World War I memorials, Maine's Sailors and Soldiers Monument in Kittery "portrays the suffering and anguish of womanhood; the terror of childhood; the sacrifice of manhood," according to Gov. Percival P. Baxter. In the spirit of Francisco Goya's *The Disasters of War*, a mother protects her child with two dead figures at her feet as she gazes at a line of soldiers marching into battle.

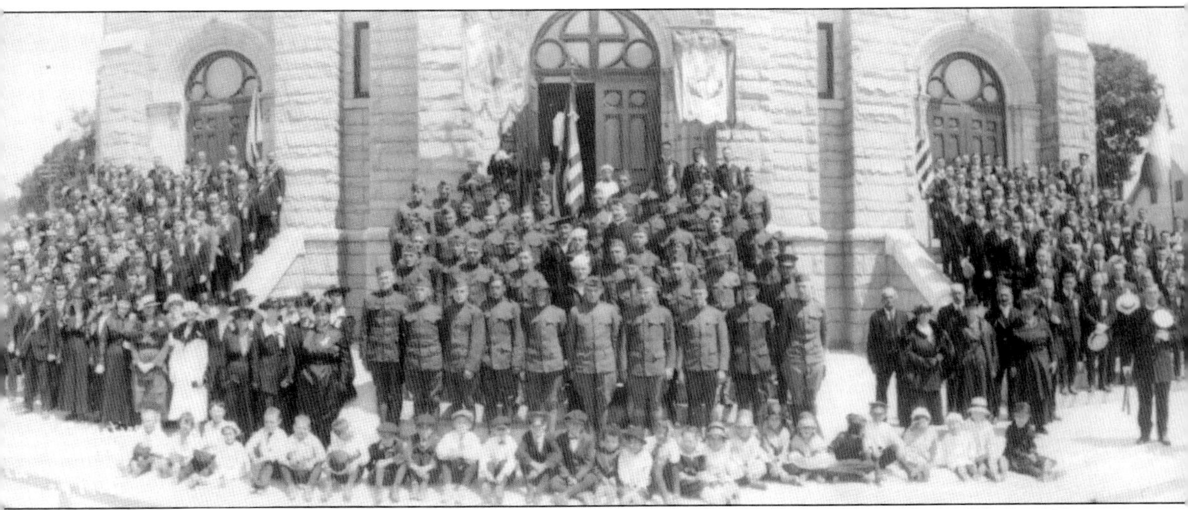

On Sunday, June 29, 1919, St. Augustine's Catholic Church in Augusta honored its parishioners who had served in World War I. Uniformed soldiers and sailors stood proudly on the steps of the church, home to a large congregation of French-Canadian descent. Their contribution to the war would be marked by a bronze plaque in front of the church.

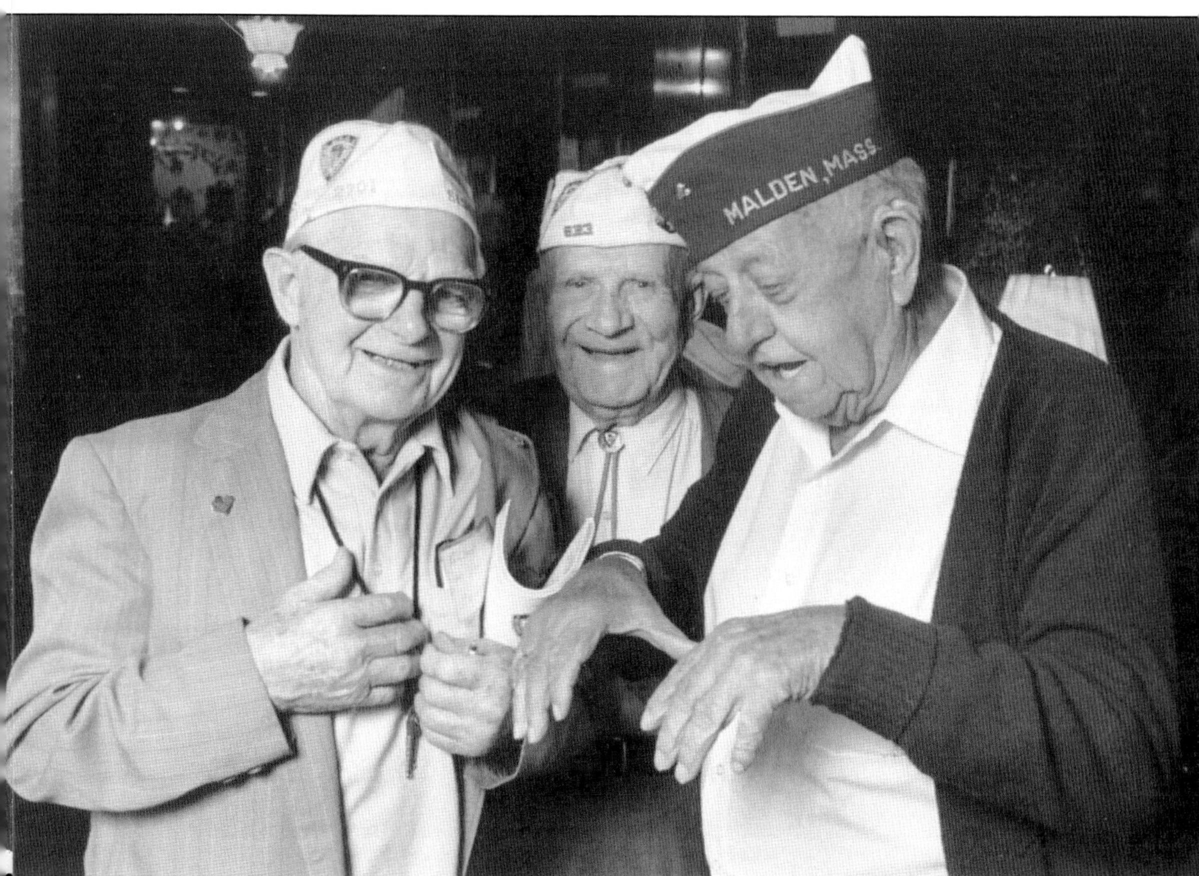

Arthur Dinsmore (center) socializes with fellow veterans at the Veterans of World War I of the USA's convention in Milwaukee in 1985. Born in Lubec, Dinsmore enlisted in the Army in December 1917 and was assigned to the 54th Coastal Artillery Corps. He went overseas with his unit and served until his discharge in March 1919. Following the war, Dinsmore returned to Maine, started a men's clothing store in the central part of the state, and became active in the veterans group. The ability to talk with those who were "over there" came to an end with the passing of Frank Buckles, the last surviving American veteran in 2011, who was followed by Florence Green of the United Kingdom less than a year later. (Libby.)

BIBLIOGRAPHY

Biddeford Weekly Journal, 1916–1919.
Cabot, Charles R., ed. *History of the 103rd US Infantry*, 1919.
Industrial Journal, The. Bangor, 1914–1918.
Lewiston Daily Sun, 1916–1919.
Lewiston Evening Journal, 1916–1919
Liaison, The Courier of the Big Gun Corps. Fort Monroe, VA: Coast Artillery School, 1919.
McIntire, Colby. *The Old Man of the 103rd: The Biography of Frank M. Hume*. Houlton, ME: Aroostook Print Shop, 1940.
Office of the Adjutant General, Roster of Maine in the Military Service of the U.S. and Allies in World War, 1917–1919, Vol. I–II, Augusta, ME: 1919.